Optical Disks vs. Magnetic Storage

Optical Disks vs. Magnetic Storage

William Saffady

Meckler

Westport • London

Library of Congress Cataloging-in-Publication Data

Saffady, William, 1944-
    Optical disks vs. magnetic storage / William Saffady.
      p. cm.
    Includes bibliographical references and index.
    ISBN 0-88736-703-8 : $
    1. Optical disks. 2. Optical storage devices. 3. Magnetic disks.
    4. Magnetic tapes. I. Title.
    TA1635.S34   1990
    621.39'76--dc20   90-38102
                                           CIP

British Library Cataloguing in Publication Data

Saffady, William *1944-*
    Optical disks vs. magnetic storage.
    1. Storage devices. Computer systems. Direct access
    storage devices
    I. Title
    004.53

    ISBN 0-88736-703-8

Meckler Corporation, 11 Ferry Lane West, Westport, CT 06880.
Meckler Ltd., Grosvenor Gardens House, Grosvenor Gardens,
   London SW1W 0BS, U.K.

Printed on acid free paper.
Printed and bound in the United States of America.

Contents

Preface

This report provides a detailed comparison of optical and magnetic devices and media as computer storage technologies, emphasizing similarities and differences in recording technology, storage capacity, performance characteristics, and costs. Intended for computer specialists, information systems analysts, adminstrative managers, and others responsible for computer system planning and selection, the report will hopefully help such readers clarify their thinking about the competitive and complementary relationship of magnetic and optical storage technologies. While it is designed as a standalone publication that can be read without reference to other works, this report also serves as a companion piece to the author's *Optical Disks vs. Micrographics as Document Storage and Retrieval Technologies*, published by Meckler Corporation in 1988. As its title suggests, that work provides a competitive analysis of optical disk and microfilm systems in image-oriented records management applications. This report emphasizes the competitive relationship of optical disks and magnetic technologies for the storage of computer-generated data and text, although the discussion is also applicable to image storage.

The report is divided into three parts:

• PART ONE provides a detailed comparison of optical disk and magnetic disk drives and media. It compares and contrasts the storage capacities, performance characteristics, and costs of typical optical and magnetic disk configurations. The analysis of magnetic disk systems includes both fixed and removable magnetic media.

• PART TWO provides a similar comparison of optical disk and magnetic tape technologies. It also includes a brief discussion of optical tape systems which were not commercially available at the time this report was written.

• PART THREE discusses hierarchical storage systems that integrate magnetic and optical components. It begins with an overview of hierarchical storage concepts, followed by a description of typical hierarchical storage configurations.

This report is based on a detailed analysis of available magnetic and optical disk products, many of which are cited as examples of particular characteristics and capabilities. Major points raised in the narrative discussion are summarized in a series of graphs that compare specific optical and magnetic storage configurations. To facilitate additional research and encourage readers to examine specific topics in greater depth, a lengthy bibliography contains references to books, articles, and other publications. References are cited at appropriate points in the discussion.

As a final point, this report contains cost analyses that are based on equipment and media prices prevailing in early 1990. While specific costs are likely to change in the future, the cost comparisons presented in PART ONE and PART TWO should retain their methodological significance, enabling users to recalculate the cost comparisons to reflect changing prices.

William Saffady
School of Information Science
and Policy
State University of New York
at Albany

Part One: Optical Disks vs. Magnetic Disks

The idea that optical disk and magnetic disk systems are competing technologies is well established in the computer industry and predates the commercial availability of optical storage products. Over 15 years ago, Bruun (1973) cited optical storage as one of two future alternatives to magnetic disks; the other was bubble memory, a form of magnetic storage that attracted much publicity in the 1970s but never gained the widespread acceptance predicted by many industry analysts. Citing the advantages of higher capacity, greater durability, the convenience of removability, and lower cost, Surden (1977) contended that optical disks would rival magnetic storage in certain applications, while King (1983) enthusiastically praised optical storage as a revolutionary "trend of the future" for applications requiring high storage capacity at low cost. Similar views have been expressed by Scannell (1980), Neary (1982), Schmidt (1982), Banks (1983), Boyer-Chamard and Moussy (1983), Moore (1984), Lipoff (1985), Silva (1985), Chadwick (1986), Popovich et al (1986), Ruy et al (1986), Hecht (1987), Steinbrecher (1987), Bate (1989), Bloom (1989), Deverell (1989), and Simpson (1989). Perlman (1988) questions the viability of magnetic storage industry from the investment standpoint, noting that optical disks are challenging the role of magnetics as the dominant computer storage technology. Expressing a view shared by many industry analysts, Allin (1989) predicts that optical storage products will significantly expand their market share at the expense of magnetic disk drives.

The competitive relationship between optical and magnetic disk systems is clear: each provides direct, online access to computer processible data. Any information that can be stored on magnetic disks can be stored on optical disks. Since optical disk drives are available for most computer equipment configurations, data processing installation managers increasingly view them as an alternative to magnetic disk systems. To facilitate evaluation of the two technologies, the following discussion compares the characteristics and capabilities of commonly encountered magnetic and optical disk products. It begins with a description of magnetic and optical recording technology, followed by detailed comparisons of storage capacities, performance characteristics (access time and data transfer rates), and storage costs. The discussion is limited to a comparison of magnetic disks with read/write optical disks of the write-once and erasable type. Like their magnetic counterparts, such optical disks are purchased blank and permit the direct recording of machine-readable data generated by keyboards, document scanners, or other computer input devices. They can also record information transferred from magnetic disks or other optical disks. Comparisons of magnetic disks with read-only optical disks, notably CD-ROM systems, are intentionally omitted from this discussion. Produced by a mastering process, such disks contain prerecorded information and have no direct recording properties. They consequently compete with certain types of magnetic disks in a relatively narrow range of applications involving the publication or other distribution of machine-readable data bases, text files, and software. Unlike read/write optical disks, however, they do not offer an alternative to magnetic disks in the broad spectrum of computer applications.

TECHNOLOGY

All data storage and retrieval systems incorporate storage media, energy sources for recording and retrieving information, and control mechanisms. Differ-

3

ences in the implementation of these fundamental components determine the performance characteristics of particular devices and influence their competitive positions with respect to alternative products. While they both utilize platter-shaped storage media, magnetic and optical disk drives differ in recording technology and equipment design. The following discussion of magnetic and optical disk technology emphasizes factors that influence equipment performance. Specific competitive advantages associated with one or the other technology will be discussed in detail in subsequent sections.

The theoretical foundations and historical development of magnetic recording technology have been discussed, in varying degrees of detail, by Hoagland (1963), Mee (1964), Renwick (1964), Speliotis (1967), Loeschner (1968), Mallinson (1971), Renwick and Cole (1971), Lowman (1972), Speliotis and Johnson (1972), Fuller (1975), Matick (1977), Miller (1977), Altman (1978), Stevens (1981), Majumder (1983),

Herda (1985), White (1985), Wood (1986), Hirayama (1987), Mallinson (1987), Wohlfarth (1987), Bate (1988), Camras (1988), Jorgensen (1988), Mee and Daniel (1989), Bhushan (1990), and others. As their name suggests, magnetic disks are platter-shaped media coated with a magnetizable compound dispersed in a binder material. The earliest magnetic coatings relied on ferric oxide particles suspended in a solvent and attached to a rigid or flexible substrate by an epoxy. Various other oxides -- including magnetite, cobalt-substituted ferric oxide, and cobalt-substituted magnetite -- have been utilized as magnetic disk coatings, but they have generally proven less useful than ferric oxide. High density magnetic recording requires a very thin storage medium that contains small particles. The magnetic properties of such particulate materials are discussed by Speliotis (1980, 1987, 1987a), Akashi (1982), Hirota et al (1982), Nunnelley (1984), Stubbs and Alexander (1986), Takahashi et al (1986), Fujiwara (1987), and Simmons and Lee

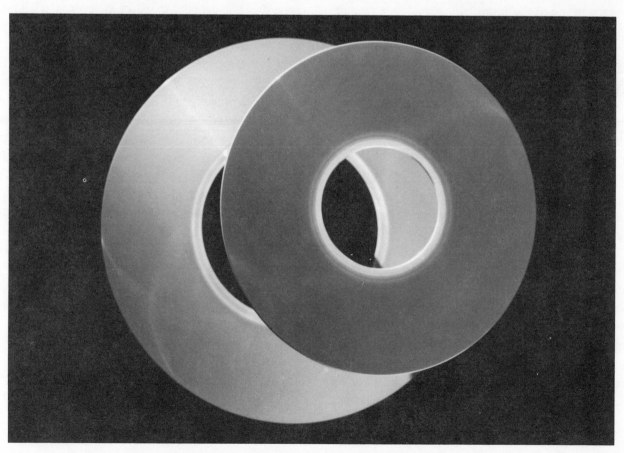

Magnetic disks are available in various diameters. Mainframe-oriented 10.8-inch and 14-inch platters are depicted here. (Courtesy: IBM Corporation)

(1988). Ferric oxide magnetic media have been successfully utilized for data, audio, and video recording for many years, and particle sizes and coating thicknesses have decreased substantially over the last four decades. Such reductions -- as will be discussed in the next section -- have been accompanied by steady and significant improvements in the storage density of magnetic disks. Among particulate materials, cobalt-alloyed ferric oxide and barium ferrite media offer especially good prospects for high density recording.

With particulate materials, however, reductions in coating thicknesses are accompanied by diminished magnetic flux that results from the dilution of particles in non-magnetic binder materials. While ferric oxide media remain in widespread use, manufacturers of high performance magnetic disk drives increasingly employ iron, nickel, cobalt, or other metals or alloys that are applied to a substrate, such as a rigid aluminum platter, in a thin film layer. Such thin film technology is discussed by Lee (1973), Inagaki (1976), Speliotis and Chi (1976), Hattori et al (1979), Shinohara et al (1979), McArthur (1981), Ishi et al (1982), Yoshii (1982), Yoshimura and Ishii (1983), Pingry (1984), Abe (1985), Desserre (1985), Futamoto et al (1985), Morisako et al (1985, 1986), Nakagawa et al (1985), Tagami (1985), Arnoldussen (1986), Chen (1986), Hoffman (1986), Howard (1986), Koiwa et al (1986), Roll (1986), Hitzfeld et al (1987), Ishii et al (1987), Morisako et al (1987), Naoe et al (1987), Sato (1987), Chen and Yamashita (1988), Chen et al (1988), Christener et al (1988), Hatano and Hashimoto (1988), Kehr et al (1988), Liou and Chien (1988),

Winchester-type magnetic disk drives contain media and read/write components in a sealed module.
(Courtesy: Core International)

Natarajan and Murdock (1988), Shibaya (1988), Shiroishi et al (1988), and Nasu et al (1989). Metallic thin films offer excellent magnetizable properties and can be applied to substrates without dilution using electroplating, chemical deposition, or vacuum deposition techniques. Compared to ferric oxide coatings, metallic thin films are much more durable, a characteristic that gives them a potentially important advantage in desktop and portable computer equipment configurations where rough handling is commonplace.

Whether particulate coatings or thin metallic films are utilized, magnetic disk drives record information by magnetizing small areas of a disk's surface in a manner corresponding to the bit patterns associated with digitally-coded text, quantitative values, images, or other information. For recording purposes, magnetic disks are divided into tracks. Individual bits are typically recorded in linear -- sometimes termed, longitudinal or horizontal -- fashion within each track,

although future magnetic disk systems, as discussed later in this report, may utilize perpendicular or vertical recording to increase platter capacity. Actual recording is performed by a transducer, called a write head, which uses electric current to align areas of a given track in directions that correspond to the positive and negative saturation magnetization of the recording medium. Positive saturation magnetization may, for example, be used to record one bits, while negative saturation magnetization is used to record zero bits. The resulting magnetization patterns must be capable of detection, or playback, by a read head.

While magnetic drum systems with one read/write head for each track were utilized as a form of main memory in some early computer installations, the read/write heads employed by magnetic disk drives are typically mounted on movable access arms that are controlled by an actuator mechanism. Magnetic disk drives can be configured with single or multiple

SyQuest magnetic disk cartridges can be removed from their drives. (Courtesy: SyQuest Technology)

platters and read/write component assemblies. Currently available in diameters of two to 14 inches, the platters may be fixed or removable. Fixed magnetic disk drives, the oldest type, are invariably equipped with rigid platters; they are popularly termed hard disks. Such disks typically feature highly polished aluminum substrates, although several manufacturers employ glass substrates for their superior smoothness and light weight. Depending on the device that will utilize them, removable magnetic disks may consist of rigid or flexible substrates, floppy disks being the most widely encountered example of the latter category.

Whether their storage media are rigid or flexible, fixed or removable, the highest capacity magnetic disk drives have multiple platters and one read/write head for each recording surface. Since the early 1970s, Winchester technology has dominated the design of fixed hard disk drives, supplanting the disk-and-spindle socket assemblies utilized by older products. Taking their names from an IBM internal product designation, Winchester-type drives combine one or more magnetic disk platters, read/write heads, access arms, and actuators, in a sealed module that minimizes contamination, enhances reliability, and virtually eliminates preventative maintenance requirements. The technology has been described by Hopkins (1981), Elphick and Parker (1983), McNeill (1985), and many

others. Because their read/write heads have low mass and fly very close to the platter surface, Winchester drives permit much higher recording densities than older disk storage devices.

IBM introduced the first magnetic disk drive to utilize removable recording media in 1962. Such devices were originally designed for smaller mainframe installations that could not afford enough fixed disk drives to meet their data storage requirements. Removable 14-inch disk packs, consisting of multiple platters mounted on a common spindle, were commonly encountered in mainframe and minicomputer installations through the early 1980s. While no longer popular, drives that accept such removable magnetic disk packs are still available for sale, and many older devices remain in use in mainframe and minicomputer sites. When not mounted in their drives, the disk packs are stored under a protective, translucent plastic cover that resembles a hat box. A variant form of removable hard disk system employs 14-inch platters encapsulated in opaque plastic cartridges. While minicomputer-oriented disk cartridge systems are rarely encountered, removable hard disk cartridges -- as discussed in the next section -- are widely available for microcomputer installations.

As noted above, floppy disk drives are the most widely utilized example of removable magnetic disk technology. Floppy disks -- various called flexible disks or, simply, diskettes -- are circular pieces of polyester coated with ferric oxide or other magnetizable compounds. Eight-inch and 5.25-inch floppy disks are usually enclosed in square paper envelopes that offer some protection against contaminants and rough handling, although several systems employ plastic-encapsulated media.

A removable Winchester drive contains media and read/write components in a plastic cartridge. (Courtesy of Plus Development Corporation)

3.5-inch and two-inch diskettes are invariably packaged in protective plastic cartridges. Most floppy disk drives support double-sided recording.

An interesting group of removable magnetic disk drives employs Winchester technology but separates the read/write head assembly from the recording medium, enclosing the latter in a removable plastic cartridge. Such drives are described as hard disk cartridge systems. The best known example, manufactured by SyQuest, is sold under various names by many vendors. A variant equipment configuration packages a complete disk drive, including read/write components as well as recording media, in a self-contained, removable module. Termed removable Winchester drives, such products are available for various microcomputer systems.

Magnetic recording materials based on ferric oxide compounds have been in widespread use for over three decades; thin metallic films have been utilized in magnetic disk recording since the 1970s. While neither technology is static, both are well developed and well understood. Optical recording is comparatively new, and -- while optical disk drives have been commercially available since the early 1980s -- the technology is still developing. As briefly noted earlier in this report,

Optical disk cartridges are encapsulated in protective plastic cartridges. A WORM cartridge is depicted here with its top cover removed and the recording medium exposed. (Courtesy: Laser Magnetic Storage International)

read/write optical disks can be divided into write-once and erasable varieties. Write-once optical disks record unalterable, unremovable information, while erasable optical disks, like their magnetic counterparts, are rewritable -- that is, they permit the reuse, by overwriting, of previously recorded media segments.

Whether write-once or erasable technology is involved, optical disk drives use lasers to record digitally-coded information by selectively altering the light reflectance characteristics of a platter-shaped storage medium. As with magnetic disks, digitally-coded data is recorded on a given optical platter in tracks, the individual bits that encode textual characters, quantitative values, and images following one another in linear fashion. Areas of altered reflectivity are subsequently detected by a laser operating at a different wavelength. Functioning in this manner, lasers are the counterparts of the read/write heads employed in magnetic disk recording.

At the time this report was written, five write-once technologies were being used by commercially available optical disk drives.

1. In ablative recording, a laser burns microscopic holes in a thermally-sensitive tellurium thin film coated on a glass or plastic substrate. The holes typically represent the one bits in digitally-coded data; to represent the zero bits, spaces are left in disk areas where holes might otherwise have been burned. When read by a laser, the holes reflect light differently than spaces. Because tellurium is unstable, it is usually alloyed with other compounds and hermetically-sealed to protect it from oxidation and contaminants. Ablative recording technology is employed in write-once optical disk drives manufactured by a number of companies, including Hitachi, Toshiba, Laser Magnetic Storage International, Optimem, Information Storage Incorporated, and Fujitsu. The technology is described in various publications, including McFarlane et al (1977), Takenaga et al (1982), Hoekstra (1983), Gittleman and Arie (1984), Kanazawa et al (1984), Vriens and Jacobs (1984), Chen et al (1985), Jacobs (1985), Suh (1985), Gittleman et al (1986), Abe et al (1987), Thomas (1987), Yamazaki et al (1987), and DiGuilio et al (1988).

2. In thermal bubble recording, a laser evaporates a polymer to selectively form bubbles in a thin film composed of precious metals, such as gold or platinum. As described by Robbins et al (1981) and Freese et al (1982), the bubbles open to form pits which reveal a reflective substrate. Areas with the exposed substrate represent the one bits in digitially-coded data, while unexposed areas represented the zero bits. Thermal bubble recording is utilized in write-once optical disk drives manufactured by ATG.

3. Bi-metallic alloy recording, which is utilized in write-once optical disk drives manufactured by Sony, employs a disk with two alloy layers -- one composed of tellurium and bismuth, the other of selenium and antimony. As described by Nakane et al (1985), a laser beam records the one bits in digitally-coded data by joining the alloys into a four-element layer with altered reflective properties. The layers remain unfused in areas that record the zero bits.

4. Dye-based recording technology utilizes thermal and photochemical effects to form pits or bubbles in areas of a disk surface that are irradiated by a laser. Described by Howe and Marchant (1983), Gravesteijn and Van der Veen (1984), Gupta (1984), Umehara et al (1985), Oba et al (1986), Graham (1987), Miceli et al (1987), Tai-Shung (1987), Couture and Lessard (1988), Molaire (1988), and Shephard (1988), dye-based recording is utilized in write-once optical disk drives manufactured by Eastman Kodak, Pioneer, and Ricoh.

5. In phase-change recording, areas of an optical disk are selectively converted from a crystalline to an amorphouse state, thereby altering their reflectivity characteristics. The technology is described by Van der Poel et al (1986), Gravesteijn (1987, 1988), Gravesteijn et al (1987), Tyan et al (1987), and Van Tongeren and Sens (1987). Phase-change technology is utilized in write-once optical disk drives manufactured by Panasonic.

Write-once optical disk systems have been utilized as alternatives to paper files and microfilm technology in document image storage applications where erasability is seldom required and may not be desired. For general data and text storage, proponents note that write-once optical recording technology can prevent the inadvertent destruction of information and provide a useful, unalterable audit trail in financial and other applications. Computer specialists, however, are accustomed to rewritable magnetic recording media. Erasability offers significant advantages in transaction processing, data base management, and other applications where data is updated frequently. To accommodate such updating requirements, write-once optical disk systems must rely on software which maintains pointers to the storage locations of replacement data -- a technique that can significantly increase access times with a resulting degradation of system performance. As a result, some industry analysts consider write-once optical disk drives an interim product group that will eventually be supplanted by erasable systems.

At the time this report was prepared, all commercially available erasable optical disk drives utilized magneto-optical (MO) -- sometimes termed thermo-magneto-optical (TMO) --recording technology. A hybrid process, magneto-optical recording utilizes a laser to selectively heat areas of a magnetic disk coated with iron combined with such rare-earth transition metals as cobalt, gadolinium, berbium, and dysprosium. When a magnetic field is applied, the heated areas will have a polarity, or magnetic direction, opposite that of the remainder of the disk. The recorded information is read by a laser which detects differences in the polarization of light transmitted through the recording material. Data is erased by applying a more powerful laser beam which reverses the magnetization in recorded areas. Magneto-optical technology is described in a large and rapidly growing body of technical literature. Examples include Hartmann et al (1984), Heitmann et al (1985), Kryder (1985), Mansuripur et al (1985), Connell (1986), Meiklejohn (1986), Asano et al (1987), Asari et al (1987), Bate (1987), Funkenbusch et al (1987), Jipson (1987), Kokubu et al (1987), Sato et al (1987), Bell (1988), Katayama (1988), Omachi (1988), Oochi (1988), Torazawa et al (1988), Bartholomeusz (1989), Crasemann et al (1989), Hansen et al (1989), Iijima et al (1989), Ishii et al (1989), Schultz and Kryder (1989), and Yamaoka (1989).

Whether write-once or erasable, all optical disk drives utilize removable recording media encapsulated in protective plastic cartridges. Depending on the technology employed, optical recording materials may be coated on rigid glass, plastic, or aluminum substrates. Platter sizes range from 5.25 to 14 inches in diameter; 3.5-inch optical disks have been demonstrated in prototype versions but were not commercially available at the time this report was prepared. Most optical disk drives utilize double-sided recording media, although -- as discussed in the next section -- only one side of a given disk can be accessed at a time. While several vendors have proposed flexible optical disks, such products were not commercially available at the time this report was prepared.

STORAGE CAPACITY

As platter-shaped recording media, magnetic and optical disks store computer-processible, digitally-coded information in a series of concentric or spiralling tracks. As cited in manufacturers' product specifications, storage capacity measurements may apply to a single recording surface or to multiple recording surfaces for those disk systems that employ double-sided media and/or multiple platters. In either case, such measurements denote the online storage capacity supported by magnetic or optical disk drives with recording media installed. Such measurements are typically expressed in megabytes (MB) or gigabytes (GB) for rigid magnetic disks and optical disks. Flexible disk capacities may be expressed in kilobytes (KB) or megabytes.

Product specification sheets may cite either formatted or unformatted capacities for a given disk system. Because it indicates the amount of storage space available to the user after control signals, error correction codes, and other system-specific information has been recorded, formatted capacity is the more meaningful of the two measurements. Where unformatted capacities are cited, they must usually be reduced by 10 to 20 percent, depending on the computer system with which the disks will be utilized. Whether formatted or unformatted, storage capacity measurements are often nominal, meaning that they are approximations of a given disk system's capacity. Thus, a magnetic or optical

disk drive advertised as having 800 megabytes of formatted capacity may actually store 793, 795, or 798 megabytes.

Storage capacities of magnetic and optical disks vary principally with platter sizes and recording densities, the latter being strongly influenced by the recording technology employed by a particular disk drive. With their greater surface areas, large platters can usually store more data than smaller ones. Areal density measurements, however, facilitate the comparison of disks of different sizes. For a given magnetic or optical disk, areal recording density is computed by the formula:

$$AD = LD \times TD$$

where:

AD = the areal recording density in bits per square inch of recording surface;

LD = the linear recording density in bits per inch within a given track; and

TD = the track density in tracks per inch.

In most cases, linear recording densities are fixed, successive bits being more closely spaced within a given disk's innermost tracks which have smaller circumferences than tracks near the disk's outer edges. Areal recording densities consequently vary from one part of a disk's surface to another. Unless otherwise indicated in product specifications, areal density calculations are typically based on linear densities measured at the innermost tracks.

Since the 1950s, magnetic disk platter sizes have decreased steadily, while technological innovations and improved product designs -- particularly reductions in head-to-disk spacing, read/ write gap dimensions, and the thickness of magnetic coatings -- have significantly enhanced recording densities and storage capacities. A survey of IBM disk drives -- the products that defined the state of the art in magnetic disk storage from the late 1950s through the early 1980s -- illustrates this point.

Historical reviews of IBM disk technology and

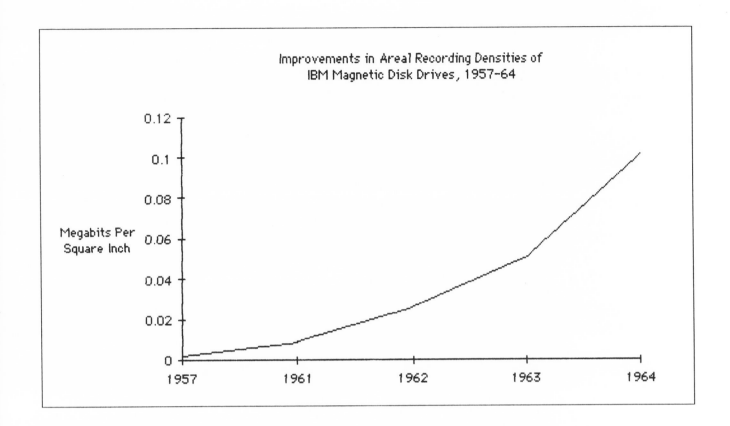

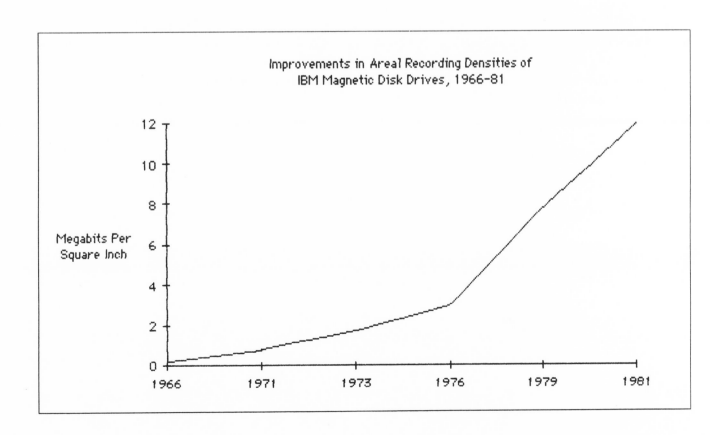

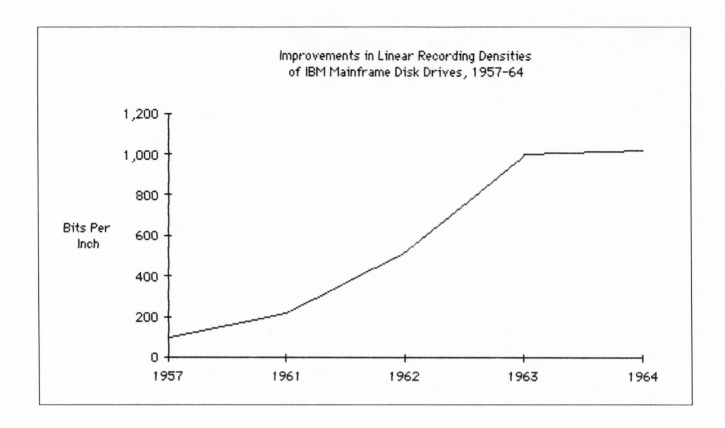

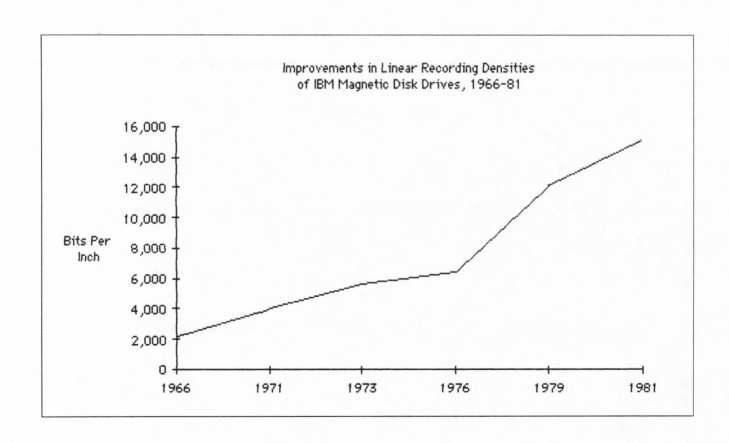

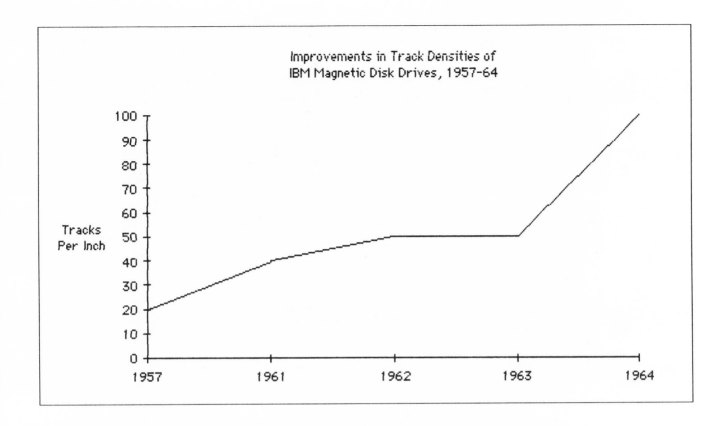

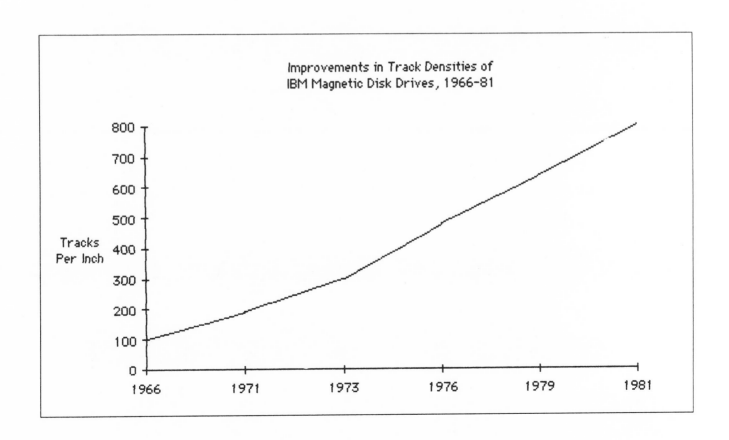

The IBM 1301 disk drive stored data on 100 24-inch platters. (Courtesy: IBM Corporation)

products are provided by Ahearn et al (1972), Mulvany (1974), Bohl (1981), Harker et al (1981), Mulvany and Thompson (1981), and Haas (1988). The accompanying graphs summarize the characteristics of selected IBM magnetic disk drives and depict the steady improvement in areal, linear, and track densities from 1957 through 1981. Announced in 1956 but actually introduced in 1957, the IBM 350 utilized 24-inch platters and stored a total of five megabytes of data on 100 surfaces. With a linear density of 100 bits per inch and a track density of 20 tracks per inch, its areal recording density was 2,000 bits per square inch. The IBM 1405 disk drive, which became commercially available in 1961, utilized the same 100-platter configuration to store 20 megabytes. With a linear density of 220 bits per inch and a track density of 40 tracks per inch, its area recording density was 8,800 bits per inch. Introduced in the following year, the IBM 1301 -- the last of the 24-inch, 100-platter disk systems -- offered 56 megabytes of online storage with an areal recording density of 26,000 bits per inch, based on a linear recording density of 520 bits per inch with 50 tracks per inch.

During the next ten years, linear recording densities supported by IBM disk drives increased eight-fold, while track densities quadrupled and areal densities increased by a factor of 32. The IBM 1311 -- a 14-inch disk system introduced in 1963 -- featured an areal density of 51,250 bits per inch based on a linear recording density of 1,000 bits per inch with 50 tracks per inch. Areal recording density increased to 102,500 bits per square inch -- based on a linear recording density of 1,025 bits per inch and a track density of 100 tracks per inch -- with the introduction of the IBM 2311 in the following year. Two years later, the IBM 2314 -- which utilized removable disk packs -- featured an areal recording density of 220,000 bits per inch, based on a linear recording density of 2,200 bits per inch and a track density of 100 tracks per inch. With 25.9 megabytes per disk pack and nine drives per controller, it offered online access to 233 megabytes of data. The IBM 3330, introduced in 1971 for use with System 370 mainframe computer systems, featured an areal recording density of 775,6800 bits per square inch based on a linear recording density of 4,040 bits per inch with 192 tracks per inch. Widely utilized in

the early 1970s, its popularity spurred the development of various plug-compatible products.

Successive models in the IBM 3300 series offered progressively improved recording densities and online storage capacities. Introduced in 1973, the IBM 3340 -- the first 14-inch drive to utilize Winchester technology -- supported a linear recording density of 5,636

While no longer popular, removable magnetic disk packs were once widely utilized in mainframe and minicomputer installations. (Courtesy: IBM Corporation)

bits per inch and a track density of 300 tracks per inch, yielding an areal recording density of 1.69 million bits per square inch. With 35 megabytes per removable disk pack and four packs per drive, it offered online access to 140 megabytes of data. The IBM 3350, introduced in 1976, supported an areal recording density of 3.07 million bits per square inch, based on a linear recording density of 6,425 bits per inch with 478 tracks per inch. It offered 317.5 megabytes of online storage per drive. The IBM 3370, introduced in 1979, featured thin-film read/write heads and supported an areal recording density of 7.8 million

An IBM 3990, in the foreground, offers storage capacity equivalent to a much larger IBM 3880 configuration in the background. (Courtesy: IBM Corporation)

bits per square inch, based on a linear recording density of 12,134 bits per inch with 635 tracks per inch. At the time this report was prepared, IBM continued to offer one model in the 3370 series. It provides online access to 1.5 GB of data.

The various disk drives in the IBM 3380 product family -- and their plug-compatible equivalents manufactured by Amdahl, Hitachi Data Systems (formerly, National Advanced Systems), StorageTek, Memorex Telex, and others -- have dominated IBM mainframe computer installations throughout the 1980s, and they are likely to remain in use well into the 1990s. Designed for IBM 43xx, 303x, 308x, and 309x processors, the 3380 and plug-compatible disk systems feature 14-inch platters and utilize thin film technology for read/write heads and/or recording surfaces. Several disk drives are usually combined in a configuration termed a storage "string." A typical 3380 equipment configuration includes a storage control unit, one or

two head-of-string disk drives, and one or more additional disk drives. Depending on the controller selected, a 3380 installation can support one or two strings of disk drives, each containing a maximum of four storage units. As discussed below, some 3380-compatible disk systems can significantly increase on-line storage capacity by supporting more than four drives per string and more than two strings per controller.

Introduced in 1981, the first model in the 3380 series featured a single head-disk assembly (HDA) with a storage capacity of 1.26 gigabytes. With a linear recording density of 15,200 bits per inch and a track density of 800 tracks per inch, its areal density exceeded 12 million bits per square inch. Among currently available 3380 products, only the Model CJ2 is configured with a single HDA. The other 3380 models, and their plug-compatible counterparts, feature two head-disk assemblies per drive. They are available in single-density, double-density, and triple-density storage capacities:

1. Single-density drives -- including the IBM 3380 Models D and J, the Amdahl 6380A and 6380J, the StorageTek 8380 and 8380P, and the NAS 7380 Models A and J -- provide 1.26 gigabytes of storage capacity per HDA and 2.52 gigabytes per drive. A string of four single-density drives provides online access to 10.08 gigabytes. A two-string configuration supports 20.16 gigabytes of online storage.

2. Double-density drives -- including the IBM 3380 Model E, the Amdahl 6380E, the NAS 7380 Models E and JX, the StorageTek 8380E, and the Memorex Telex 3682 -- provide 2.52 gigabytes of storage capacity per HDA and 5.04 gigabytes per drive. Compared to the single-density version, the increased storage capacity is achieved by doubling the track density to 1,600 tracks per inch. The resulting areal recording density is 24.3 million bits per square inch. A single string of four double-density drives provides online access to 20.16 gigabytes. A two-string configuration supports 40.32 gigabytes.

3. Triple-density drives -- including the IBM 3380 Model K, the Amdahl 6380K, the NAS 7380 Model K, and the StorageTek 8380F -- provide 3.78 gigabytes of storage capacity per HDA and 7.56 gigabytes per drive. Compared to their single-density counterparts, the increased storage capacity is achieved by tripling the track density to 2,400 tracks per inch. The resulting areal recording density is 36.5 million bits per square inch. A single string of four triple-density drives provides online access to 30.24 gigabytes. A two string configuration supports 60.48 gigabytes. As noted above, several plug-compatible vendors have introduced controllers that can support larger drive configurations. As an example, the Amdahl 6100 Storage Processor can support up to 32 storage units.

2.5-inch fixed magnetic drives, shown here with 3.5-inch diskettes, provide very compact storage in laptop computer configurations. (Courtesy: PrairieTek Corporation)

When configured with triple-density disk drives, it provides online access to 241.92 gigabytes.

Similar high-capacity disk drives are available for non-IBM mainframes. The various MSU series disk drives designed for use with Honeywell Bull DPS 90, 8000, and 9000 computers, for example, provide 1.1 to 3.3 gigabytes of online storage capacity. The Unisys 9494 disk systems offer up to 1.7 gigabytes of formatted storage capacity per drive. They are intended for Unisys V Series computer installations. NCR offers the 6099 Series disk drive for use with its 8800 and 9800 mainframes. Depending on the model selected, it can store up to 1.6 gigabytes per drive.

Ibis Systems offers several high-capacity magnetic disk drives for supercomputer, mainframe, and large minicomputer installations. Employing thin film technology and 14-inch platters, the Ibis Model 1012 provides 1.01 gigabytes of unformatted storage. Utilizing three disks and five data surfaces, it features an areal recording density of 26.18 million bits per square inch, based on a linear recording density of 32,000 bits per inch with 818 tracks per inch. The Model 2812 offers 2.83 gigabytes of unformatted storage on nine disks and 16 surfaces.

Like their mainframe counterparts, minicomputer manufacturers have long offered 14-inch fixed magnetic disk drives for use in large installations. Digital Equipment Corporation's RA82, for example, offers 855 megabytes of unformatted storage capacity (622 megabytes formatted) on eight recording surfaces. Designed for VAX installations, its areal recording density is 13.34 million bits per square inch, based on 12,545 bits per inch with 1,063 tracks per inch. Increasingly, however, computer and peripheral equipment manufacturers view 14-inch magnetic disk drives as older technology to be replaced by smaller but denser devices. IBM itself selected 10.8-inch media for the 3390 disk drive, the company's newest and highest-capacity direct access storage device for mainframe computer installations. Introduced in late 1989, the IBM 3390 is available in single- and double-density configurations. The single-density Model 1 stores 1.89 gigabytes per head/disk assembly. Model 1 units are available with two, four, or six head/disk assemblies that offer approximate online recording and storage capacities of 3.8, 7.6, or 11.4 gigabytes, respectively.

The double-density Model 2 stores 3.78 gigabytes per head/disk assembly. At approximately 61 million bits per square inch, its areal recording density is the highest of any magnetic disk drive that was commercially available at the time this report was prepared. Model 2 units are available with two, four, or six head/disk assemblies that offer approximate online recording and storage capacities of 7.6, 15.1, or 22.7 gigabytes, respectively. When configured with an IBM 3990 controller, two multi-drive strings of Model 1 and Model 2 units can provide up to 120 gigabytes of online recording and storage capacity.

IBM employs nine-inch drives in its AS/400 minicomputer configurations. Among other minicomputer manufacturers, Data General -- which offered 14-inch drives with storage capacities of 592 and 862 megabytes -- has discontinued development of 14-inch products in favor of eight-inch drives with 700 megabytes to more than one gigabyte of storage capacity. Introduced in late 1989, the company's Model 6621 disk system offers 1.2 gigabytes of storage capacity and can be configured in a storage array totalling 9.6 gigabytes.

Reflecting the state-of-the-art in nine-inch magnetic disk technology, the Hitachi DK816 offers two gigabytes of unformatted storage capacity. Featuring metal oxide recording media and thin film read/write heads, its areal recording density is 44.6 million bits per square inch, based on a linear density of 35,470 bits per inch with 1,256 tracks per inch. Tomono and Nishida (1987) and Naruse and Nakagoshi (1988) discuss its most important characteristics, emphasizing the advantages of compactness and lower energy consumption when compared to 14-inch magnetic disk drives. For VAX installations, Digital Equipment Corporation's RA90 drive -- described by Crane (1989) and Sidman (1989) -- employs nine-inch platters and offers 1.6 gigabytes of unformatted storage capacity (1.2 gigabytes formatted) on 13 surfaces. Utilizing thin film technology for both media and read/write heads, its areal recording density is 39.97 million bits per square inch, based on a linear density of 22,839 bits per inch with 1,750 tracks per inch. Sabre Series disk drives -- manufactured by Imprimis Technology, a subsidiary of Control Data Corporation -- are compatible with various mainframes and larger minicomputers. Utilizing eight-inch platters, three of the Sabre models can store more than one gigabyte of data. The Sabre 1230, for example, offers an unformatted storage capacity of 1.236 gigabytes utilizing nine disks and 15 recording surfaces.

Reflecting the trend toward smaller form factors and more compactly designed equipment, the newest 5.25-inch magnetic disk drives offer impressive areal recording densities and storage capacities that approach or exceed those of larger platters. While citing the advantages of eight-inch drives in minicomputer, McMahon (1988) concedes that 5.25-inch Winchester drives can prove less expensive than eight-inch models in many situations. Employing thin film technology for media and/or read/write heads, several manufacturers have developed gigabyte-level 5.25-inch magnetic disk drives. As discussed by Davies (1986), Voelker (1987) and others, these products provide a 200-fold increase in capacity when compared to the earliest Winchester models. The highest capacity 5.25-inch magnetic disk drives typically employ run-length limited (RLL) coding schemes to increase platter capacities when compared to drives that utilize modified frequency modulation (MFM) techniques. RLL coding concepts are discussed by Yencharis (1981), Adler et al (1985, 1985a), Siegel (1986), Ashley and Siegel (1987), Lin and Wolf (1988), and Howell (1989). Siegel (1985) compares coding schemes utilized in optical and magnetic disk recording.

Among the newest 5.25-inch drives available at the time this report was prepared, Maxtor Corporation's Panther product line offers unformatted storage capacities up to 1.7 gigabytes with linear recording densities exceeding 52,000 bits per inch. The Wren VII, a 5.25-inch disk drive from Imprimis Technology, provides an unformatted storage capacity of 1.2 gigabytes. The Micropolis 1510 offers similar recording capacity. Given the rapid development of this product group, Dodge (1988) and Patterson et al (1988) suggest that arrays of high-capacity 5.25-inch disk drives offer a viable alternative to larger disk systems in mainframe and large minicomputer installations.

For small-to-mid-size minicomputer installations, 5.25-inch magnetic disk drives offer storage capacities that range from 150 to 800 megabytes, with nominal capacities of 200, 400, and 800 megabytes being wide-ly encountered. In the highest capacity group, for example, the Maxtor XT-8000 Series supports an areal density of 43.5 million bits per square inch, based on a linear recording density of 31,596 bits per inch with 1,376 tracks inch. Utilizing eight disks and 15 recording surfaces, the largest model in the XT-8000 Series provides 769 megabytes of unformatted storage capacity. A five-disk model offers 410 megabytes of unformatted capacity on eight recording surfaces. Among other high-density 5.25-inch magnetic disk drives, the Toshiba MK-358FA provides 765 megabytes of unformatted storage capacity on 15 recording surfaces. Its areal recording density is 42.83 million bits per square inch, based on a linear recording density of 32,200 bits per inch with 1,330 tracks per inch. 5.25-inch products with similar capacities include the Priam 676 and 776, Hitachi DK515-78, and Hewlett-Packard 97540.

Since the mid-1980s, rigid magnetic disk systems have virtually replaced floppy disk drives as the principal data storage peripherals in business-oriented personal computer and desktop workstation installations. While the earliest microcomputer-based hard disk drives offered as little as five megabytes of online storage, capacities of currently available products range from 20 megabytes to several hundred megabytes. Hard disk drives with online capacities of 60 to 80 megabytes are now commonplace in desktop microcomputer configurations, while 160- and 340-megabyte models are increasingly utilized as file server components in local area network installations. More compact 20- and 40-megabyte models remain popular in laptop computers where one-inch installation slots limit the number of platters that a given drive can contain.

Invariably employing Winchester technology, microcomputer-based fixed magnetic disk drives typically utilize 5.25- or 3.5-inch platters. At the time this report was prepared, 5.25-inch systems were the most common, but 3.5-inch drives may eventually supplant them. Even smaller products -- designed initially for laptop computers -- should play an increasingly important role in the 1990s. Pearce et al (1988), for example, describe a 2.5-inch fixed magnetic disk drive developed by Domain Technology. Several companies -- including PrairieTek Corporation, Areal Technology, and JVC Information Products -- have recently introduced 2.5-inch magnetic disk drives with 20 to 40 megabytes of storage capacity. Higher-capacity models are expected in the near future.

Regardless of media size, areal recording densities supported by microcomputer-based fixed magnetic disk drives range from less than 10 million to more than 50 million bits per square inch. A typical 20-megabyte, 5.25-inch fixed magnetic disk drive, like the Ricoh RH5260, supports an areal density of 13.3 million bits per square inch, based on a linear recording density of 10,894 bits per inch with 1,222 tracks per inch. Some high-capacity models support areal densities that are comparable to their lower-capacity counterparts, but they increase the number of recording surfaces. This is the case, for example, with the 190-megabyte Maxtor XT-2190 which records data on 15 surfaces at an areal density of 11.2 million bits per square inch, based on a linear recording density of 10,470 bits per inch with 1,070 tracks per inch. Other

models achieve high capacity through increased areal density. The Maxtor XT-4170, for example, stores approximately 180 megabytes on seven surfaces at an areal density of 22.5 million bits per square inch, based on a linear recording density of 21,064 bits per inch with 1,070 tracks per inch. Similarly, the Toshiba MK-355FA offers 459 megabytes of unformtted storage capacity on nine 5.25-inch recording surfaces. Its areal density is 42.8 million bits per square inch, based on a linear recording density of 26,229 bits per inch with 1,330 tracks per inch. As noted above, the Toshiba MK-358FA employs the same density to offer 765 megabytes of unformatted storage capacity on 15 recording surfaces.

With their small form factors, 3.5-inch fixed magnetic disk drives permit compact equipment design. Obviously well suited to laptop systems, they also address the microcomputer purchaser's increasingly strong preference for desktop devices with small footprints. At the time this report was prepared, 3.5-inch

A dual-drive Bernoulli Box II configuration provides online access to 88 megabytes of data. (Courtesy: Iomega Corporation)

fixed magnetic disk drives were available in storage configurations ranging from 20 megabytes to over 200 megabytes, although higher capacity models are expected in the early 1990s. Among low-capacity models, the Rodime 3058A can store 45 megabytes of data at an areal density of 32.9 million bits per square inch, based on a linear recording density of 23,875 bits per inch with 1,380 tracks per inch. Representative of higher-capacity 3.5-inch products, the Maxtor LXT-200 can store 207 megabytes and supports an areal recording density of 43.6 million bits per square inch, based on a linear recording density of 27,370 bits per inch and a track density of 1,591 tracks per inch. Other 200-megabyte, 3.5-inch magnetic disk drives include the Rodime RO3259A, the Hitachi DK312C, and the CP-3200 from Connor Peripherals.

While their overall storage capacities are constrained by relatively small surface areas, 2.5-inch fixed magnetic disk drives feature high recording densities. The Prairie 220 from PrairieTek Corporation, for example, supports an areal recording density of 25.9 million bits per square inch, based on a linear density of 22,500 bits per inch with 1,150 tracks per inch. Offering 20 megabytes of online storage capacity, it is configured with two platters and four recording surfaces. Announced in late 1989, the 40-megabyte Prairie 240 supports an areal recording density of 51.9 million bits per square inch, based on a linear density of 38,452 bits per inch with 1,350 tracks per inch. As discussed by Wood et al (1984), magnetic disk drives with such high areal densities were still considered experimental just half a decade ago.

The superior performance and reliability of fixed magnetic disk drives have made them the dominant online storage devices in mainframe, minicomputer, and microcomputer installations. IBM, for example, introduced its last mainframe-based removable disk drive -- the 3340 -- in 1973, and other computer and peripheral equipment manufacturers likewise emphasize fixed disk systems. As a potentially significant constraint, however, fixed disks can become full, ne-

12-inch optical disk drives offer two to 6.6 gigabytes of double-sided recording capacity in a desktop device. (Courtesy: Sony Corporation)

cessitating the purchase of additional drives, the deletion of data, or its transfer to magnetic tape or other media. Addressing this limitation, magnetic disk systems that utilize removable media provide infinite storage capacity with a given hardware configuration, although some data will necessarily be stored offline at any given moment.

As a group, magnetic disk drives that utilize removable media offer significantly lower areal recording densities and online storage capacities than equivalently sized fixed disk systems. The earliest 14-inch magnetic disk cartridges, for example, stored as little as 2.5 megabytes, while higher capacity models encountered in minicomputer installations during the 1970s stored about 16 megabytes. Storage capacities of newer drives that utilize removable disk packs range from 80 megabytes to 300 megabytes. Among available products for minicomputer installations, Digital Equipment Corporation's RA60 supports 205 megabytes of formatted storage capacity on five, 14-inch platters. With a linear density of 9,668 bits per inch and 779 tracks per inch, its areal recording density is a relatively low 7.5 million bits per square inch. By way of comparison, Digital Equipment's RA70, a fixed 5.25-inch magnetic disk drive with 280 megabytes of storage capacity, has an areal recording density is 30.4 million bits per square inch, based on a linear density of 22,437 bits per inch with 1,355 tracks per inch.

Much recent attention has been given to removable magnetic disk systems for microcomputer installations where floppy disks are currently the most widely encountered removable storage media. Floppy disk technology and recording characteristics are discussed by Engh (1981), Zschau (1973), Murphy (1974), Bowers (1977), Rampil (1977), Sollman (1978), Harman (1979), Bate (1980), Nathanson et al (1980), Adachi and Yano (1983), Jarrett (1983), Katoh et al (1983), Krass (1983), Hirshon (1984), Myers (1984), Pingry (1984), White (1984), Tsugawa (1987), Williams (1987), Highland (1988), and Takasaki (1988). Like their rigid counterparts, floppy disk capacities have increased steadily and significantly since the 1970s. The earliest eight-inch diskettes, introduced in 1971, stored just 81.6 kilobytes and supported a linear recording density of just 1,594 bits per inch -- about one-fourth the linear density of hard disk systems available at the

time. Within several years, however, improved head designs and thinner magnetic coatings permitted linear recording densities exceeding 3,000 bits per inch and overall storage capacities approaching 250 kilobytes per recording surface. With a linear recording density of 3,268 bits per inch and 48 tracks per inch, such eight-inch diskettes supported an areal density of just 156,864 bits per square inch. In 1976, IBM introduced a dual-sided floppy disk drive with approximately half a megabyte of storage capacity per eight-inch diskette. A 1.2-megabyte, eight-inch diskette -- with an areal density of 327,312 bits per square inch, based on a linear recording density of 6,816 bits per inch with 48 tracks per inch -- became available in the following year, and such media were widely utilized in minicomputer, microcomputer, and word processing installations through the early 1980s.

Introduced in the late 1970s, 5.25-inch minifloppy disk drives were initially utilized by relatively low performance microcomputer systems -- including the Apple II product line, Commodore PET series, and Atari 400/800 -- many of which were intended for educational or consumer markets rather than business applications. Most employed single-sided media with storage capacities in the 70 kilobyte to 120 kilobyte range. Business-oriented computer and word processing system vendors continued to favor eight-inch media until IBM selected 5.25-inch minifloppy disk drives for its Personal Computer, which was introduced in 1981. The first version of the IBM Personal Computer utilized single-sided 5.25-inch diskettes with just 160 kilobytes of storage capacity, but the introduction of double-sided drives and a slight change in formatting soon increased media capacity to the 360-kilobyte total familiar to MS-DOS users. With 5,900 bits per inch and 96 tracks per inch, such diskettes support an areal recording density of 566,400 bits per square inch. For use with the PC/AT, IBM introduced a high-density 5.25-inch floppy disk drive with 1.2 megabytes of double-sided recording capacity. It supports an areal density of 926,400, based on a linear recording density of 9,640 bits per inch with 96 tracks per inch.

IBM PS/2 series computers and compatible products utilize 3.5-inch microfloppy disk drives that offer 720 kilobytes or 1.44 megabytes of double-sided stor-

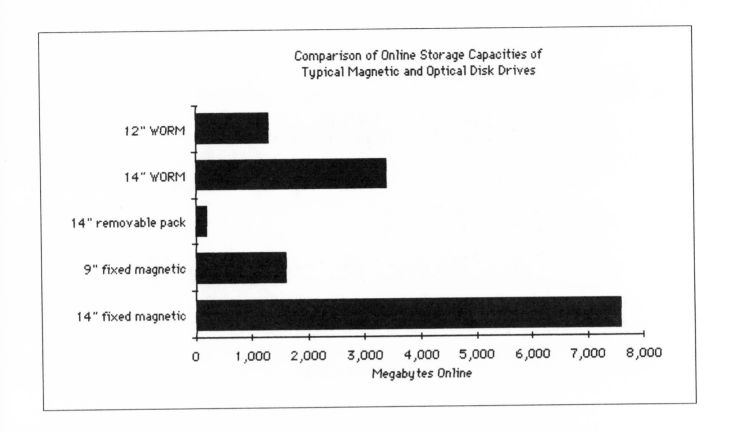

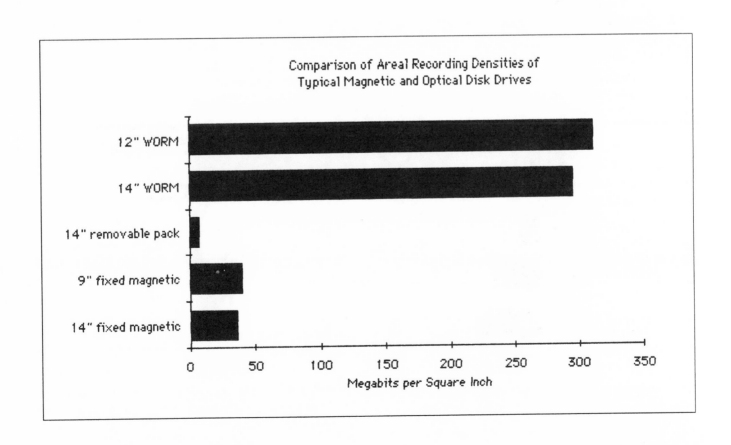

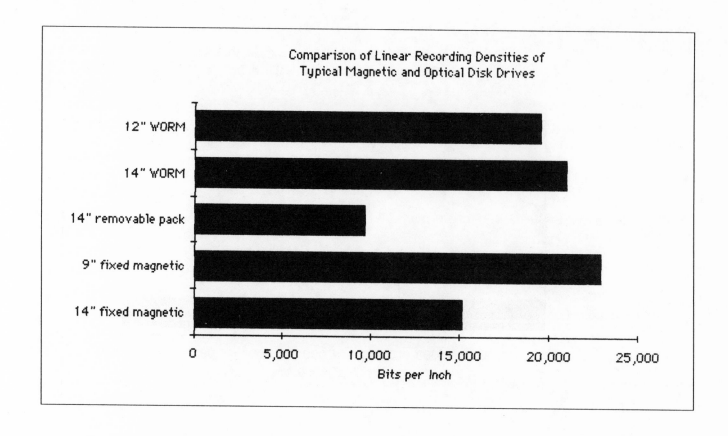

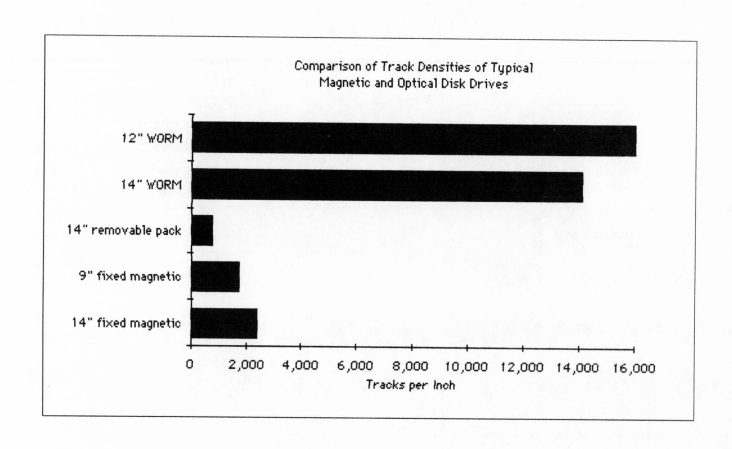

age capacity. With 8,717 bits per inch and 135 tracks per inch, the 720-kilobyte model supports an areal recording density of 1.18 million bits per square inch. By increasing the linear recording density to 17,434 bits per inch, the 1.44-megabyte model supports an areal density of 2.45 million bits per square inch. Macintosh computers can be equipped with 3.5-inch diskette drives that provide double-sided storage capacities of 800 kilobytes or 1.44 megabytes. In 1989, several companies introduced two-inch floppy disk drives intended primarily for use in laptop computer systems. Like the 3.5-inch media they are designed to replace, the earliest models offer a double-sided, formatted storage capacity of 720 kilobytes. The areal recording density is 3.64 million bits per square inch, based on a linear density of 14,340 bits per inch with 254 tracks per inch.

As an alternative to standard hardware in IBM-compatible and/or Macintosh personal computer installations, several companies have introduced floppy disk systems with higher storage capacities. The PRACTIDISK EXD Series from Practical Computer Technology, for example, offers 2.88 megabytes of formatted capacity per double-sided, 3.5-inch diskette. Designed for IBM-compatible computer configurations, it supports an areal recording density of 4.7 million bits per square inch, based on a linear density of 34,868 bits per inch with 135 tracks per inch. As described by Yamamori et al (1983, 1986), Enoki et al (1984), Nakayama et al (1984), Imamura et al (1985, 1986), Ozue et al (1985), Okuwaki et al (1985), Matsuda et al (1986), Killmann and Frohmader (1987), Ozue et al (1987), Wadatani and Harada (1987), Yamada et al (1987), and Tsuya et al (1988), several companies have developed high-capacity 3.5-inch floppy disk drives that employ perpendicular rather than longitudinal recording technologies. As discussed later in this report, such perpendicular magnetic recording systems typically utilize dual-layer media. Maxell, for example, offers high-density diskettes with four and 12 megabytes of recording capacity. Designed for use in drives manufactured by To-

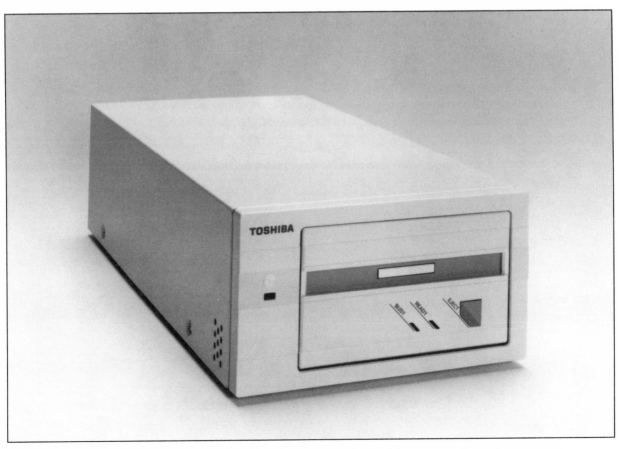

5.25-inch WORM drives are available in external configurations for attachment to various microcomputers or workstations. Internal models are also available. (Courtesy: Toshiba America)

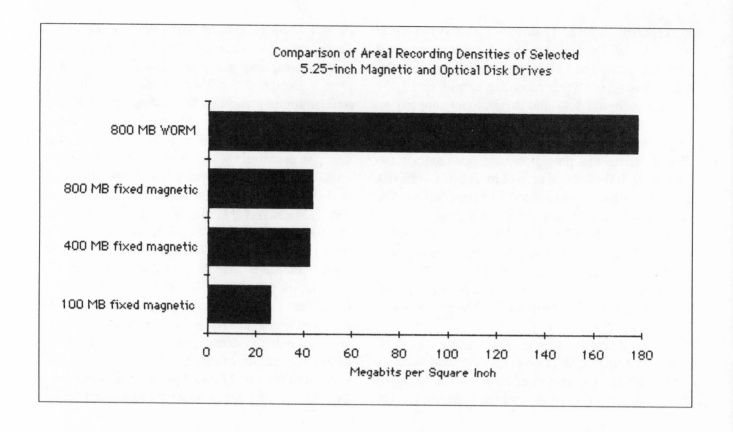

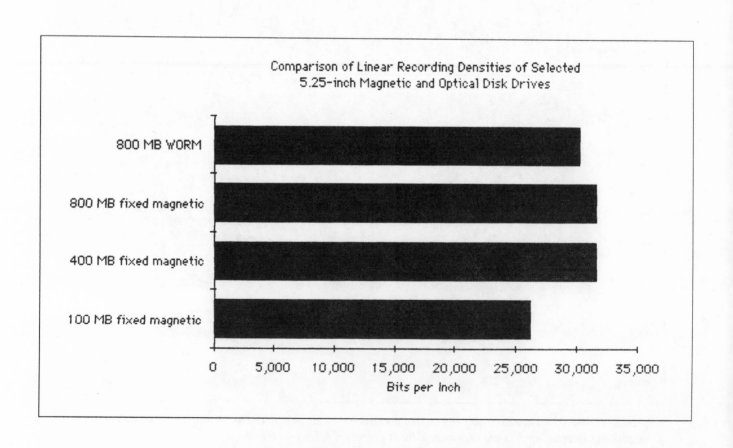

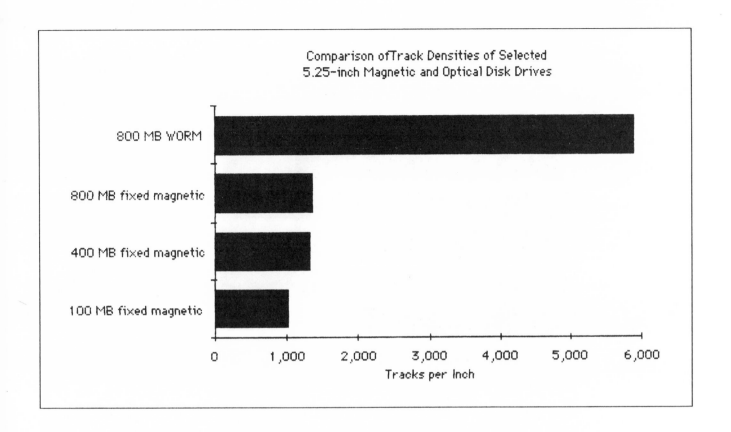

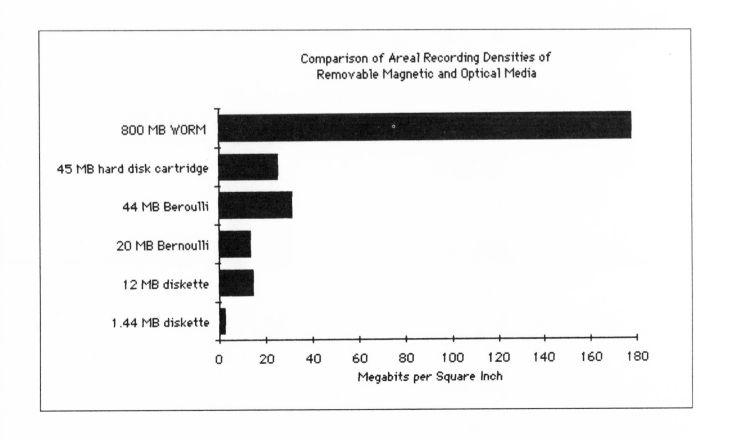

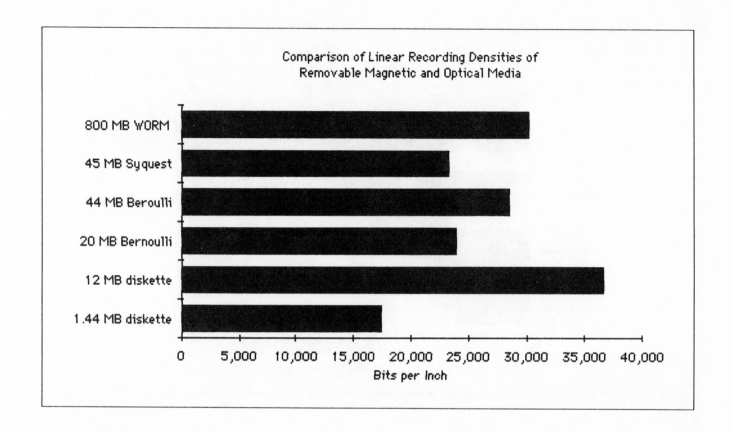

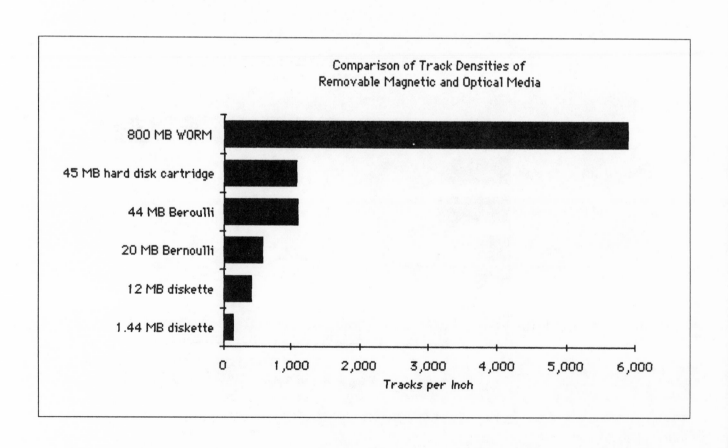

shiba, Teac, Mitsubishi, and others, the four-megabyte diskette supports an areal recording density of 4.73 million bits per square inch, based on a linear density of 35,000 bits per inch with 135 tracks per inch. Its recording surface consists of either barium ferrite or ferric oxide combined with cobalt. The 12-megabyte diskette is intended for use in drives manufactured by NEC and Y.E. Data. It features a metallic powder coating and supports an areal recording density of 14.9 million bits per square inch, based on a linear density of 36,700 bits per inch with 406 tracks per inch. NEC has also demonstrated prototype versions of a 50-megabyte floppy disk drive that utilizes 3.5-inch media composed of a very thin recording film. Among U.S. manufacturers, Brier Technology has developed a 3.5-inch floppy disk drive which employs dual layer media that stores high-frequency data signals in the top layer and low-frequency control signals in the bot-

tom layer. Its areal density is 20.2 million bits per square inch, based on a linear recording density of 26,000 bits per inch and a track density of 777 tracks per inch.

Perhaps the best known of high-capacity floppy disk drives, the Bernoulli Box, takes its name from a fluid-dynamics theorem formulated by a nineteenth century Swiss physicist. Within a Bernoulli drive, spinning motion creates air pressure that lifts a flexible magnetic storage medium toward read/write heads. The technology has been described by Cope et al (1977), Perrone (1985), Radman and Cornaby (1985) and Yasuda and Kaneko (1985). Available in eight-inch and 5.25-inch diameters, Bernoulli disks are encapsulated in a protective plastic cartridge. Designed for Macintosh and IBM-compatible microcomputer installations, Bernoulli drives are manufactured by Iomega Corporation and sold, under private labels, by various

All erasable optical disk drives available at the time this report was prepared utilized magneto-optical cartridges. (Courtesy: Ricoh)

companies. The original eight-inch model, which remains commercially available and widely utilized, can store 10 or 20 megabytes per disk. The 10-megabyte model supports an areal recording density of 7.2 million bits per square inch, based on a linear density of 24,000 bits per inch with 300 tracks per inch. The 20-megabyte model supports an areal recording density of 15.3 million bits per square inch, based on a linear density of 24,000 bits per inch with 639 tracks per inch.   When first introduced, 5.25-inch Bernoulli drives were limited to just five megabytes per cartridge, but newer models offer 20 or 44 megabytes of

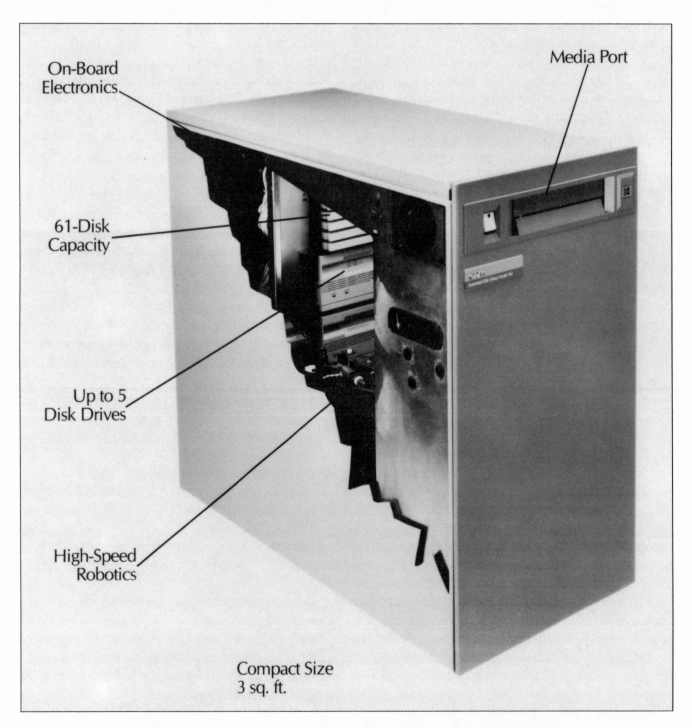

An optical disk jukebox, shown here in a cutaway view, can provide unattended access to gigabytes of data. (Courtesy: Eastman Kodak)

online storage. The 20-megabyte version supports an areal density of 13.4 million bits per square inch with a linear recording density of 24,000 bits per inch and a track density of 570 tracks per inch. The 44-megabyte model supports an areal density of 31.3 million bits per square inch with a linear density of 28,500 bits per inch and a track density of 1,096 tracks per inch.

Other vendors offering removable flexible disk systems with similar storage capacities include Verbatim, Qume, and Peripheral Land. The Verbatim drives, for example, can store 12 or 24 megabytes per 5.25-inch cartridge. Like the Bernoulli Box, they are available from various systems integrators and value-added resellers for IBM-compatible and Macintosh personal computers. Insite Peripherals has announced a high capacity, 3.5-inch floppy disk drive that uses optically-encoded control information to greatly increase the track density. Termed a "floptical" disk drive, its head carriage includes both a magnetic read/write head and an optical sensor, the latter adapted from devices employed in CD-ROM drives. As described by Phillips (1988) and Williams and Adkisson (1989), the floptical recording medium is a preformatted diskette with a storage capacity of 20.8 megabytes. Its areal density is 30.2 million bits per square inch, based on a linear recording density of 24,145 bits per inch with 1,250 tracks per inch.

Where higher storage capacity is desired, several vendors offer removable magnetic disks with rigid media encapsulated in a protective plastic shell. As noted above, the best known of such hard disk cartridge systems is the SyQuest SQ555 which is sold under various names by many vendors. Available for IBM-compatible and Macintosh microcomputers, it offers approximagely 44 megabytes of formatted storage capacity per 5.25-inch cartridge. The areal recording density is 25.3 million bits per square inch, based on a linear density of 23,316 bits per inch with 1,086 tracks per inch. Removable Winchester-type drives -- which combine recording media and read/write components in a removable module -- are available in storage capacities of 20 to 200 megabytes. The most commonly encountered models store less than 45 megabytes per cartridge. Their recording densities are comparable to those of fixed Winchester-type drives of equivalent capacity.

Like the magnetic media described above, optical disks are encapsulated in removable plastic cartridges. As their most distinctive characteristic, write-once and erasable optical disk systems offer much greater areal densities and storage capacities than equivalently-sized magnetic platters. As previously described, areal recording densities supported by magnetic disk systems currently peak at slightly more than 60 million bits per square inch. Optical disk systems routinely offer areal densities exceeding 150 million bits per square inch, and some products support densities that exceed 400 million bits per square inch. It is important to note, however, that the impressive storage capacities cited in manufacturers' product literature are typically based on double-sided media, although only one side of an optical disk cartridge is accessible at any given moment. Such cartridges must be ejected and turned over to access data recorded on their opposite sides. For a fair comparison with magnetic disk systems, the following discussion is consequently based on single-sided storage capacities.

Like their magnetic counterparts, 14-inch optical disks are designed for high-volume data storage in mainframe and large minicomputer installations. At the time this report was prepared, Eastman Kodak was the only manufacturer of such products. Its decision to produce a 14-inch write-once optical disk system was reportedly influenced by the availability of 14-inch aluminum platters which are widely utilized in magnetic disk drives. The Kodak Model 6800 optical disk drive can store 3.4 gigabytes on each side of a double-sided write-once cartridge. At 296 million bits per square inch, the optical disk's areal recording density far exceeds that of 14-inch magnetic disk platters and is attributable to a track density of 14,111 tracks per inch, which is almost seven times greater than track densities supported by the highest-capacity IBM 3380 magnetic disk drives. The Model 6800's linear recording density of 21,000 bits per inch is exceeded by many magnetic disk drives. In late 1989, Eastman Kodak announced its intention to manufacture a second-generation 14-inch, double-sided WORM cartridge capable of storing 4.1 gigabytes per recording surface.

Depending on the model selected, 12-inch optical disk drives can store between one and 3.3 gigabytes on each side of a write-once cartridge. The popular Hitachi OC301 optical disk cartridge, for example, can store 1.3 gigabytes per disk surface. Its areal recording density is 312 million bits per inch, based on a linear density of 19,500 bits per inch with 16,000 tracks per inch. As previously noted, the Hitachi cartridge's substantial storage capacity is largely attributable to its high track density; its linear recording density is exceeded by some low-capacity magnetic disk systems.

Steady improvements in recording capacity have been demonstrated by those manufacturers who have produced two or more generations of 12-inch optical disk drives. As an example, the Optimem 1000 -- a first-generation optical disk drive drive introduced in 1984 -- could store one gigabyte on each side of a 12-inch, write-once cartridge. Still utilized, it supports an areal recording density of 221.85 million bits per inch, based on a linear density of 15,300 bits per inch with 14,500 tracks per inch. With the Optimem 2400, announced in 1987, storage capacity increased to 1.2 gigabytes per recording surface at an areal density of 258.57 million bits per square inch, based on a linear recording density of 15,300 bits per inch with 16,900 tracks per inch. The Optimem 4000, introduced in 1989, can store 1.96 gigabytes per disk surface at an areal density of 373.32 million bits per square inch, based on a linear recording density of 22,090 bits per inch with 16,900 tracks per inch.

Taking its name from its recording capacity, the original Gigadisc 1001 could store one gigabyte per side of a 12-inch WORM cartridge when it was introduced by Alcatel Thomson in 1983. Its successor, introduced by ATG in 1989, can store 3.15 gigabytes per side of a 12-inch WORM cartridge. Among the 12-inch optical storage products of other vendors, Toshiba's DF-0210 write-once optical drive could store just 400 megabytes per recording surface when it was introduced in Japan in 1981. By 1983, its successor, the DF-0300, could store 1.2 gigabytes on each side of a 12-inch WORM cartridge. The DF-0450, introduced in 1984, increased the storage capacity to 1.8 gigabytes per recording surface. The WM-500, the latest addition to Toshiba's 12-inch product line, was initially introduced with two gigabytes of single-sided recording capacity, but an upgrade has since increased the capacity to 2.5 gigabytes per recording surface.

Sony's WDD-3000 and WDD-600 WORM drives offers a choice of recording formats, giving the user the option of sacrificing performance to increase storage capacity. In the constant angular velocity (CAV) mode, the WDD-3000 can store 1.05 gigabytes on each side of a 12-inch write-once optical disk cartridge. In the constant linear velocity (CLV) mode, it can store 1.6 gigabytes per recording surface. With their variable rotation speeds, however, CLV-format disks suffer slow access times, as discussed later in this report. Introduced in late 1989, Sony's WDD-600 drive can store 3.275 gigabytes per recording surface in the CLV mode. At the time this report was prepared, it offered the highest storage capacity of any 12-inch optical disk system. In the CAV format, the WDD-600 can store 2.1 gigabytes per recording surface.

At the time this report was prepared, only one manufacturer -- Pioneer -- offered an eight-inch optical disk system for sale in the United States. It can store 750 megabytes per recording surface. Eight-inch disks with similar capacities have been available in Japan from other vendors.

Like their 12-inch counterparts, storage capacities of 5.25-inch write-once optical disk drives have increased steadily and significantly since the mid-1980s. The ISI 525WC, announced in 1985, offered 115 megabytes of single-sided storage capacity, while the Optotech 5984 could store 202 megabytes per recording surface. Both models were initially introduced with single-sided media, but double-sided cartridges soon became available. Since 1987, Hitachi, Fujitsu, Laser Magnetic Storage International, Mitsubishi, and other manufacturers have introduced write-once optical disk drives based on the ISO standard for 5.25-inch optical disk cartridges. Employing ablative recording of tellurium-based thin films, such ISO-compatible systems can store 300 to 328 megabytes on each side of a 5.25-inch write-once cartridge, depending on the specific recording format utilized. In the 300-megabyte capacity, the areal recording density is approximately 403 million bits per square inch, based on a linear density of 25,400 bits per inch with 15,875 tracks per inch.

Among non-standard 5.25-inch optical disk drives, the Panasonic LF-5010 can store 470 megabytes per recording surface. Its predecessor, the LF-5000, was limited to just 200 megabytes per single-sided cartridge. Utilizing dye-based recording technology, the Pioneer DD-S5001 can store 327 megabytes per recording surface. The Maxtor RXT-800 offers 400 megabytes of single-sided storage capacity. With 30,200 bits per linear inch and 5,900 tracks per inch, its areal recording density is 178 million bits per square inch. Introduced in 1988, the ISI 525GB can store 640 megabytes on each side of a 5.25-inch optical disk cartridge. Like the Sony WDD-3000 drive discussed above, the Toshiba WM-D070 offers a choice of recording modes. When the ISO-compatible CAV format is selected, it can store 300 megabytes per 5.25-inch recording surface. When Toshiba's proprietary Modified CAV (MCAV) format is utilized, the WM-D070 can store 450 megabytes per recording surface, but access time will be degraded.

Erasable optical disk drives offer storage capacities similar to certain comparably-sized write-once products without sacrificing the rewritability that magnetic disk users have come to expect. Conforming to ISO standards for 5.25-inch magneto-optical media, the erasable optical disks utilized by the Sony SMO-D501, Ricoh RO-5030E, and Hitachi OD112-1 drives can store 298 or 325 megabytes per side, depending on the sector capacity selected. With approximately 24,000 bits per linear inch and 16,000 tracks per inch, their areal recording density is 384 million bits per square inch. When operating in the ISO-compatible mode, Maxtor's Tahiti drive can likewise store 298 or 325 megabytes per recording surface. The Tahiti drive also supports a proprietary Zoned CAV (ZCAV) mode that can store 466 or 512 megabytes per recording surface. In that mode, its areal recording density is 423 million bits per square inch, based on a linear density of 25,000 bits per inch with 16,933 tracks per inch.

Among lower capacity magneto-optical products, Canon offers a drive that can store 256 megabytes per single-sided, 5.25-inch cartridge. Verbatim, which introduced two 5.25-inch magneto-optical systems in late 1989, has demonstrated a 3.5-inch magneto-optical disk drive in various prototype versions since the mid-1980s. Capable of storing 60 megabytes per single-sided cartridge, it was not commercially available at the time this report was prepared. Maxtor has suspended development of a 3.5-inch erasable optical disk drive with 160 megabytes of single-sided recording capacity, but other manufacturers are reportedly developing similar products.

As discussed above, magnetic disk controllers designed for mainframe and minicomputer installations commonly support multiple drives, thereby providing online access to gigabytes of data. Many write-once and erasable optical disk systems are equipped with SCSI or other controllers that can support four or eight drives. Depending on the devices employed, a four-drive, 12-inch, write-once optical disk configuration can provide online access to over 12 gigabytes of data. When high-density products are utilized, such multi-drive optical disk configurations offer online capacity equivalent to one string of single-density IBM 3380 magnetic disk drives. In microcomputer installations, multi-drive optical disk configurations offer online capacity comparable to that of magnetic disk storage arrays. Several manufacturers of 5.25-inch optical disk systems offer preconfigured dual-drive configurations that provide online access to as much as 1.28 gigabytes of data. Their storage capacities exceed those of comparably configured magnetic disk devices, such as dual-drive Bernoulli Box II systems which provide online access to 88 megabytes.

Where greater online recording and storage capacity is desired, optical disk autochangers -- popularly described as "jukeboxes" -- can access hundreds of gigabytes of data without manual intervention. Since the demise of the IBM 3850 Mass Storage System described by Harris et al (1975), Johnson (1975), Muller-Raab (1977), and Russell (1987), no comparable direct access device has been available for magnetic disk storage. As described by Ammon and Siryj (1983), Bonini (1985), Miyazaki and Nishi (1985), Altman et al (1986), Zellinger (1987), Trapp (1988), Yochum (1988), and Schewe (1989), a typical jukebox unit includes one or more optical disk drives, a collection of optical disk cartridges arranged in stacks or bins, a microprocessor which receives instructions from an external computer, and a robotic retrieval mechanism that responds to the received instructions by extracting a specified cartridge and mounting in a drive. Specific data storage implementations are described by Donsbach (1988) and Thompson et al

(1988).

Jukebox capacities range from approximately 30 gigabytes for tabletop models utilizing 5.25-inch media to more than one terabyte for floor-standing units configured with 14-inch cartridges. As its name suggests, FileNet's OSAR 64, one of the most widely encountered jukebox units, can store 64 optical disk cartridges, providing online access to 166.4 gigabytes of data. Other FileNet jukeboxes can store as many as 288 optical disk cartridges and provide online access to up to almost 750 gigabytes of data. Modular in design and construction, jukeboxes manufactured by Cygnet Systems vary with the type and number of optical disk drives employed. When configured with one Optimem 2400 drive, for example, the Cygnet 1800 Series Expandable Jukebox can store 141 optical disk cartridges for an approximate online capacity of 340 gigabytes. Designed for 5.25-inch optical disk cartridges, the Cygnet 5000 Series offers up to 36 gigabytes of online storage capacity. At the time this report was prepared, jukeboxes for erasable optical disk cartridges provided online access to more than 20 gigabytes of data.

As corporations, government agencies, and other organizations expand the range of computer applications and generate ever greater quantities of machine-readable data, the value of high-capacity storage peripherals is increasingly apparent. As the foregoing discussion indicates, optical disks support much greater areal recording densities than fixed or removable magnetic disk systems. While certain magnetic disk systems -- triple-density IBM 3380 drives and double-density IBM 3390 drives, for example -- offer greater online storage capacity than optical disk drives, they obtain that capacity through multi-platter media and multiple head/ disk assemblies. Optical disks currently provide much greater storage capacity per recording surface than any magnetic media. This capacity advantage makes optical disk drives a potentially attractive alternative to magnetic disk systems in text storage and retrieval systems, electronic document imaging, and other storage-intensive applications that involve voluminous amounts of computer-processible information.

Broadly defined, text storage and retrieval systems -- variously called full text retrieval systems or text information management systems -- are computer programs that store the complete contents of books, reports, business correspondence, memoranda, policy statements, and other textual documents in machine-readable, character-coded form for retrieval or other processing. The character-coded text may be produced by word processing programs, converted from human-readable information by optical character recognition devices, derived from computerized typesetting systems, or generated by other methodologies. Regardless of the information's source, text storage and retrieval programs create indexes to every significant word in stored documents. The indexes permit the rapid identification and retrieval of text segments containing specified character strings. Retrieved text segments, or the complete documents which contain them, can be displayed or printed to satisfy specified user requirements. Introduced in the 1960s, text storage and retrieval programs are currently available for computers of all types and sizes. Saffady (1989) surveys the technology, discusses the published literature dealing with text storage and retrieval methodologies, and describes typical products.

Because each alphanumeric character, punctuation mark, or other symbol in textual documents occupies one byte of storage, disk capacity requirements will vary with the typographic characteristics of the documents to be stored and with the indexing methodology employed by a given text storage and retrieval program. A letter-size, double-spaced typewritten page, for example, contains about 1,700 characters, assuming a page format of 25 lines with 68 characters per line, including embedded spaces and carriage returns. Most text storage and retrieval programs employ inverted index structures which consist of alphabetical lists of index terms accompanied by pointers to their document locations. Typically, disk storage requirements must be increased by a factor of 2.5 to accommodate such inverted indexes, working files, and other overhead data. For double-spaced, typewritten, letter-size documents, the actual storage requirement is approximately 4,250 bytes per page, and one megabyte of disk space can store 235 double-spaced, typewritten pages.

Text storage and retrieval programs are increasingly available for microcomputer implementations, but the most commonly utilized microcomputer-based magnetic disk drives cannot accommodate large document collections. As an example, an 80-megabyte fixed magnetic disk drive, a typical medium-capacity device that is widely encountered in microcomputer installations, can store the character-coded contents of approximately 19,000 double-spaced, typewritten pages -- the equivalent of just two four-drawer, vertical-style filing cabinets -- assuming that the entire drive is available for text storage. With their unlimited storage capacities, drives that employ removable media are better suited to such applications. A 1.44-megabyte floppy disk, however, can only store 340 double-spaced, typewritten pages, and 30 disks would be required to accommodate the contents of a single vertical-style filing cabinet. Among higher-capacity magnetic storage products, a 20-megabyte Bernoulli cartridge can store less than 5,000 double-spaced, typewritten pages -- the approximate contents of two file drawers -- while a 42-megabyte SyQuest cartridge or a

letter-size filing cabinets. The highest capacity, 5.25-inch WORM cartridges can store over a quarter of a million double-spaced, typewritten pages. Depending on the configuration selected, jukebox retrieval units for 5.25-inch optical disks can provide unattended access to more than eight million pages.

With their higher storage capacities, fixed magnetic disk drives intended for minicomputer and mainframe installations can accommodate much larger document collections than their microcomputer counterparts. For double-spaced, typewritten documents of the type described above, an 800-megabyte drive, such as the Maxtor XT-8000, can store the character-coded contents of approximately 190,000 pages -- the equivalent of 19 filing cabinets. A number of text storage and retrieval programs are available in VAX implementations, and, with 1.6 gigabytes of storage capacity, Digital Equipment Corporation's RA90

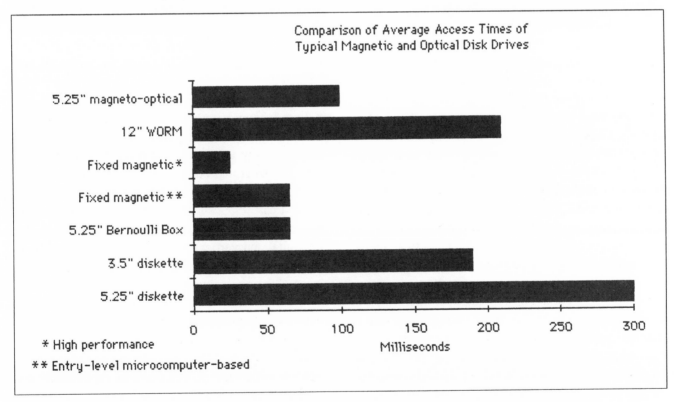

Comparison of Average Access Times of Typical Magnetic and Optical Disk Drives

* High performance
** Entry-level microcomputer-based

44-megabyte Bernoulli cartridge can store approximately 10,000 such pages, the equivalent of four file drawers. A 600-megabyte, 5.25-inch write-once optical disk cartridge, on the other hand, can store the character-coded text of over 140,000 double-spaced, typewritten pages -- the equivalent of 14 vertical-style,

magnetic disk drive can accommodate almost 380,000 pages, but prospective text storage and retrieval applications can involve several or many times that number of pages. To accommodate such voluminous applications, 12-inch WORM cartridges can store the character-coded contents of 450,000 to 1.3 million double-spaced, typewritten pages. A typical jukebox installation, configured with 64 WORM cartridges capable of storing 2.6-gigabytes each, can provide unattended access to almost 40 million double-spaced, typewritten pages. Higher-capacity jukeboxes can provide unattended access to more than four times that total.

Among the highest-capacity mainframe-based magnetic disk drives, triple-density IBM 3380 and compatible models can store the character-coded contents of 1.7 million double-spaced, typewritten pages, and an eight-drive string can provide online access to over 13 million pages. With approximately 1.6 million pages of storage capacity per double-sided cartridge, however, 14-inch WORM disks are equally well-suited to the highest volume applications, and a 14-inch WORM jukebox unit can provide unattended access to approximately 235 million pages -- the equivalent of 23,500 vertical-style, letter-size filing cabinets.

With their high capacities, optical disks are currently the computer storage media of choice in electronic document imaging applications. As their name suggests, electronic document imaging systems convert paper documents to digitized images suitable for computer storage. The digitized images -- in effect, electronic pictures of documents -- are generated by a scanner which divides documents into a series of closely spaced horizontal lines, each of which is subdivided into small scannable units called picture elements or pixels. The scanner measures the amount of light reflected by successively encountered pixels and transmits a corresponding electrical signal to an image processing unit which converts the signal to digital codes. In the most common implementations, documents are divided into 200 scan lines per inch with 200 pixels in each inch of scan line. Pixels which reflect light in excess of some specified amount are considered white and are encoded as either a one or a zero bit. Where the amount of reflected light is lower than the predetermined threshold amount, the scanned pixels are considered black and are represented by the opposite bit value. More complicated digitization systems can encode grey tonal values or color information by utilizing multiple bits to represent individual pixels.

Electronic document imaging systems are storage-intensive. Although data compression algorithms are

typically utilized to minimize storage requirements, a digitized image of a single letter-size page scanned at 200 pixels per horizontal and vertical inch will occupy approximately 47 kilobytes of disk space. Images of large documents and/or those generated at higher scanning resolutions will require significantly more storage space. If the scanning depth is increased to 300 pixels per horizontal and vertical inch, for example, a document image produced from a letter-size page will require over 105 kilobytes of storage. As a result, magnetic disk capacities that are appropriate for character-coded text and data files can easily be overwhelmed by image storage applications. An 80-megabyte fixed magnetic disk drive, for instance, can store about 1,700 digitized images of letter size pages, while a 42-megabyte SyQuest cartridge or a 44-megabyte Bernoulli cartridge can store just slightly more than half that amount. While high-capacity mainframe- and minicomputer-based magnetic disk drives can store 30,000 to more than 150,000 pages in digitized form, electronic document imaging applications involving millions of pages are routinely encountered.

With their higher capacities, optical storage media will prove more practical than their magnetic counterparts in such applications. A file of 30,000 pages that would occupy an entire RA90 fixed magnetic disk drive can be stored on three 650-megabyte magneto-optical disk cartridges. A 2.6-gigabyte, twelve-inch WORM cartridge can store over 50,000 digitized images of letter-size pages scanned at 200 pixels per horizontal and vertical inch. A 64-disk jukebox unit can provide unattended access to over 3.2 million pages -- the equivalent of 320 four-drawer, vertical-style filing cabinets. Higher capacity optical disk jukeboxes can provide unattended access to more than 20 million document images.

While optical disks currently enjoy unquestioned capacity advantages in the types of applications described above, reports by Koshimoto et al (1987, 1988), Mitsuya and Takanami (1987), Mitsuya et al (1987), Tachiwada (1987), Thapar and Patel (1987), Sato et al (1988), Feig (1989), and other researchers indicate that magnetic recording technology is still developing. As previously discussed, magnetic disk areal densities and storage capacities increased steadily and significantly since 1957. During the 1980s, the continued refinement of equipment components and recording methodologies increased the areal recording densities of fixed magnetic disk drives by a factor of five, from 12 million bits per square inch to more than 60 million bits per square inch. During the same period, areal recording densities of removable magnetic disks also increased by a factor of five, while storage capacities of flexible magnetic media increased by a factor of 275 when the 160-kilobyte, single-sided diskettes utilized by the original IBM Personal Computer are compared to 44-megabyte Bernoulli cartridges. If comparable improvements in technology and equipment are achieved during the next decade, areal recording densities of fixed magnetic disks will approach 200 million bits per square inch by the year 2000, at which time nine-inch drives -- if that form factor is still in use -- will offer nine gigabytes of storage capacity, while 3.5-inch and 5.25-inch fixed magnetic disk drives will routinely store several gigabytes. Similarly, flexible magnetic media will be able to store several hundred megabytes. Few researchers believe that the maximum storage capacity of magnetic disks will be reached soon. Grau (1988), for example, cites areal densities of 250 million bits per square inch as a possibility.

Ragle et al (1978), Touchton (1982), Freedman (1983), Miller and Freese (1983), White (1983), Bell and Marrello (1984), Yonge (1984), Hoagland (1985), Kaneko (1985), Kryder (1985a), Mallinson (1985), Sikorav (1986), Ohura et al (1987), Ito et al (1988), Bloom (1989), Brindza (1989), Myers (1989), Rossum (1989, 1989a), and other researchers and industry analysts note that continuing improvements in magnetic disk capacity can be expected from refinement of existing recording technologies, including reductions in the flying height of read/write heads, higher-quality recording media, tighter mechanical tolerances, and expanded application of data compression algorithms. The technical challenges associated with such refinements are significant, however. As discussed by Rabinowicz (1988), reductions in the flying heights of read/write heads -- which currently currently measure less than 13 microinches as compared with 800 microinches for the earliest fixed magnetic disk drives -- require very smooth media, but smoothness increases "stiction", the tendency of smooth surfaces to stick to each other. Similarly, track densities can be increased by reducing the widths of read/write heads, but signal levels will be correspondingly re-

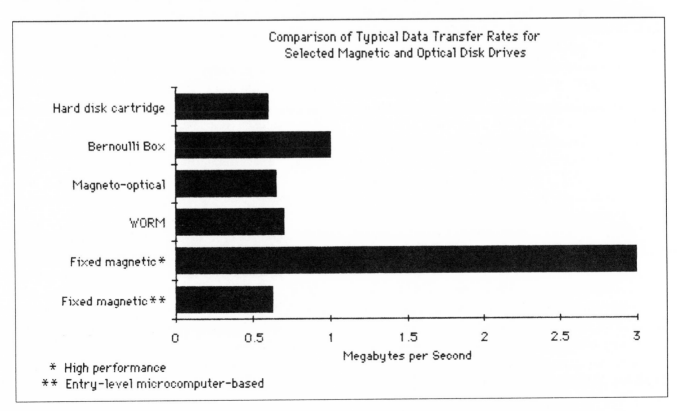

duced.

Addressing these difficulties, perpendicular magnetic recording offers the most dramatic prospects for increased media capacity. As previously described, existing magnetic disk drives record data longitudinally, the magnetic domains that store individual bits following one another in a given track. In perpendicular recording, magnetic domains are aligned vertically, usually within multi-layer magnetic media. As previously noted, several manufacturers of high-density floppy disk drives currently employ perpendicular recording technology with barium ferrite diskettes. Various companies have demonstrated perpendicular recording systems for fixed and removable magnetic disk drives utilizing double-layered media composed of cobalt-chromium or other cobalt or chromium alloys. These developments are reflected in the large and rapidly growing number of publications that discuss perpendicular recording technology and describe prototype products. Examples include Dy (1983), Kobayashi et al (1983, 1987), Kobayashi (1984), Nakamura and Iwasaki (1984), Nakayana et al (1984), Suzuki (1984), Ouchi and Iwasaki (1984, 1984a, 1988), Tatsuta and Ishida (1984), Fujiwara (1985, 1985a), Nakamura (1985), Sasaki et al (1985), Shiraki et al (1985), Shiroishi et al (1985), Yamamoto et al (1985, 1988), Bolzoni et al (1986), Koiwa et al (1986), Nicholson and Khan (1986), Bernards et al (1987), Bernstein (1987), Fukizawa (1987), Honda et al (1987), Inoue et al (1987), Koiwa and Osaka (1987), Muratomi et al (1987), Nakamura et al (1986, 1987), Osaka et al (1987), Sugita (1987), Takeda et al (1987), Tsutsumi et al (1987), Jeanniot (1988), Katz and Brechtlein (1988), Kishi et al (1988), Rupp and Hulsing (1988), Sakata et al (1988), Schewe (1988), Takahashi (1988), and Zieren et al (1988).

While longitudinal magnetic recording employs ring-shaped read/write heads, perpendicular recording utilizes a probe-shaped, single-pole mechanism to read and record information. Because probe-shaped heads minimize side-fringing -- the migration of a given signal to adjacent tracks where they interfere with data recorded there -- track densities can be increased. Censtor Corporation, for example, has demonstrated 3.5-inch fixed magnetic disk drives with areal densities approaching 80 million bits per square inch, based on a

linear recording density of 40,000 bits per inch with 2,000 tracks per inch. Perpendicular areal recording densities exceeding 200 million bits per square inch are considered possible by many researchers

While anticipated developments in magnetic recording disk technology could raise media storage capacities to levels associated with today's optical disks, optical recording technology is itself far from static. As previously discussed, the areal recording densities supported by 12-inch WORM drives have almost doubled since 1983, and storage capacities of available products increased three-fold during the same period. Since 1985, storage capacities of 5.25-inch WORM products have more than quintupled. Storage capacities of 5.25-inch, magneto-optical cartridges have increased by more than 50 percent since their commercial introduction in 1988. As discussed by Rugar et al (1987), Ando et al (1988), Furukawa et al (1988), Saito et al (1988), and Yamanaka et al (1988), the refinement of existing technologies should result in continued improvements in the recording capacities of future optical storage products.

Alternative optical recording technologies promise even higher storage capacities. As the optical counterpart of perpendicular magnetic recording, various companies are reportedly developing systems that will use laser beams of different wavelengths to achieve areal densities approaching 100 billion bits per square inch. Such systems, which are based on photochemical hole burning (PHB) technologies, have been the subject of laboratory experiments since the 1970s. IBM scientists, for example, have experimented with frequency domain technologies that employ two laser sources to record multiple bits within the same focal diameter on an optical storage medium composed of photon-gated compounds. A laser beam excites those molecules in the exposed area that are sensitive to the laser's specific frequency. A second beam provides sufficient additional energy to record a bit by bleaching the excited molecules. The presence and absence of such bleached molecules represent the one and zero bits which encode data. By slightly varying the color of the read/write beam, other groups of molecules can be selectively excited and bleached, thereby recording thousands of bits in the same exposed area.

Several Japanese companies are also developing

photochemical hole burning systems that utilize multiple laser beams of different wavelengths to irradiate a polymer material, creating photochemical reactions which record multiple signals in a given spot. Mitsubishi, for example, has used PHB technology to demonstrate optical disk recording at 600 times currently attainable areal densities. Similarly, Sony has demonstrated an experimental optical recording system that may increase areal densities by a factor of 1,000 or more. Other PHB research and development activities are described by Haarer (1979, 1987), Volker and Macfarlane (1979), Levenson et al (1980), Bjorklund et al (1981, 1982, 1984), Levenson (1981), Alvarez and Burland (1982), Tani (1983), Bjorklund et al (1984), Moerner (1985), Lenth et al (1986), Schellenberg et al (1986), Moerner et al (1987), Tani et al (1987), Babbitt and Mossberg (1988), Desmarais (1988), Itoh and Tani (1988), Rebane et al (1988), and Yoshimura (1988).

PERFORMANCE CHARACTERISTICS

While magnetic disks provide far less storage capacity than equivalently sized optical media, most magnetic disk drives are significantly faster than their optical disk counterparts. As direct access storage devices, magnetic and optical disk drives write data onto, and retrieve data from, particular tracks within a platter's recording surface. To accomplish these tasks, the drive's read/write head assembly must be moved to the proper track. The plater then revolves to bring the desired track area under the read/write head. As a combination of the time required for each of these operations, the average access time supported by a given magnetic or optical drive is calculated by the formula:

$$A = S + L$$

where:

A = the average access time, typically measured in milliseconds;

S = the seek time, in milliseconds, required to move the read/write head to the proper track for recording or retrieval;
  and

L = latency, the average time, in milliseconds, required for the desired part of the track to revolve around to the read/write head.

Seek time is measured from the receipt of a motion command until a ready command is sent to the drive's controller. The average latency is one half the time required for one disk revolution. Where a given manufacturer's product specifications report the disk speed in revolutions per minute (rpm), the formula to calculate the average latency is:

$$0.5 \times \frac{60 \text{ (seconds per minute)}}{\text{revolutions per minute}}$$

Because access times vary from one product to another, the following discussion can only indicate and compare typical access times for particular categories of magnetic and optical disk drives. The discussion necessarily relies on access times reported in manufacturers' product specifications. As Maggio (1984), Scranton et al (1984), Peckham and Campbell (1987), Hospodor (1988), and others have pointed out, however, manufacturers' specifications do not always clearly indicate the manner in which particular performance characteristics are measured. Variations will consequently be noted where appropriate.

Among fixed magnetic disk drives intended for mainframe installations, the IBM 3390 rotates at over 4,200 revolutions per minute. Its average latency is 7.1 milliseconds. Average seek times range from 9.5 milliseconds for the 3390 Model 1 to 12.5 milliseconds for the 3390 Model 2. With average access times ranging from 16.6 to 19.6 milliseconds, it was the fastest disk drive available at the time this report was prepared. The IBM 3380 and compatible products rotate at 3,600 revolutions per minute, yielding an average latency of 8.3 milliseconds. Average seek times range from 12 seconds for the single-density 3380 Model J to 17 milliseconds for the double-density 3380 Model E. The triple-density 3380 Model K, with its faster head positioning mechanism, supports an average seek time of 16 milliseconds. The

3380-compatible disk drives of other manufacturers support comparable seek times. Taken together, these latencies and seek times yield average access times of 20.3 to 25.3 milliseconds for IBM 3380 and compatible installations. Magnetic disk drives designed for Unisys, NCR, and other non-IBM mainframes offer identical average latencies with comparable or slightly greater seek times than their IBM-compatible counterparts. Typical average access times range from 22 to 28.3 milliseconds.

Among minicomputer-oriented magnetic disk drives with greater than 200 megabytes of storage capacity, Digital Equipment's RA90 -- a nine-inch drive with 1.2 gigabytes of formatted storage capacity -- supports an average seek time of 18.5 milliseconds with an average latency of 8.3 milliseconds. At 26.8 milliseconds, its average access time is comparable to that of mainframe-based products. Digital Equipment's RA82, an older 14-inch drive that remains available for VAX installations, offers an average seek time of 24 milliseconds and an average latency of 8.3 milliseconds, for a total average access time of 32.2 milliseconds. The RA70 -- a 5.25-inch drive with 280 megabytes of formatted storage capacity -- offers an average seek time of 19.5 milliseconds. Spinning at 4,000 rev-

olutions per minute, its average latency is just 7.5 milliseconds, and its average access time is 27 milliseconds.

Seek times for the various drives in the widely utilized Wren series from Imprimis Technology range between 14 and 28 milliseconds, although one model offers a seek time of just 10.7 milliseconds. Spinning at 3,600 revolutions per minute, all Wren models offer an average latency of 8.3 milliseconds. The resulting average access times range between 19 and 36.3 milliseconds. Other high performance magnetic disk drives offer seek times in the 14 to 16 millisecond range. Assuming 3,600 revolutions per minute, average access times of 22.3 to 24.3 milliseconds are typical. Similar access times are supported by comparable products manufactured by Maxtor, Toshiba, Hitachi, Micropolis, Priam, and others.

Average access times for minicomputer- and microcomputer-based magnetic disk drives with less than 200 megabytes of storage capacity range from less than 20 milliseconds to more than 60 milliseconds. With typical entry-level 20- to 40-megabyte hard disk drives intended for IBM PC/XT and compatible microcomputer systems, access times can approach 65 milliseconds. Higher performance, 60-to-

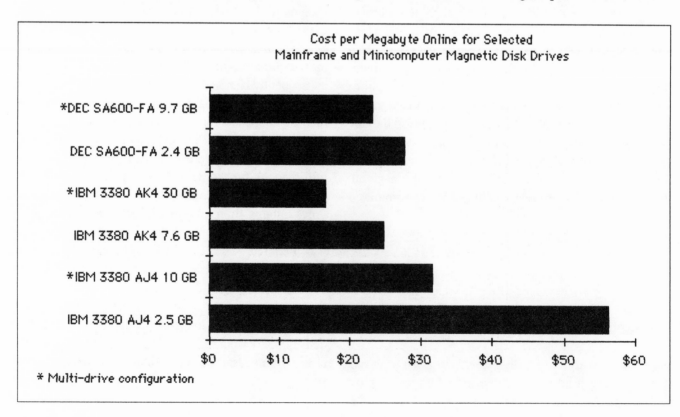

80-megabyte drives intended for PC/AT and compatible hardware configurations typically support average access times of 25 to 28 milliseconds. Typical access times for drives with 100 to 200 megabytes of storage capacity range between 22 and 25 milliseconds, although some manufacturers claim average access times as low as 18 seconds. Such devices typically feature voice coil actuators and dedicated servo heads and surfaces to reduce access times.

The slow access times historically associated with floppy disk drives are partly attributable to long average latencies resulting from low rotation speeds. The earliest eight-inch floppy disk drives, for example, operated at just 90 revolutions per minute, although subsequent eight-inch models supported 360 or 720 revolutions per minute. The 5.25-inch floppy disk drives encountered in many IBM-compatible microcomputer installations revolve 360 times per minute. At 85 milliseconds, their average latencies are ten times longer than latencies associated with many hard disk drives. When the average latency is added to average seek times of 80 to 250 milliseconds, the average access times supported by 5.25-inch floppy disk drives range from 165 to 335 milliseconds. Operating at 300 revolutions per minute, 3.5-inch floppy disk drives have an

average latency of 100 milliseconds. With average seek times ranging from 80 to 95 milliseconds, average access times of 180 to 195 milliseconds are typical.

Among other removable magnetic disk systems, drives that utilize SyQuest hard disk cartridges compare favorably with conventional magnetic disk drives in supporting average access times in the 25 millisecond range. Bernoulli systems feature an average seek time of 40 milliseconds with an average latency of 25 milliseconds for an average access time of 65 milliseconds -- the equivalent of slower fixed magnetic disk systems.

Measured by average access time, write-once and erasable optical disk drives are generally much slower than their magnetic disk counterparts -- a performance limitation that can place them at a significant disadvantage in disk-intensive applications. Like floppy disk drives, their slow access times are partly attributable to long latencies resulting from disk rotation speeds as low as 360 revolutions per minute, but optical disk drives are also burdened by relatively long seek times. As an example, the Kodak Model 6800, a high-capacity 14-inch write-once optical disk drive intended for mainframe and large minicomputer in-

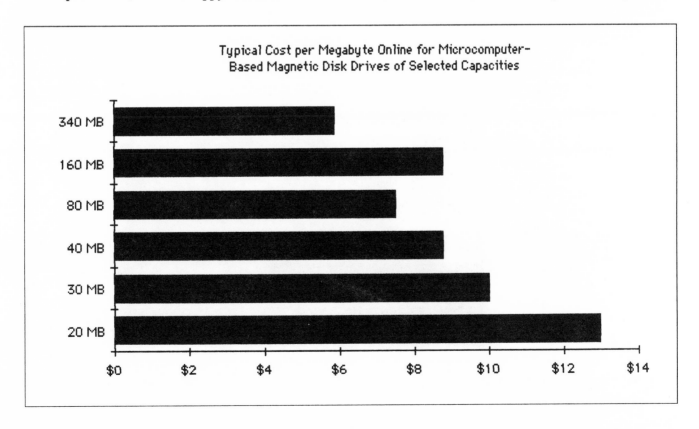

stallations, features a seek time of 400 milliseconds with a latency of 27 milliseconds. At 427 milliseconds, the drive's average access time is almost 20 times slower than high performance, 14-inch magnetic disk drives.

Among 12-inch optical drives, older write-once models -- such as the ATG 1001, Optimem 1000, and Hitachi 301-A1 -- offer average access times in the 250 millisecond range -- about ten times longer than high performance magnetic disk drives. Newer 12-inch WORM products, like the ATG GD6000 and Optimem 4000, support access times in the 120 to 180 millisecond range, but they remain much slower than their magnetic disk counterparts. When operating in the CAV mode, the Sony WDD-3000 drive offers an average access time of 190 milliseconds. In the higher-capacity CLV mode, however, the average access time increases to 500 milliseconds. The Toshiba WM-S500 supports average seek times in the 160 millisecond range, but -- because the Toshiba disk rotates at just 617 revolutions per minute -- the average latency is 48.6 milliseconds. The resulting average access time exceeds 208 milliseconds.

The earliest 5.25-inch WORM drives were likewise relatively slow. The Optotech 5984, for example, offered average an access time of 350 milliseconds. Among newer products, the ISI 525GB supports an average access time of 127 milliseconds -- an unquestionable improvement over older WORM models -- but it still remains two to five times slower than 5.25-inch magnetic disk drives. Newer 5.25-inch WORM drives from Hitachi, Fujitsu, and Laser Magnetic Storage International support access times in the 90 to 125 millisecond range. The Pioneer DD-5001 claims a seek time of 60 milliseconds with an average latency of 16.7 milliseconds for an average access time of 76.7 milliseconds. The Toshiba WM-D070 offers an average seek time of 90 milliseconds. When spinning at 1,800 revolutions per minute in the CAV mode, the average latency is just 16.7 milliseconds and the average access time is 106.7 milliseconds. In the higher-density CLV mode, however, the disk spins at just 900 revolutions per minute, average latency increases to 33.3 milliseconds, and the average access time is 123.3 milliseconds.

Access times for magneto-optical disk drives compare very favorably with the fastest WORM models but are generally much slower than magnetic disk drives. The Sony SMO-D501, for example, offers an average seek time of 95 milliseconds with an average

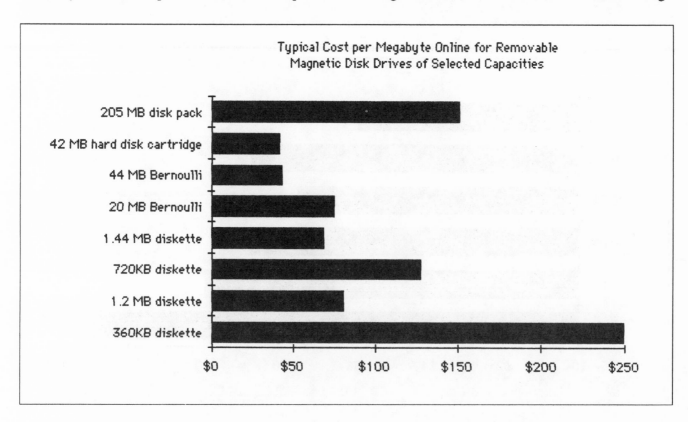

Typical Cost per Megabyte Online for Removable Magnetic Disk Drives of Selected Capacities

latency of just 12.5 milliseconds for an average access time of 107.5 milliseconds. Several models claim average access times under 100 milliseconds. The Ricoh RO-5030E supports an average seek time of 75 milliseconds with an average latency of 16.7 milliseconds, yielding an average access time of 91.7 milliseconds. Maxtor claims an average seek time of 35 milliseconds and for its Tahiti magneto-optical disk drive, but -- unlike many manufacturers -- it defines average seek time as one-third rather than one-half of a full stroke. A number of manufacturers have demonstrated magneto-optical disk drives with average access times lower than 80 milliseconds, although such products were not commercially available in North America at the time this report was prepared. Examples are described by Ishibashi et al (1987), Itao et al (1987), Hara et al (1988), Inouye and Hatayama (1988), Shimuzu et al (1988), Tanaka et al (1988), Tereshima and Yamaoka (1988), Hosokawa et al (1989). Ito et al (1987) and Ogawa et al (1987) describe a high-speed prototype WORM drive.

The foregoing comparisons of average access times for magnetic and optical disk drives are most meaningful in situations where successive recording or retrieval operations involve geographically separate areas of a given magnetic or optical disk. This is the case, for example, in many transaction processing and data base management applications where information requests are received in an unpredictable sequence, successive operations require access to non-contiguous tracks, and the typical access operation involves the recording or playback of a relatively small amount of data -- perhaps a small fraction of a given track's capacity. In such situations, optical disk drives, as previously noted, are burdened by slow read/write head movements and consequently long seek times.

Where large amounts of data will be consecutively recorded onto or retrieved from adjacent tracks, however, optical disk access times compare favorably with their magnetic disk counterparts. On a track-to-track basis, both optical and magnetic disk drives routinely support average seek times of three to five milliseconds. Optical disk drives likewise offer competitive average seek times in data recording and retrieval operations involving less than 100 contiguous tracks. In such situations, average access times of 20 milliseconds or less are supported by newer optical disk drives. Such devices can consequently perform very effectively in applications involving sequential data, text, or image files.

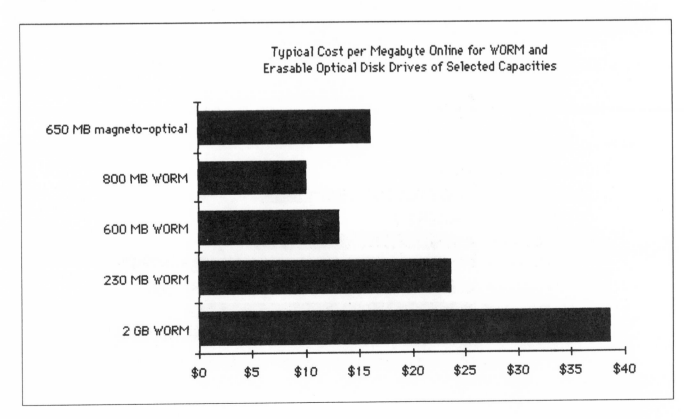

To improve optical disk drive performance in access-intensive applications, an increasing number of optical disk drive manufacturers, systems integrators, and value-added resellers offer models that employ caching methodologies. Broadly defined, a cache provides a relatively small amount of temporary, fast storage for data transferred from a slower storage medium. Some optical disk subsystems employ all or part of a magnetic disk drive as a cache memory unit to store frequently utilized data transferred from an optical disk, thereby reducing the time required to access or re-access such information. Typically, such cache-oriented optical disk drives employ a "read-ahead" approach which transfers to a magnetic disk the data stored in the sectors which immediately follow those requested by a given operation. Where retrieval operations access sectors sequentially, such anticipatory reading can effectively reduce access time. To satisfy subsequent requests for information stored on an optical disk, the magnetic disk cache is first checked to determine whether it contains the desired data. If the data is present, it is transferred to the program at magnetic disk speed; otherwise, the optical disk is accessed. When the cache becomes full, old data is automatically discarded on a least-frequently-used basis.

To improve recording speed by minimizing head movements, some systems also use cache storage to consolidate data to be recorded in a given track. In such configurations, data is only transferred to an optical disk drive when the cache fills to a specified level. As an example of a cache-oriented optical storage product, the LaserCache software that supports the LaserStore optical disk subsystems marketed by Storage Dimensions utilizes one megabyte to 128 megabytes of space on a magnetic disk drive resident in a microcomputer's system unit. Alternatively, a LaserStore optical disk subsystem can be configured with an external 155-megabyte magnetic disk drive.

While such cache configurations may improve access times in an optical disk installation by a factor of four or five, they do not necessarily give optical disk drives parity with their magnetic disk counterparts, since magnetic disk access times can be improved by utilizing random-access memory as a cache for frequently utilized data. As discussed by Brady (1987), Goldman (1984), Nishigaki and Yamamoto (1984), Grossman (1985), Rosenberry (1986), Salsburg (1987, 1988), Fuld (1988), Menon and Hartung (1988), Glass (1989), and Jalics and McIntyre (1989), such cache configurations are encountered in main-

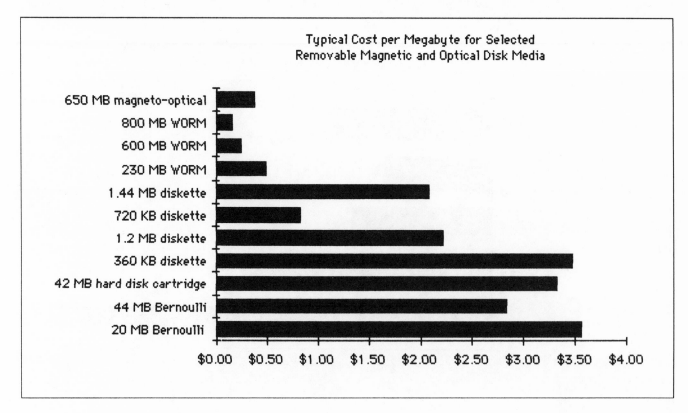

frame, minicomputer, and microcomputer installations. In applications where disk sectors are accessed sequentially, cache-based magnetic disk implementations can reduce access time to a few milliseconds.

As previously discussed, optical disk jukeboxes offer unattended access to very large amounts of data stored on multiple WORM or magneto-optical cartridges. Typical access times range from six to fifteen seconds (6,000 to 15,000 milliseconds), including the time required to retrieve a designated optical disk cartridge, insert into a drive, and access the start of a desired file. Average access times will prove faster by several seconds in jukebox configurations equipped with multiple optical disk drives, but the additional drives occupy space that might otherwise be used by optical disk cartridges, thereby reducing the jukebox unit's storage capacity. The long access times supported by optical disk jukeboxes are rarely a source of complaint in electronic document imaging applications, since they compare very favorably with access times supported by such competing storage methodologies as paper filing systems and computer-assisted microfilm retrieval systems. Compared to magnetic disk drives, however, optical disk jukeboxes can be properly described as providing "nearline" rather than online data access.

Once a desired data area on a magnetic or optical disk is located, information must be transferred between the drive and the central processing unit. A given drive's reading or recording rates are typically measured in kilobytes or megabytes per second. Most product specifications indicate the sustained rate for data transfers from a disk drive to its controller. To improve operating efficiency, some magnetic and optical disk controllers collect data for transmission in a burst to or from the central processor. Such burst transfer rates, which are often reported separately, may be 50 to 100 percent higher than sustained data transfer rates.

With magnetic disk drives, transfer rates improved steadily and significantly from the late 1950s through the early 1980s. Among IBM disk drives intended for mainframe installations, transfer rates rose from 8.8 kilobytes per second to 312 kilobytes per second in 1966, 1.2 megabytes per second in 1976, and three megabytes per second by 1981. Three megabytes per second is currently the transfer rate for IBM 3380 disk drives and compatible products operating with 3880-type controllers. High performance disk drives intended for Unisys, NCR, Honeywell, and other mainframes likewise transfer data at a maximum of three megabytes per second. When configured with the 3990 controller and certain 3880 controller models, IBM 3380 and 3390 disk drives can support transfer rates exceeding four megabytes per second. While most disk drives employ serial data transfers, the Ibis Model 1012 uses two six-megabyte channels, operating in parallel, to support multicylinder transfer rates up to 9.75 megabytes per second. Burst data transfer rates can approach 12 megabytes per second.

Among minicomputer- and microcomputer-based magnetic disk drives with greater than 200 megabytes of storage capacity, typical data transfer rates range from 500 kilobytes to three megabytes per second. In VAX installations, for example, Digital Equipment's RA90 can transfer 2.8 megabytes per second. The RA82 operates at 2.4 megabytes per second, while the RA70 can transfer data at 1.4 megabytes per second. Among similar magnetic disk drives of other manufacturers, data transfer rates of 1.25 to two megabytes per second are quite common. As an example, the IBM 9332 Direct Access Storage Unit -- which is designed for IBM AS/400, System/36, and System/38 computer installations -- supports a transfer rate of 1.4 to 1.9 megabytes per second.

A large number of magnetic disk drives intended for IBM-compatible personal computer installations support a transfer rate of 625 kilobytes per second. As discussed by Glass (1989a), such devices are typically equipped with the ST506/412 interface developed by Seagate Technology. IBM-compatible magnetic disk drives equipped with an ST506/RLL interface can support transfer rates approaching one megabyte per second. Where faster operation is desired, drives equipped with an Enhanced Small Device Interface (ESDI) can transfer data at speeds of 1.25 to 1.875 megabytes per second, and future ESDI drives can be expected to operate at speeds up to 2.5 megabytes per second. Typical transfer rates for Macintosh-compatible magnetic disk drives equipped with a Small Computer Systems Interface (SCSI) range from 500 kilobytes to 1.5 megabytes per sec-

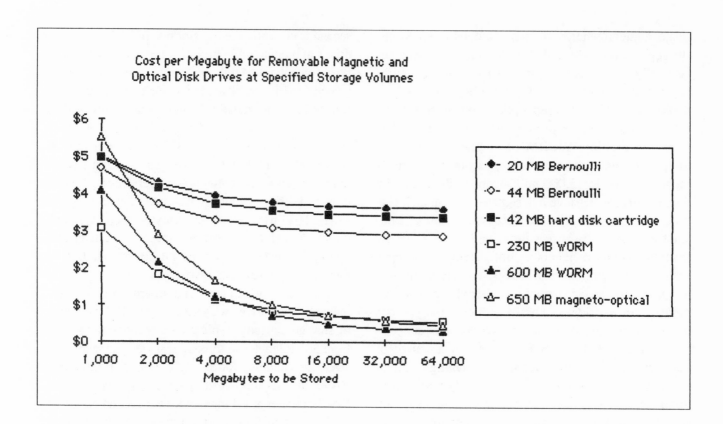

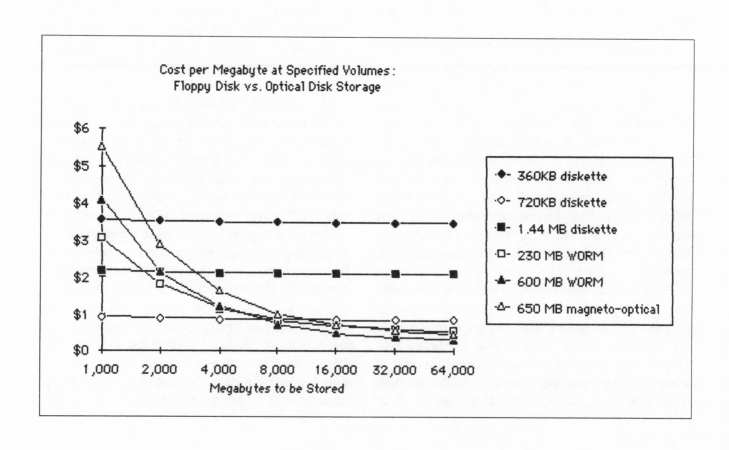

ond. Among removable disk systems, drives that utilize SyQuest hard disk cartridges can transfer data at 600 kilobytes per second, with burst rates up to 1.25 megabytes per second. Bernoulli Box systems can transfer data at speeds up to 1.13 megabytes per second, depending on the host computer's capabilities.

Optical disk drives' transfer rates are generally lower than their magnetic disk counterparts. The earliest 12-inch WORM drives -- like the Toshiba DF-0450, ATG Gigadisc 1001, Optimem 1000, LMS LaserDrive 1200, and Hitachi 301A-1 -- supported sustained data transfer rates ranging from 250 to 480 kilobytes per second, although relatively high burst rates improved performance. The Sony WDD-3000, for example, supports a sustained data transfer rate of 300 kilobytes per second with a burst rate of 1.1 megabytes per second. Similarly, the Toshiba WM-S500A supports a sustained data transfer rate of 500 kilobytes per second and a burst rate of one megabyte per second. Several second- and third-generation 12-inch models can operate at faster sustained transfer rates than their predecessors. The Optimem 2400 and 4000, for instance, support sustained transfer rates of 625 and 766 kilobytes, respectively. The ATG Gigadisc 6000 supports a sustained data transfer rate of one megabyte per second. The Kodak Model 6800, which likewise operates at a sustained rate of one megabyte per second, can transfer data in bursts of 64 kilobytes at 10 megabytes per second.

Transfer rates supported by 5.25-inch write-once and erasable optical disk drives are comparable to those of medium-performance magnetic disk products. Like their 12-inch counterparts, data transfer rates for the earliest WORM models ranged from about 250 to more than 400 kilobytes per second. With a sustained data transfer rate of 694 kilobytes per second, the Fujitsu M2505A is typical of newer WORM drives. Among magneto-optical drives, the Sony SMO-D501 operates at sustained transfer rates of 620 or 680 kilobytes per second, depending on the number of bytes per sector. Its burst rate for controller-to-host transfers is 1.2 megabytes per second. In its standard CAV configuration, the Maxtor Tahiti drive can transfer data at 700 kilobytes per second. In the proprietary ZCAV format, its sustained transfer rate is 1.25 megabytes per second.

STORAGE COSTS

Any comparison of magnetic and optical disk storage costs is necessarily complicated by variations in equipment configurations, application characteristics, the availability of discounts for specific products or customers, and other factors. In addition, costs are subject to change over time, the prices of newer products -- such as erasable optical disk drives -- being particularly likely to decline as the technology becomes more widely available. Based on manufacturers' retail price lists in effect in late 1989, the following discussion compares equipment and media cost associated with typical magnetic and optical disk configurations. Comparisons of fixed magnetic disk drives with optical disk drives are based on the cost per megabyte online. The comparison of removable magnetic disk drives with optical disk drives considers the cost per megabyte online and media costs associated with offline data storage.

The cost of fixed magnetic disk drives varies with the type of computer system for which the drives are intended. As might be expected, high-capacity, high-performance fixed disk drives for mainframe installations are the most expensive to purchase. As previously discussed, the IBM 3380 is available in single- and multi-drive configurations with storage capacities that range from 2.6 to 60.48 gigabytes. At the time this report was prepared, 3380 drive prices ranged from $59,000 for a single-density slave unit to $128,000 for a triple-density, head-of-string model. All IBM 3380 drives require a controller that must be purchased separately at prices ranging from $60,000 to $850,000. The most expensive controllers can support up to eight drives and offer random-access memory caches for high-speed operation.

An entry level, single-density 3380 configuration -- consisting of an IBM 3990, Model 001 controller and a Model AJ4 head-of-string disk drive -- costs $142,000 and provides 2.52 gigabytes of online recording and storage capacity at a relatively high cost of $56.35 per megabyte online. The addition of Model BJ4 slave drives, priced at $59,000 each, raises the total configuration cost but reduces the cost per megabyte online. Priced at $201,000, a two-drive string offers 5.04 gigabytes of online recording and storage capacity at a cost of $39.88 per megabyte on-line. A three-drive string offers 7.56 gigabytes of on-line recording and storage capacity at a cost of $35.81 per megabyte online, while a four-drive string provides online access to 10.08 gigabytes at a cost of $31.64 per megabyte online.

As might be expected, double- and triple-density 3380 models are more expensive than their single-density counterparts but offer a much lower cost per megabyte online. As an example, a triple-density 3380 configuration -- consisting of an IBM 3990, Model 001 controller priced at approximately $60,000) and a head-of-string Model AK4 disk drive priced at approximately $128,000 -- costs $188,000 and provides 7.56 gigabytes of online recording and storage capacity at a cost of $24.86 per megabyte. A four-drive string, including three BK4 slave drives priced at $105,000 each, provides online access to 30.24 giga-bytes at a cost of $16.63 per megabyte. A dual-string, eight drive configuration -- consisting of an IBM 3990, Model 002 controller (priced at $110,000), two 3380 Model AK4 head-of-string, triple-density drives, and six BK4 triple-density slave drives -- costs $996,000 and offers 60.48 gigabytes of online recording and storage capacity at a cost of just $16.47 per megabyte online.

These cost calculations are based on the lowest priced 3990 controllers -- the single-string Model 001 and the dual-string Model 002 -- without cache memo-ry. For a four-drive, triple-density configuration that includes a Model J03 controller (priced at $290,000) with 64 megabytes of cache memory, the retail price is $733,000. Such a configuration provides 30.24 giga-bytes of online recording and storage capacity at a cost of $24.24 per megabyte online versus $20.10 for the same drives with a Model 001 controller. For an eight-drive, triple-density configuration, the retail price is $1,176,000. It provides 60.48 gigabytes of online recording and storage capacity at a cost of $19.45 per megabyte online versus $16.47 for the same drives with a Model 002 controller.

As might be expected, some 3380-compatible prod-ucts are less expensive than their IBM counterparts. As an example, a four drive, single-density Amdahl 6380 system -- including a Model 6880-G2 controller ($47,200), a Model 6380-A4 head-of-string disk drive ($64,100), and three Model 6380-B4 slave drives

($46,100 each) -- sells for $249,600 and offers 10.08 gigabytes of online recording and storage capacity at a cost of $24.76 per megabyte online versus $31.64 per megabyte online for a comparable IBM 3380 equipment configuration. A four-drive, triple-density NAS 7380 system -- including a Model 7980-1 con-troller ($57,000), a Model 7380-AK head-of-string disk drive ($121,600), and a three Model 7380-BK slave drives ($99,750 each) sells for $477,850 and provides 30.24 gigabytes of online recording and stor-age capacity at a cost of $15.80 per megabyte online versus $16.63 for a comparable IBM 3380 equipment configuration.

Prices for minicomputer-based fixed magnetic disk drives vary with storage capacity, performance char-acteristics, and the specific computer configuration for which the drives are intended. For the various models in Digital Equipment Corporation's fixed magnetic disk product line, for example, costs range from less than $25 to more than $32 per megabyte on-line. Intended for medium-size and larger VAX in-stallations, the Model SA600-FA Storage Array Building Block system configured with two RA90 disk drives provides 2.43 gigabytes of online record-ing and storage capacity for $67,320 or $27.70 per megabyte online. Each additional RA90 drive adds 1.2 gigabytes of disk capacity for $30,000 or $24.67 per megabyte online. A fully populated SA600-FA system, configured with eight RA90 drives, provides 9.7 gigabytes of online recording and storage capacity for $225,000 or $23.20 per megabyte.

Among other DEC magnetic disk drives, the RA82 provides 622 megabytes of online recording and stor-age capacity for $17,340 or $27.88 per megabyte on-line. In VAX installations, it can be used alone or combined with the RA90 in a storage array. The RF71, a 400-megabyte drive intended primarily for MicroVAX installations, is priced at $11,000 or $27.50 per megabyte online. The RA70, a 280-megabyte drive which can be used alone or combined with the RA90 or RA82 in a storage array, is priced at $9,180 or $32.79 per megabyte online.

Due to volume sales, considerable competition, and widespread discounting by both computer stores and mail order suppliers, prices for microcomputer-based fixed magnetic disk drives have declined steadily and significantly since the early 1980s. Such devices offer significantly lower storage costs than their mainframe and minicomputer counterparts, although their overall storage capacities -- as previously discussed -- are lower as well. Among low-capacity (20-to-40-megabyte) drives for IBM-compatible microcomputer installations, typical storage costs range from $10 to $15 per megabyte online. An entry-level, 20-megabyte hard disk drive -- such as the ST-225 from Seagate Technology -- can be purchased for about $260 or $13 per megabyte online, including the drive controller, cables, and mounting screws. The Seagate ST-238, a 30-megabyte model, can be purchased for about $300 or $10 per megabyte online. With an average access time of 65 milliseconds, however, it is relatively slow. Where improved performance is desired, the Seagate ST-125 supports an average access time of 40 milliseconds and offers 20 megabytes of online recording and storage capacity for $300 or $15 per megabyte online. For disk drives that support a given access time, the cost per megabyte declines as storage capacity increases. The Seagate ST-251-0, a 40-millisecond drive, provides 40 megabytes of online recording and storage capacity for $350 or $8.75 per megabyte online. The faster ST-251-1 drive, which offers the same storage capacity with an average access time of 28 milliseconds at a cost of $440 or $11 per megabyte online.

Among medium-capacity (60-to-100-megabyte) fixed magnetic drives for IBM-compatible microcomputers, the Seagate ST-277R-1 supports an average access time of 40 milliseconds and offers 60 megabytes of online recording and storage capacity at a cost of $400 or $6.67 per megabyte online. The higher-performance Seagate ST-4096 supports an average access time of 28 milliseconds and offers 80 megabytes of online recording and storage capacity at a cost of $600 or $7.50 per megabyte online. Most high-capacity (100-megabytes or more) fixed magnetic disk drives for IBM-compatible microcomputer installations support access times lower than 20 milliseconds. As noted above, storage costs vary inversely with capacity. A Miniscribe M3180, for example, provides 160-megabyte of online recording and storage capacity for about $1,400 or $8.75 per megabyte online, while a Miniscribe M9380E, a 340-megabyte drive, can be purchased for about $2,000 or $5.88 per megabyte online.

As is the case with most Macintosh peripheral devices, fixed magnetic disk drives intended for Macintosh installations are more expensive than their IBM-compatible counterparts. Taking the Integra product line from Dolphin Systems as an example, a 20-megabyte model can be purchased for $550 or $27.50 per megabyte online. Supporting an average access time of 65 milliseconds, it is more than twice as expensive as comparable products for IBM-compatible microcomputers. Costs for other Integra disk drives range from $600 or $20 per megabyte online for a 30-megabyte model to $1,180 or $14.75 per megabyte for an 80-megabyte model. All models are housed in external cabinets and include a Small Computer Systems Interface. Prices for Macintosh-compatible internal disk drives are lower. As an example, the XL30 from Cutting Edge offers 30-megabytes of online recording and storage capacity for $467 or $15.63 per megabyte. The XL45 provides 45 megabytes of storage capacity for $645 or $14.33 per megabyte online. Both XL models are based on components acquired from Seagate Technology, although prices are higher than Seagate drives for IBM-compatible microcomputer installations.

Fixed magnetic disk drives for workstations and other high-end microcomputer systems are significantly more expensive than those for IBM-compatible and Macintosh personal computers. As an example, the DEC RD32 -- a 42-megabyte drive for MicroVAX 2000, VAXstation, and MicroPDP-11 installations -- costs $1,650 or $39.29 per megabyte online. The RD54, a 159-megabyte model, sells for $4,590 or $28.87 per megabyte online.

Prices cited in the preceding discussion of fixed magnetic disk devices include the cost of the disks themselves which are integrated with, and inseparable from, the drives that utilize them. With removable magnetic disk drives, hardware and media are purchased separately. As previously noted, such removable disk systems provide unlimited recording capacity, although some data will typically be stored offline at any given moment. To be consistent with the preceding discussion, the cost of removable magnetic disk storage must be calculated with a single recording medium installed in the drive.

Measured solely by equipment prices, floppy disk

drives are the least expensive disk storage devices, but, in terms of cost per megabyte online, they are the most expensive. At the time this report was prepared, a 5.25-inch, double-sided, double-density floppy disk drive with 360 kilobytes (0.36 megabytes) of online recording and storage capacity could be purchased for about $90 in a half-height configuration intended for installation in the system unit of an IBM-compatible microcomputer. Assuming that double-sided, double-density diskettes can be purchased for $1.00 each, the cost per megabyte online for a 360-kilobyte floppy disk drive with one diskette installed is $252.78.

Higher capacity floppy disk drives offer more attractive storage costs, but the cost per megabyte remains much higher than that obtainable with fixed magnetic media. As an example, a 5.25-inch, double-sided, high-density floppy disk drive with 1.2 megabytes of online recording and storage capacity can be purchased for about $95 in a half-height configuration intended for installation in the system unit of an IBM PC/AT or compatible microcomputer. Assuming that double-sided, high-density diskettes can be be purchased for $1.25 each, the cost per megabyte online for a 1.2-megabyte floppy disk drive with one diskette installed is $80.63. Among newer floppy disk drives for IBM-compatible microcomputers, a 3.5-inch, double-sided unit with 720 kilobytes (0.72 megabytes) of online recording and storage capacity can be purchased for about $90 in a half-height internal configuration. Assuming that diskettes can be purchased for $2.00 each, the cost per megabyte online for a 720-kilobyte floppy disk drive with one diskette installed is $127.78. A 3.5-inch, double-sided, high-density floppy disk drive with 1.44 megabytes of online recording and storage can be purchased for about $95 in a half-height internal configuration. Assuming that high-density, 3.5-inch diskettes can be purchased for $5.00 each, the cost per megabyte online is $69.44.

Prices are higher for external floppy disk drives designed for attachment to IBM-compatible desktop or portable microcomputers. An external 3.5-inch, 1.44-megabyte model, for example, can be purchased for about $270. When loaded with a single high-density diskette, priced at $5.00, the cost per megabyte online is $190.97. Similarly, an external, 800-kilobyte Macintosh-compatible floppy disk drive can be purchased

for about $150. When loaded with a single, 3.5-inch diskette priced at $2.00, the cost per megabyte online is $190. Floppy disk storage for other types of computers is even more expensive. As an example, Digital Equipment Corporation's RX33 -- a 1.2-megabyte, 5.25-inch floppy disk drive designed for MicroVAX, VAXstation, and MicroPDP-11 installations -- costs $400. With one diskette installed, the cost per megabyte online is $334.36.

Among special floppy disk drives with higher storage capacities, an external 5.25-inch, 20-megabyte Bernoulli Box system equipped with a non-bootable adapter card for IBM-compatible microcomputer installations can be purchased for about $1,425. Assuming that Bernoulli media cartridges can be purchased for $78 each, the cost per megabyte online for a Bernoulli drive with one cartridge installed is $75.15. An external Bernoulli Box II/44 drive, with 44 megabytes of online recording and storage capacity, can be purchased for about $1,800. Assuming that media cartridges can be purchased for $125 each, the cost per megabyte online for a 44-megabyte drive with one cartridge installed is $43.75. Available at discount for about $2,500, a dual drive Bernoulli Box II/44 system provides online access to 88 megabytes at a cost of $33.52 megabytes online.

In mainframe and minicomputer installations, the storage costs associated with removable magnetic disk packs are much higher than those obtainable with fixed magnetic disk drives. As an example, Digital Equipment Corporation's RA60 drive, configured with cabinet and controller, can be purchased for $29,900. Disk packs are priced at $984 each. A single drive with a disk pack installed provides 205 megabytes of online recording and storage capacity at a cost of $150.65 per megabyte -- almost five times the cost associated with Digital's RA70, a 280-megabyte fixed magnetic disk drive. Three additional drives, priced at $20,700 each, can be added to a single controller. Adding $984 for a magnetic disk pack, each additional drive offers online access to 208 megabytes of recording and storage capacity at a cost of $104.25 per megabyte online. A four-drive configuration offers an online recording and storage capacity of 832 megabytes at a cost of $147.76 per megabyte online.

In IBM-compatible and Macintosh microcomputer

installations, magnetic disk drives that utilize SyQuest removable cartridges can be purchased for $1,000 to $1,900, with $1,300 being a typical discounted selling price for such devices. Prices for SyQuest hard disk cartridges range from $100 to $170 each, depending on the procurement source. If a cartridge is purchased for $140, a SyQuest removable magnetic disk drive drive with one cartridge installed provides 42 megabytes of online recording and storage capacity for $1,440 or $34.29 per megabyte online.

As a complicating factor in cost calculations and comparisons, manufacturers of optical disk drives sell their products to systems integrators, value-added resellers, and other OEM clients who typically combine them with additional hardware components and/or software in plug-and-play configurations or turnkey systems intended for sale to end users. The cost of the optical disk drive is never quoted separately, since it cannot be purchased alone. Because they incorporate distinctive added-value components, the end-user configurations offered by different vendors are subject to considerable pricing variations, even when they incorporate the same optical disk drives. The following discussion consequently reflects the general tendency in optical disk drive and media prices. While the prices cited here do not apply to all optical disk implementations, they do provide a useful comparison between optical and magnetic disk storage costs.

As previously discussed, proponents of optical storage systems typically claim cost advantages when compared to products that utilize magnetic recording technology, but comparisons based on the cost per megabyte online for specific optical and magnetic disk drives indicate that magnetic disk storage is often less expensive than its optical counterpart. This is invariably the case when optical disk drives are compared to fixed magnetic disk drives intended for specific computer configurations. As an example, Digital Equipment Corporation offers its RV20 optical storage system as a complement, supplement, or alternative to magnetic storage devices in VAX installations. Based on the LaserDrive 1200 from Laser Magnetic Storage International, the RV20 uses 12-inch, write-once optical disk cartridges with two gigabytes of double-sided storage capacity. The RV20 can be purchased for $38,250 in a configuration that includes a controller,

cabinet, cables, and software. Double-sided WORM cartridges are priced at $400 each. A single RV20 drive with a cartridge installed provides one gigabyte of online recording and storage capacity -- as previously discussed, optical disk drives can only access one side of a cartridge at a time -- at a cost of $38,650 or $38.65 per megabyte. Up to three additional RV20 drives, priced at $25,500 each, can be supported by a single controller. A dual-drive configuration with a cartridge installed in each drive provides two gigabytes of online recording and storage capacity at a cost of $64,550 or $32.27 per megabyte online. As previously discussed, Digital Equipment Corporation's SA600-FA Storage Array Building Block system provides 2.43 gigabytes of online magnetic disk capacity at a cost of $27.70 per megabyte. The lowest cost attainable in an RV20 optical storage equipment configuration -- $29.08 per megabyte online for a four-drive, four-gigabyte system -- is almost $6.00 per megabyte higher than the cost of fully configured SA600-FA installation.

Subject to significant product-specific variations, online data storage costs associated with 5.25-inch write-once optical disk drives are much higher than their fixed magnetic disk counterparts for IBM-compatible microcomputers. They compare favorably, however, with online storage costs associated with the lowest capacity (20-megabyte) fixed magnetic disk drives for Macintosh computers. As an example, the ISI 525WC WORM drive can be purchased for about $2,600. It utilizes 5.25-inch optical disk cartridges with 230 megabytes of double-sided capacity. The cartridges sell for $115 each. A single 525WC drive with one WORM cartridge installed provides online access to 115 megabytes of recording and storage capacity at a cost of $23.60 per megabyte online. It is more than twice as expensive as online storage costs associated with some IBM-compatible fixed magnetic disk drives, but it is about about $4.00 per megabyte less expensive than a typical entry-level, 20-megabyte fixed magnetic disk drive for Macintosh computers.

Other 5.25-inch WORM drives are more expensive than the 525WC, but their higher media capacities yield lower storage costs per megabyte online. As an example, the Corel 600, which is based on the Hitachi

OD101, costs $3,800 and utilizes WORM cartridges with 600 megabytes of double-sided capacity. The cartridges can be purchased for $145 each. With a cartridge installed, the Corel 600 provides 300 megabytes of online recording and storage capacity at a cost of $13.15 per megabyte, making it competitive with most Macintosh magnetic disk drives and some IBM-compatible drives. Similarly, the Maxtor RXT-800S can be purchased for about $3,900 and utilizes 5.25-inch WORM cartridges with 800 megabytes of double-sided capacity. The cartridges can be purchased for $125 each. With a cartridge installed the RXT-800S provides 400 megabytes of online recording and storage capacity at a cost of $10.06 per megabyte. As previously discussed, fixed magnetic disk drives for IBM-compatible microcomputers offer 340 megabytes of online recording and storage capacity at costs below $6.00 per megabyte. The ISI 525GB, the highest capacity 5.25-inch optical disk drive available at the time this report was prepared, can be purchased for about $6,300 and utilizes WORM cartridges with 1.28 gigabytes of double-sided capacity. With a cartridge installed, it provides 640 megabytes of online recording and storage capacity at a cost of $10.39 per megabyte. Where equivalent storage capacity is desired, two 340-megabyte fixed magnetic disk drives can be purchased for less.

As might be expected of a relatively new product group, prices for erasable optical disk drives and media are higher than those of write-once systems. At the time this report was prepared, a 5.25-inch magneto-optical disk drive, like the Sony SMO-D501, could be purchased from a systems integrator or value-added reseller for $5,000 to $6,000, including software and cables suitable for IBM-compatible or Macintosh microcomputer installations. Magneto-optical disk cartridges, with 650 megabytes of double-sided capacity, could be purchased for $250 to $300 each. With a cartridge installed, such a magneto-optical disk drive provides 325 megabytes of online recording and storage capacity at a cost of $16.15 to $19.39 per megabyte -- more than twice as expensive as a 340-megabyte fixed magnetic disk drive.

Comparisons based on costs per megabyte online assume that optical disk drives will be utilized, in the traditional magnetic disk drive manner, as direct access storage devices. That assumption necessarily ignores the advantages of removable optical disk cartridges which provide virtually unlimited storage capacity -- at a very low cost per megabyte -- in applications where some data can be stored offline. As an example, Digital Equipment Corporation's RV20 12-inch WORM drive can store 10 gigabytes (10,000 megabytes) of data at a cost of approximately $40,300 or $4.03 per megabyte, assuming that the data is maintained on five double-sided WORM cartridges with nine gigabytes being offline at any given moment. In microcomputer installations, a 5.25-inch Maxtor RXT-800S WORM drive can store 10 gigabytes of data at a cost of $5,525 or just 55 cents per megabyte, assuming that the data is maintained on 13 double-sided WORM cartridges with 9.6 gigabytes being offline at any given moment.

Data access times may, of course, prove unacceptably long in such storage configurations, since offline optical disk cartridges must be retrieved from their storage locations and mounted when needed. Removable optical media are well suited, however, to the storage of backup files, the archiving of data recorded on fixed magnetic disk drives, and the distribution of data bases, text files, CAD/CAM files, digitized document images, or other machine-readable information. In such applications, optical disk systems compete most directly and compare most favorably with floppy disk drives, Bernoulli Box systems, hard disk packs, hard disk cartridge drives, and other products that utilize removable magnetic media. As will be discussed in Part Two of this report, optical storage products also compete with magnetic tape systems in data backup and archiving applications.

Measured by media cost alone, write-once and erasable optical disk systems offer a significantly less expensive alternative to removable magnetic disk media. Among products for minicomputer installations, the previously discussed RV20 optical disk drive from Digital Equipment Corporation employs WORM cartridges with two gigabytes (2,000 megabytes) of double-sided storage capacity. The cartridges cost $400 each or 20 cents per megabyte. The same company's RA60 magnetic disk drive utilizes removable disk packs with 205 megabytes of data storage capacity. At $984 each or $4.80 per megabyte, such removable magnetic disk packs are 24 times more expensive than their optical disk counterparts. Media costs are similarly high with other removable magnetic disk drives. Disk packs intended for CDC 9762 drives, for example, provide 80 megabytes of recording capacity at an approximate cost of $340 per pack or $4.25 per megabyte. The 300-megabyte disk packs utilized by CDC 9766 drives cost approximately $900 each or $3.00 per megabyte. Removable disk cartridges encountered in some older minicomputer installations are even more expensive. The 16-megabyte cartridges employed by CDC Phoenix drives, for example, cost approximately $130 each or $8.13 per megabyte.

Among microcomputer-based removable magnetic media, double-sided, high-density, 5.25-inch floppy disks of the type encountered in PC/AT-compatible installations provide 1.2 megabyte of storage capacity at an approximate media cost of $1.25 per disk or $1.03 cents per megabyte. On a per-megabyte basis, other flexible magnetic media are more costly. Double-sided, double-density, 5.25-inch floppy disks, for example, provide 360 kilobytes (0.36 megabytes) of storage capacity at an approximate media cost of $1.00 per disk or $2.78 per megabyte, although quantity discounts combined with the purchase of off-brand disks can reduce costs to as little as 50 cents per disk or $1.39 per megabyte. When formatted by IBM-compatible microcomputers, double-sided, double-density, 3.5-inch floppy disks provide 720 kilobytes (0.72 megabytes) of storage capacity at an approximate media cost of $2.00 per disk or $2.78 per megabyte. When formatted by Macintosh computers, the same disks provide 800 kilobytes (0.8 megabytes) of storage capacity an an approximate media cost of $2.50 per megabyte. Volume discounts can reduce these costs by perhaps 20 percent. Double-sided, high-density, 3.5-inch floppy disks provide 1.44 megabytes of storage capacity an approximate media cost of $5.00 or $3.47 per megabyte, although quantity discounts can reduce media costs to $4.00 per disk or $2.78 per megabyte. Among specially-designed flexible magnetic media, 20-megabyte Bernoulli cartridges can be purchased for $78 each or $3.90 per megabyte, while 44-megabyte Bernoulli cartridges cost $125 each or $2.84 per megabyte. SyQuest hard disk cartridges provide 42 megabytes of storage at a cost of $140 or $3.33 per megabyte.

On a cost-per-megabyte basis, the 5.25-inch cartridges employed by microcomputer-based optical disk drives are invariably and significantly less expensive than removable magnetic media. Typical costs range for write-once optical media range from 50 cents per megabyte for the 230-megabyte tellurium-alloy cartridges employed by the ISI 525WC to 16 cents per megabyte for the 800-megabyte dye-based media utilized by the Maxtor RXT-800S. Regardless of the recording technology employed, newer write-once products routinely offer media costs below 30 cents per megabyte. Priced at $145 per disk or 24 cents per megabyte, the 600-megabyte WORM cartridges employed by the Hitachi OD101 are typical. Among high-capacity, 5.25-inch media, the 1.28-gigabyte WORM cartridges utilized by the ISI 525GB cost $349 each or 27 cents per megabyte. As might be expected of a relatively new product group, erasable optical disks are more expensive than their write-once counterparts, but they compare favorably with magnetic media. The 650-megabyte magneto-optical cartridges utilized by the Sony SMO-D501 erasable optical disk drive, for example, cost $250 each or 39 cents per megabyte.

As the preceding examples indicate, optical storage technology can yield substantial savings in media costs. In a desktop microcomputer installation, a Maxtor RXT-800S optical disk drive can store 800 megabytes at a media cost of just $125. To store an equivalent amount of data would require 556 high-density, 3.5-inch floppy disks at a total media cost of $2,224, assuming that such disks could be purchased for $4.00 each. To store 800 megabytes with other microcomputer-oriented removable magnetic disk systems would require 40 20-megabyte Bernoulli cartridges at a total media cost of $3,120, 19 44-megabyte Bernoulli cartridges at a total media cost of $2,356, or 19 42-megabyte SyQuest hard disk cartridges at a total media cost of $2,660.

While they reflect the cost saving potential of optical storage technology, the foregoing comparisons are based on media costs alone and do not reflect the substantial hardware cost advantage enjoyed by magnetic storage products. As discussed earlier in this section, magnetic disk drives are typically much less expensive than their optical disk counterparts. Prices for 5.25-inch WORM drives, for example, routinely exceed $2,500, while a 5.25-inch, double-sided, high-density floppy disk drive can be purchased for less than $100. In applications involving removable media, a given optical storage system will only prove less expensive than a given magnetic storage system when and if the accumulated savings in media costs exceed the hardware cost differential. With their lower equipment costs, removable magnetic storage systems are more economical in low-volume applications; optical storage's cost savings potential increases, however, with the amount of data to be stored. For any two equipment configurations, the point at which optical storage becomes less expensive than removable magnetic disk storage can be calculated by the following formula:

$$V = \frac{D_{od} - D_{md}}{M_{md} - M_{od}}$$

Where:

V = the data storage volume, in megabytes, required for optical storage to be less expensive than magnetic disk storage;

D_{od} = the purchase price of an optical disk drive and its associated hardware and software components;

D_{md} = the purchase price of a magnetic disk drive and its associated hardware and software components;

M_{md} = the cost per megabyte for magnetic disk storage media; and

M_{od} = the cost per megabyte for optical disk storage media.

This formula can be used to quickly compare costs for specific optical and magnetic storage products. Write-once optical disk drives, for example, are often cited as cost effective alternatives to Bernoulli Box systems in applications where software, data bases, text files, CAD/CAM files, or other voluminous machine-readable information will be archived or distributed on removable media. An ISI 525WC WORM drive, as previously described, can be purchased for $2,600. Media costs are 50 cents per megabyte. A 20-megabyte Bernoulli Box system can be purchased for $1,425. Media costs are $3.90 per megabyte. Applying the above formula, the calculation:

$$V = \frac{2600 - 1425}{3.90 - .50}$$

indicates that, based on the indicated hardware and media costs, an ISI 525WC WORM drive will prove less expensive than a 20-megabyte Bernoulli Box system where the amount of data to be stored exceeds 345 megabytes. Similar calculations can be performed for other optical and magnetic disk products. The formula can also be used to compare two magnetic or two optical disk systems.

Part Two: Optical Disks vs. Magnetic Tape

Broadly defined, magnetic tape consists of long strips of polyester film coated with a magnetizable material. Characteristics of the polyester base material and coating technology are described by Dallman and Hasback (1987), Schaake et al (1987), Berry and Pritchet (1988), and Muller (1988). Magnetizable layers composed of particulate materials, such as the gamma form of ferric-oxide, have been utilized since the inception of magnetic tape technology. Their recording properties have been discussed in various technical publications. Examples, some of which were previously cited in Part One of this report, include Hoagland (1963), Mee (1964, 1986), Renwick (1964), Speliotis (1967), Loeschner (1968), Mallinson (1971), Renwick and Cole (1971), VanderGeissen (1973), Matick (1977), Miller (1977), Altman (1978), Izumi (1985), Sharrock and Bodnar (1985), Mee and Daniel (1987, 1989), Oseroff et al (1987, 1988), Staals et al (1987), Aoyama et al (1988), Hibst (1988), Paul and Finkelstein (1988), Spratt et al (1988), and Williams (1988). Other recording materials employed in or proposed for magnetic tape systems are described by Fujiwara (1982), Chubachi and Tamagawa (1984), Eiling and Pott (1985), Matsuda et al (1985), Corradi et al (1987), Kurokawa et al (1987), Nishikawa et al (1987), Umeda et al (1987), Satoh et al (1988), Yonezawa et al (1988), Isesaka et al (1989), and Iwasaki (1989).

At the time this report was prepared, tape widths encountered in data processing applications ranged from 4mm to 0.5 inches. Tape carriers include open reels, cartridges, and cassettes in various sizes and shapes that are described more fully in the following sections. Tape lengths vary with the type of carrier and -- for carriers of a particular type -- from model to model. Half-inch tapes mounted on open reels in 2,400 foot lengths remain widely installed in mainframe and minicomputer sites, although they are increasingly being replaced by half-inch cartridge systems. Magnetic tape systems intended for small computer installations are typically based on cartridge and cassette formats, some of which are derived from video and audio technologies. Weide (1982) and Budo and Hasler (1984) describe systems based on continuous loops of magnetic tape. Such devices are not available for data storage, although they have been utilized for voice recording in multi-user dictation systems intended for automated office installations.

As discussed by Stevens (1981), Loovenstijn (1984), Rasek (1985), Thornley (1985), Camras (1986), Muller (1986), and Weinlein (1988), magnetic tapes have been successfully utilized for information recording since the 1920s, audio recording being their first application. Magnetic tape systems for data recording date from the 1940s; video recording applications followed in the 1950s. Magnetic tape drives were the principal auxiliary storage devices in early computer installations, but their serial access characteristics made them unsuitable for online data processing applications requiring rapid retrieval of information in unpredictable sequences. As higher performance magnetic disk technology became more widely available and less expensive, tape drives were increasingly relegated to batch processing applications, offline storage, data distribution, and backup protection.

At first glance, it would seem that magnetic tape might be more appropriately compared with optical tape than with optical disks. As its name suggests, optical tape consists of a ribbon of film coated with an optical recording material. The technical characteristics and information storage potential of such products have been discussed for more than a decade. Schmitt and Lee (1979) and Lee et al (1979) discuss research on thermoplastic optical recording tapes at Honeywell in the 1970s. As described by Drexler (1881, 1983, 1983a), Drexler Technology Corporation demonstrated optical tape products utilizing its proprietary recording material, called Drexon, in the early 1980s. In its 1988 annual report, Drexler indicated renewed interest in commercializing a Drexon-based optical tape system. Altman et al (1986) propose the development of optical tape recorders for high-volume aerospace and avionics applications, while Langeveld (1987) discusses the potential of optical tape for large-scale data collection in high-energy physics research. Dancygier (1987) describes Schlumberger's experiments with an erasable, magneto-optical tape system employing iron-terbium alloys coated on Kapton. Reporting on research performed by the 3M Company, Vogelgesang and Hartmann (1988) likewise examine the feasibility of magneto-optical tape, while Castera and Lehureau (1986) describe a device for optical reading of magnetic tape using thin-film garnet transducers.

Despite this research and development interest, optical tape systems existed only in prototype versions at the time this report was prepared. In the Netherlands, DOCdata N.V. has demonstrated an optical tape cassette with six gigabytes of data storage capacity. It employs a write-once recording material featuring a dielectric layer of nonconductive polymer containing microscopic pits that represent digitally encoded data.

Data is recorded by an array of lasers. The company has proposed an automated library system that can store 128 cassettes with a total capacity of 750 gigabytes.

Imperial Chemical Industries has announced Digital Paper, a write-once optical recording material that can be packaged in a variety of physical formats, including tapes. As discussed by Abbott (1988, 1988a), Owen (1988, 1989), Williams (1988, 1989), Desmarais (1989), Pountain (1989), Ruddick (1989), Strelitz (1989), and Vanker (1989a), Digital Paper features an infrared-sensitive, dye polymer coated on a flexible polyester substrate. ICI plans to rely on other companies to develop systems that will utilize Digital Paper technology. Directly relevant to this discussion, CREO Products Incorporated -- a Canadian company formed in 1984 to design and manufacture innovative electronic products -- is developing a very high capaci-

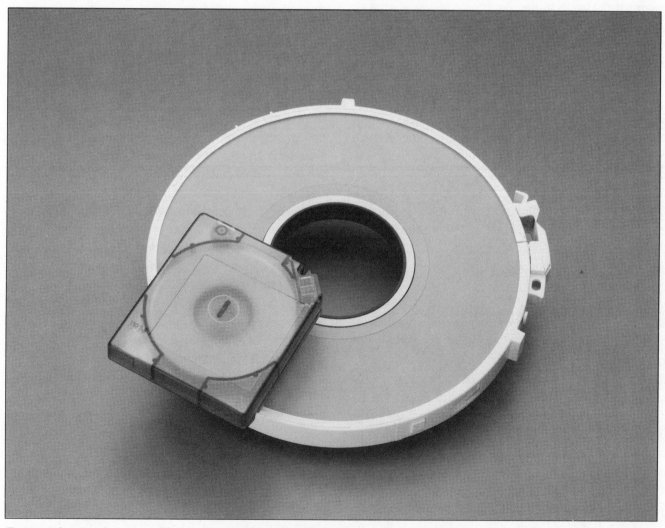

Two popular tape formats: a 10.5-inch reel and a half-inch cartridge. (Courtesy: IBM)

ty optical tape system based on Digital Paper. As described by Spencer (1988, 1988a), the CREO system features a 35mm write-once optical tape packaged on a 12-inch reel in 880-meter lengths. Designed for data collection, archiving, and backup in mainframe computer installations serving scientific, medical, and other high-volume applications, it can store one terabyte (one trillion bytes). Thorn-EMI is also reported to be developing an optical tape system that will utilize Digital Paper as its recording medium.

While the absence of commercially available products makes a comparison of magnetic and optical tape impossible, a comparison of magnetic tape with optical disks is not a contrived alternative. One of the earliest and most important applications of optical disk technology involved the replacement of magnetic tape for offline storage and data backup. Since the mid-1980s, a number of companies have developed optical disk systems that are designed to substitute for magnetic tape drives in mainframe, minicomputer, and microcomputer installations. Descriptions of such "optical archiving" systems and their intended applications are provided by Davis (1987), Lowenthal (1987), Oster-

Digital Paper, a write-once optical recording material, can be packaged as tapes, disks, or other formats. (Courtesy: ICI ImageData)

lund (1987), Rash (1987), Rosch (1987a), Williams (1987), Bican (1988), Bostwick et al (1988), Carringer (1988), Devoy et al (1988), Donsbach (1988), Francis (1988), Green (1988), Halper (1988), Hume (1988), Keele (1988), Laskodi et al (1988), Moran (1988), Owen (1988), Ramsay (1988), Replogle (1988), Slicker (1988), Waltrip and Blake (1988), Yamashita et al (1988), Yokoi et al (1988), and Ferebee and Kibler (1989).

Designed as self-contained turnkey configurations of optical storage equipment and systems software, magnetic tape replacement products require no modifications of a customer's existing computer hardware or application software. While their specific features and capabilities differ, they typically combine one or more write-once or erasable optical disk drives with host adapters, cabling, and specially-developed interface software. Magnetic tape replacement systems intended for mainframe and minicomputer installations may also include jukebox retrieval units for unattended access to multiple optical disk cartridges. Regardless of configuration, the system's interface software makes an optical disk drive appear to the host computer as a conventional magnetic tape unit -- the significant difference being that data is recorded onto and read from optical disk cartridges rather than magnetic tapes. Like the magnetic tape drive it is designed to replace, the optical disk system is fully compatible with the host computer system's existing utility programs and provides transparent, application access to recorded data.

Reaching for the broadest possible market, the first magnetic tape replacement products were developed for Digital Equipment Corporation's VAX minicomputer sites. Comparable optical disk systems have since become available for other other types of minicomputers, IBM and other mainframes, and many brands of microcomputers. To facilitate an understanding of their competitive position, the following discussion compares the characteristics and capabilities of commonly encountered magnetic tape and optical disk products. It begins with detailed comparisons of storage capacities for various magnetic tape and optical disk configurations, followed by an analysis of performance characteristics (access time and data transfer rates) and storage costs.

As was the case with Part One of this report, the dis-

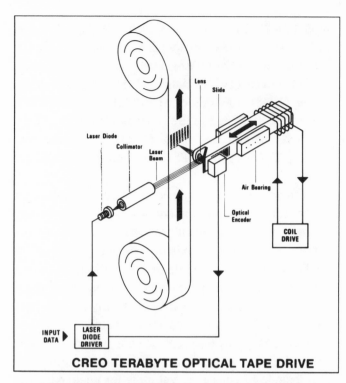

CREO TERABYTE OPTICAL TAPE DRIVE

A schematic diagram of CREO Products' optical tape system. (Courtesy: ICI ImageData)

cussion is limited to a comparison of magnetic tape with read/write optical disks of the write-once and erasable type. Like their magnetic counterparts, such optical disks are purchased blank and permit the direct recording of machine-readable data generated by keyboards, document scanners, or other computer input devices. They can also record information transferred from magnetic disks, magnetic tapes, or other optical disks. While CD-ROMs and other read-only optical disk products may compete with magnetic tapes as media for software and data base distribution, such information management applications are intentionally omitted from this report.

STORAGE CAPACITY

Magnetic tape storage capacities depend on several factors, including the tape format, length, linear recording density, and recording method. As noted above, half-inch magnetic tape of the type utilized in many mainframe and minicomputer installations is widely supplied in 2400-foot lengths mounted on plastic reels measuring 10.5 inches in diameter. Within a given reel, the bits that encode individual characters are recorded in nine parallel tracks across the width of the

tape, the individual characters following one another down the length of the tape. Eight of the tracks contain data bits, the ninth track being reserved for a parity bit that is used to reduce recording and playback errors. The tracks measure approximately .045 inches wide, and there is a separation of approximately .01 inch between tracks.

As with the magnetic disk drives described in Part One of this report, a review of IBM products reflects the historical development and improvement of half-inch, reel-to-reel magnetic tape drives. As described by Harris et al (1981), Fisher et al (1983), Pugh (1984), and Bashe et al (1986), the IBM 726 recorded data in seven parallel tracks at a linear density of just 100 bits per inch. Announced in 1952 and shipped to customers in 1953, it was designed for IBM 701 computer installations. Introduced in 1955, the IBM 727 supported a linear recording density of 200 bits per inch. With the introduction of the IBM 729 Model III tape drive in 1958, the linear recording density increased to 556 bits per inch. Introduced in 1961, the IBM 729 Model IV was the first tape drive to support a linear recording density of 800 bits per inch. Brown et al (1970) describe 800-bpi recording methodologies. The IBM 2401, which was introduced in 1966, increased the linear density to 1,600 bits per inch, using the phase encoding (PE) method of encoding. As discussed by Irwin et al (1971), subsequent models supported both 800- and 1,600-bit-per-inch recording densities with improved performance characteristics. Introduced in 1973, the IBM 3420 Model 8 was the first magnetic tape drive to support a linear recording density of 6,250 bits per inch. As described by Patel (1974), Sloan (1976), and Newton (1981), it was the first tape drive to use Group-Code Recording (GRC) technology. While 6,250 bits per inch has remained the highest linear density available in reel-to-reel magnetic tape configurations, Lemke (1979, 1982), Dolivo (1980), Spinnler and Sillers (1981), Miller and Freese (1983), Morita (1984), Phillips (1984), Sonu (1985), Tazaki and Osawa (1985), Rasek (1986), Carr and Wachenschwanz (1988), Cavellin and Callu (1988), Graubart (1988), Komatsu et al (1988), Wolf and Neuman (1989), and others note that denser tape recording is possible. Such higher densities are typically supported by the cartridge and cassette tape drives described later in this section.

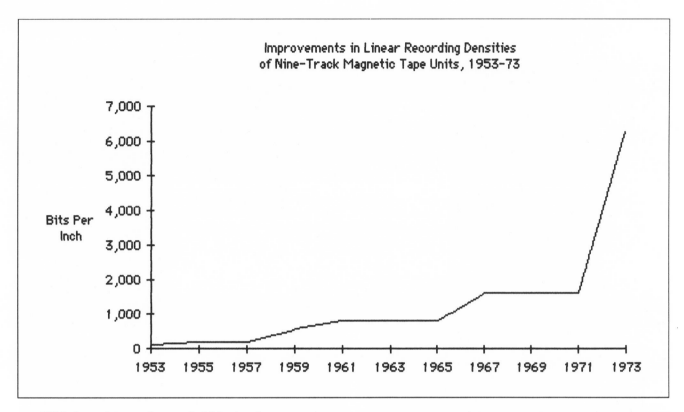

With just nine tracks per half inch of tape, a given reel's track density -- in effect, 18 tracks per inch -- is very low when compared to disks. Fixed magnetic disk systems, as described in Part One of this report, routinely support densities exceeding 1,000 tracks per inch, while optical disk track densities exceed 14,000 tracks per inch. The three commonly encountered linear recording densities of 800, 1,600, and 6,250 bits per inch are likewise much lower than their magnetic and optical disk counterparts. Applying the formula (linear density multiplied by track density) discussed in Part One of this report, areal recording densities for nine-track magnetic tape on reels range from 14,400 bits per square inch for data recorded at 800 bits per linear inch to 112,500 bits per square inch for data recorded at 6,250 bits per linear inch. At their highest, areal recording densities associated with nine-track magnetic tape on reels are comparable to those of magnetic disk drives introduced in the early 1960s. Areal densities associated with new fixed magnetic disk systems exceed 60 million bits per square inch, while optical disks routinely support areal recording densities in excess of 150 million bits per square inch. Even the lowest capacity floppy disks support areal recording densities greater than 500,000 bits per square inch.

Although a magnetic tape's recording densities is low, its relatively large surface area -- 14,400 square inches for a 2,400-foot reel of half-inch tape -- offers generous recording space. By way of contrast, one side of a 14-inch magnetic or optical disk platter only provides about 150 square inches of recordable surface. If its entire recordable surface could be used for data, a 2,400-foot reel of magnetic tape would contain 23 megabytes at a linear recording density of 800 bits per inch, 46 megabytes at a linear recording density of 1,600 bits per inch, and 180 megabytes at a linear recording density of 6,250 bits per inch. Actual capacity is limited, however, by the tape drive's operating characteristics.

Most reel-to-reel tape devices operate in the start/stop mode. When reading and recording data, blank spaces -- called inter-record gaps -- must be left between records to accommodate such start/stop actions. Such inter-record gaps reduce the tape's overall data storage capacity. Gap sizes vary from one tape drive to another and, for a given tape drive, with the linear recording density. Gap sizes of 0.6 inches at 1,600 bits per inch and 0.3 inches at 6,250 bits per inch are typical. In a magnetic tape storage application involving 1,000-character records and a linear recording density of 1,600 bits per inch, each record would require 0.63 inches of tape. Since each inter-record gap occupies

A nine-track, reel-to-reel magnetic tape drive. (Courtesy: Groupe Bull)

0.6 inches, 49 percent of the tape would be occupied by gaps. In this example, a 2,400-foot reel of magnetic tape with a raw data capacity of 46 megabytes recorded at 1,600 bits per linear inch would actually contain about 22.5 megabytes. With the same data recorded at 6,250 bits per inch, each 1,000 character record would occupy 0.16 inch. Since each inter-record gap requires 0.3 inches, gaps would consume over 60 percent of the tape's surface. A 2,400-foot reel of magnetic tape with a raw storage capacity of 180 megabytes recorded at 6,250 bits per linear inch would actually be limited to about 72 megabytes of data.

To improve the storage capacity of a given reel, multiple records are typically combined into blocks, thereby minimizing the number of gaps. When 1,000-character records are grouped into blocks of 16 records each at a linear recording density of 1,600 bits per inch, each block would occupy 10 inches of tape, and gaps would occupy less than seven percent of the tape's surface. In citing magnetic tape capacities, manufacturers' product literature often assumes that record blocking will reduce gap areas to 10 percent of the tape surface, yielding approximate storage capacities of 21 megabytes per 2,400-foot reel at 800 bits per inch, 40 megabytes per 2,400-foot reel at 1,600 bits per inch, and 160 megabytes per 2,400-foot reel at 6,250 bits per inch.

Actual tape capacities will vary, of course, with the blocking factors employed in particular applications. Kouvatsos and Wong (1984) and Kuan (1987) discuss optimal block sizes in magnetic tape recording, while Bianchi et al (1989) and Van Maren et al (1989) describe proprietary super-blocking and data compression techniques developed by Hewlett-Packard to improve tape storage capacities. While large block sizes will significantly increase the recording capacity of a given reel of magnetic tape, they can adversely affect a tape drive's performance, since entire blocks of data must be read at one time. Blocking factors aside, 9-track magnetic tape on 2,400-foot reels offers far lower storage capacity than their optical disk cartridges. As an example, a 14-inch write-once optical disk cartridge with 6.8 gigabytes of double-sided recording capacity can store the equivalent of approximately 320 reels of magnetic tape recorded at 800 bits per linear inch, 170 reels of magnetic tape recorded at 1,600 bits per linear inch, and 40 reels of magnetic tape recorded at 6,250

bits per linear inch. As described in Part One of this report, Eastman Kodak has developed a 14-inch optical disk cartridge with 8.2 gigabytes of double-sided storage capacity. Such disks can store the equivalent of approximately 390 reels of magnetic tape recorded at 800 bits per linear inch, 205 reels of magnetic tape recorded at 1,600 bits per linear inch, and 50 reels of magnetic tape recorded at 6,250 bits per linear inch.

With two gigabytes of double-sided capacity, a 12-inch write-once optical disk of the type utilized in some magnetic tape replacement systems designed for mainframe and minicomputer installations can store the equivalent of approximately 95 reels of magnetic tape recorded at 800 bits per linear inch, 50 reels of magnetic tape recorded at 1,600 bits per linear inch, and 12 reels of magnetic tape recorded at 6,250 bits per linear inch. As noted in Part One of this report, several newer 12-inch WORM systems offer much more than two-gigabytes of double-sided capacity. Six-gigabyte models, for example, can store the equivalent of approximately 285 reels of magnetic tape recorded at 800 bits per linear inch, 150 reels of magnetic tape recorded at 1,600 bits per linear inch, and 38 reels of magnetic tape recorded at 6,250 bits per linear inch.

While IBM continues to offer nine-track, reel-to-reel tape drives, its 3480 Magnetic Tape Cartridge Subsystem provides a more compact, convenient, and reliable alternative to magnetic tape reels in mainframe and minicomputer installations. Introduced in 1984, the 3480 records data on half-inch magnetic tape that is packaged in a plastic cartridge measuring four inches by five inches by one inch in size. The characteristics and significance of 3480 hardware and media are discussed by Freeman (1985), Priestley (1985), Simpson (1985), Cannon et al (1986), Collinson (1986), Cox and Taylor (1986), Morris (1986), Winarski et al (1986), Hage (1987), and Watson (1989). Following IBM's lead, vendors of plug-compatible storage equipment for IBM mainframes, as well as manufacturers of peripheral devices for other mainframe and minicomputers, have since introduced 3480-type systems as high-performance additions to their magnetic tape product lines. Digital Equipment Corporation, for example, offers the TA90 for VAX installations. Other examples include the CTS 8500 from Groupe Bull and the Unisys Model 5073.

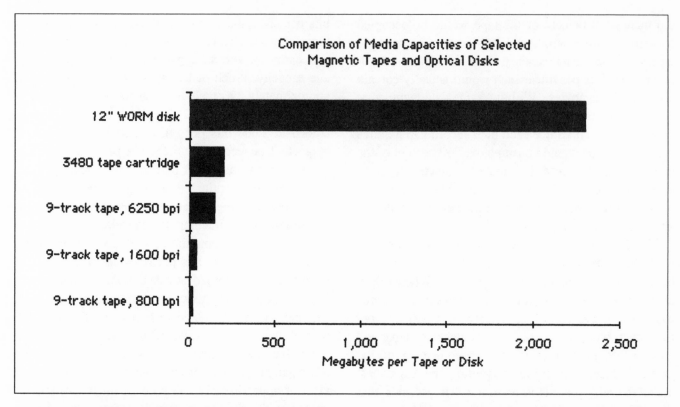

Patel (1985) describes the adaptive cross-parity (AXP) code employed by the IBM 3480 Magnetic Tape Cartridge Subsystem. To support the higher recording densities permitted by AXP coding, 3480-type cartridges utilize magnetic tape coated with chromium dioxide rather than ferric oxide employed by conventional reel-to-reel tape systems. The recording characteristics of chromium dioxide materials are discussed in various technical publications, including Bradshaw et al (1986), Honda et al (1988, 1989), and Tobin et al (1988). With 18 tracks per half-inch tape, the IBM 3480 cartridge's track density is twice that of magnetic tape reels, but it is still a small fraction of the track densities supported by magnetic and optical disk systems. At 38,000 bits per inch, however, linear recording densities compare favorably with their magnetic and optical disk counterparts. The resulting areal densities approach 1.4 million bits per square inch -- about ten times greater than reels of nine-track magnetic tape recorded at 6,250 bits per inch but a fraction of the areal densities supported by the magnetic and optical disks described in Part One of this report.

A standard 3480-type cartridge contains 550 feet of magnetic tape and offers 275 square inches of recording surface. When data is recorded in blocks of 24,000 characters, a 3480-type cartridge can store 200 mega-

bytes of data -- the equivalent of five reels of magnetic tape recorded at 1,600 bits per inch but just 1.25 reels recorded at 6,250 bits per inch. Several manufacturers of 3480-type systems employ data compression algorithms to increase the data storage capacity to 400 megabytes per cartridge. Fujita and Kakuse (1987), for example, describe such a system developed by Hitachi. While 3480 cartridges can consolidate magnetic tape collections, optical disks offer much greater storage capacities. Assuming uncompressed cartridge recording, a 12-inch write-once optical disk with two gigabytes of double-sided capacity can store the equivalent 10 3480-type cartridges. A 14-inch write-once optical disk with 6.8 gigabytes of double-sided capacity can store the equivalent of 34 3480-type cartridges.

Depending on the model selected, a 3480-type cartridge drive will be configured with two to four tape transports. To facilitate cartridge handling, each tape transport can be optionally equipped with an automatic stack loader capable of accommodating six to 10 cartridges. Such equipment configurations provide unattended access to 1.2 to two gigabytes per stack loader. For mainframe installations requiring unattended access to larger amounts of data, several companies have developed automated cartridge retrieval units with robotic components. Such devices are the magnetic tape counterparts of the optical disk jukeboxes described in Part One of this report. As described by Larson et al (1987) and Kendall (1988), the StorageTek 4400 Automated Cartridge System from Storage Technology Corporation features a cylindrical storage module for 6,000 3480-type cartridges containing up to 1.2 terabytes of data -- a total that compares favorably with the high-capacity optical disk jukeboxes employed in some magnetic tape replacement applications. On instructions from an attached controller, a robotic assembly will locate a desired cartridge and mount it in a tape drive. A single system can support up to 16 tape transports. At eleven seconds, the cartridge retrieval time is slightly longer than that of optical disk jukeboxes, some of which can retrieve and mount a cartridge in less than eight seconds. Other automated cartridge retrieval systems are described by Ito (1980), Ito et al (1980), Itao (1985), Savage (1985), and Nagatani

(1986).

The half-inch reel-to-reel and cartridge tape systems described above are primarily intended for data backup and archiving in mainframe and large minicomputer installations. Half-inch tape systems, in both reel-to-reel and cartridge formats, have been available for smaller computer installations since the early 1970s. Addleson (1986) provides a useful survey of nine-track tape drives for microcomputer installations, and a number of vendors have developed half-inch tape cartridge drives in the eight-inch form factor suitable for minicomputer and microcomputer equipment configurations. Such devices utilize 3480-type cartridges, but rather than operating in the start/stop mode associated with magnetic tape reels, they employ "streaming" techniques -- that is, they record data in a continuous format, that eliminates large interblock gaps and minimizes wasted space. Streaming tape technology is dis-

The IBM 3480 Magnetic Tape Cartridge Subsystem, shown here with automatic cartridge loaders. (Courtesy: IBM)

cussed by Aseo (1984), Oka and Ishikawa (1984), Chu (1985), Dong et al (1985), Noguchi et al (1985), Ruska et al (1985), Conti (1986), Cutler (1986, 1986a), and Winkler (1988).

Designed to back up the entire contents of commonly encountered Winchester disk drives, the capacities of half-inch streaming tape systems range from less than 90 megabytes to more than 500 megabytes per 3480-type cartridge. Among the most widely encountered examples, Digital Equipment Corporation's TK50 magnetic tape subsystem provides 95 megabytes of formatted storage capacity per 600-foot cartridge. Intended for MicroVAX installations, its areal recording density is approximately 293,500 bits per square inch, based on a linear density of 6,700 bits per inch with an effective track density of 44 tracks per inch. Where higher capacity is required, Digital's TK70 magnetic tape subsystem can store 296 megabytes per 600-foot cartridge. Its areal recording density is 960,000 bits per square inch, based on a linear density of 10,000 bits per inch with an effective track density of 44 tracks per inch. Fujitsu America offers a half-inch tape drive that can store 120 megabytes per 450-foot cartridge. The several cartridge tape drives in Cipher Data Products' 3830 Series can store 320 megabytes per 600-foot cartridge. When 1,100-foot, extended

length cartridges are utilized, the storage capacity increases to 570 megabytes.

While these and other half-inch cartridge tape products employ proprietary recording formats, standards developed by the Working Group for Half-Inch/ Tape Cartridge (HI/TC) Compatibility are designed to promote half-inch streaming tape technology by ensuring compatibility and facilitating data interchange among the products of different manufacturers. With the HI/TC-1 format, data is recorded in serpentine fashion on 24 parallel tracks, two tracks at a time. When the end of the tape is reached on one pair of tracks, the tape direction is reversed and the recording head is moved to the next pair of tracks. The recording head and tape drive must make twelve passes to fill a cartridge. The cartridge's linear recording density of 18,000 bits per inch is effectively reduced to 12,700 bits per inch after the addition of error correction and block formatting codes. Each block consists of 1,024 bytes of data plus 160 bytes of error correction codes. The track density is 48 tracks per inch, and the areal recording density is approximately 610,000 bits per square inch after error correction and block formatting codes are applied. Media storage capacity is 240 megabytes per 550-foot cartridge. HI/TC-1 systems utilize ferric oxide tape. The HI/TC-2 standard, which is based on chromium

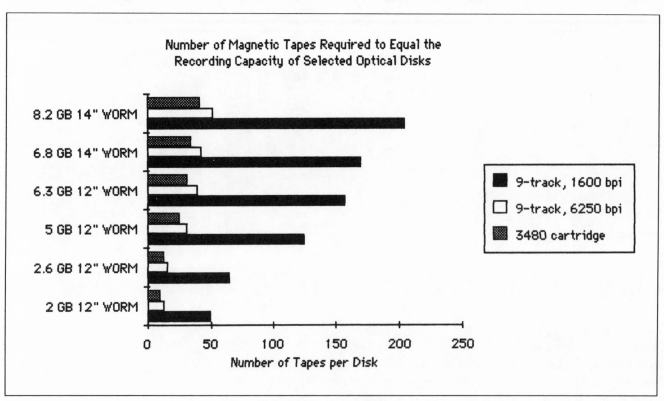

The StorageTek 4400 Automated Cartridge System provides unattended access to 1.2 terabytes of data. (Courtesy: Storage Technology Corporation)

dioxide tape, provides 480 megabytes of storage capacity per 550-foot cartridge.

In microcomputer and desktop workstation installations, half-inch streaming tape cartridge systems compete most directly with 5.25-inch optical disk products. When the HI/TC-1 format is used, a 550-foot cartridge can record slightly more data than the 230-megabyte, 5.25-inch write-once optical disk utilized by the ISI 525WC drive. A 600-megabyte, 5.25-inch write-once optical disk, however, can store the equivalent of 2.5 half-inch HI/TC-1 streaming tape cartridges, while a 1.28-gigabyte WORM disk can store the equivalent of 5.3 streaming tape cartridges. As tape length increases, however, the capacity of half-inch streaming tape cartridge approaches that of medium-capacity, 5.25-

inch optical disks.

Like their half-inch counterparts, quarter-inch magnetic tape systems are designed for streaming data recording in small computer installations. Although commonly termed data cartridges, they are actually cassettes since they house both a tape supply and a take-up spool in a single plastic shell. Half-inch, 3480-type cartridges, by way of contrast, contain only the supply spool; tape passes out of the cartridge during use and must be rewound before the cartridge is removed from the drive.

Imprecise descriptive terminology aside, quarter-inch data cartridges are available in standard and mini sizes. The standard quarter-inch data cartridge measures four inches high by six inches wide by 0.625 inch-

A streaming tape drive that utilizes half-inch cartridges. (Courtesy: Laser Magnetic Storage International)

es deep. At the time this report was prepared, tape lengths ranged from 150 to 1,000 feet, with 600-foot cartridges being the most common configuration.

Regardless of tape length, standard data cartridges are designed for use with tape drives that require a 5.25-inch installation slot in a microcomputer's system unit. External units, measuring approximately the size of a 5.25-inch magnetic or optical disk drive, are also available. Designed for use with tape drives that are compatible with 3.5-inch installation slots, quarter-inch mini data cartridges measure two inches high by three inches wide by 0.5 inches deep. At the time this report was prepared, tape lengths ranged from 140 to 308 feet.

Introduced in the early 1970s, the first quarter-inch data cartridge systems were utilized for software distribution and selective backup of data files in minicomputer applications. Development of the technology can be traced in various published product descriptions, including Aseo (1983), Domshy (1983, 1986), Armbrust (1985), Becker et al (1985), Harvey (1985), Henry and Niquette (1985), Wright (1985), DiFede (1986), Machrone (1986), Nine (1986), Rubel (1986), Stark (1986), Rosch (1987), Mayer (1988), Parkinson (1988), Swartz (1988), Gills (1989), Miller (1989), and Topham

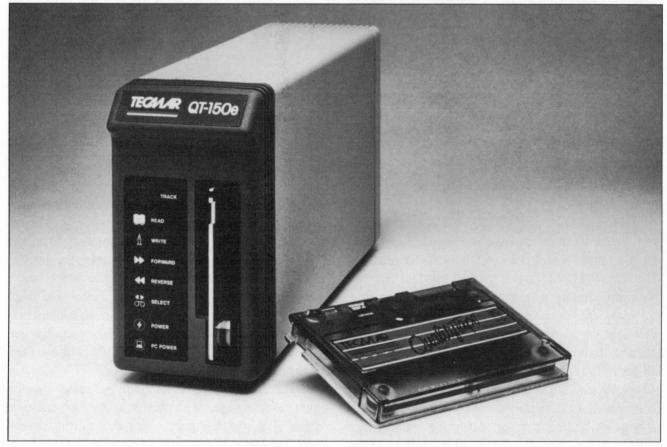

A quarter-inch tape drive and cartridge. (Courtesy: Tecmar)

(1989). Employing proprietary recording formats, the earliest quarter-inch magnetic tape drives offered less than three megabytes of storage capacity per 300-foot cartridge and supported linear recording densities of just 1,600 bits per inch. As with other types of magnetic storage products, however, cartridge capacities and recording densities have increased steadily and significantly.

Intended for microcomputer installations, newer quarter-inch tape products are typically designed to back up an entire hard disk drive in a single operation. Their recording capacities consequently reflect those of the most widely encountered microcomputer-oriented hard disk drives. To promote the technology and facilitate its acceptance, the Quarter-Inch Cartridge (QIC) Drive Compatibility Working Group has developed various recording formats for both standard-size and mini data cartridges. At the time this report was prepared, five QIC formats applied to standard data cartridges. The five formats are identified by numeric designations that reflect their approximate storage capacities:

1. The QIC-24 format, which was adopted in 1983, specifies nine-track serpentine recording at a linear density of 8,000 bits per inch. With an effective track density of 36 tracks per inch, the areal recording density is 288,000 bits per square inch. Cartridge capacity varies with tape length: 450-foot data cartridges, such as the 3M DC300XL/P or equivalent, provide approximately 45 megabytes of storage capacity, about one-fifth the amount supported by the lowest-capacity, 5.25-inch WORM disks; 600-foot data cartridges, such as the popular 3M DC600A or equivalent, offer approximately 60 megabytes of storage capacity, about one-fourth the amount supported by the lowest-

Summary of Quarter-Inch Cartridge (QIC) Formats
for Standard Data Cartridges

Format	Linear Density*	Track Density**	Areal Density†	Cartridge Type	Storage Capacity
QIC-24	8,000	36	288,000	DC300XL	45 MB
QIC-120	10,000	60	600,000	DC6150	125 MB
QIC-150	10,000	72	720,000	DC6150	150 MB
QIC-525	16,000	104	1,664,000	DC6320	320 MB
QIC-525	16,000	104	1,664,000	DC6525	525 MB
QIC-1350	38,000	120	4,560,000	DC9135	1.35 GB

Summary of Quarter-Inch Cartridge (QIC) Formats
for Mini Data Cartridges

Format	Linear Density*	Track Density**	Areal Density†	Cartridge Type	Storage Capacity
QIC-40	10,000	80	800,000	DC2000	40 MB
QIC-80	14,700	112	1,646,400	DC2080	80 MB
QIC-80	14,700	112	1,646,400	DC2120	120 MB
QIC-100	10,000	96	960,000	DC2000	86 MB
QIC-110	18,000	104	1,872,000	DC2110	110 MB
QIC-128	18,000	128	2,304,000	DC2128	128 MB

   * Bits per inch
  ** Tracks per inch
   † Bits per square inch

capacity, double-sided 5.25-inch WORM disks.

2. The QIC-120 format, which was adopted in 1985 and revised in 1987, specifies 15-track serpentine recording at a linear density of 10,000 bits per inch. With an effective track density of 60 tracks per inch, the areal recording density is 600,000 bits per square inch. With approximately 125 megabytes per 600-foot data cartridge (3M DC6150 or equivalent), the QIC-120 format offers 55 percent as much storage as the lowest-capacity, double-sided 5.25-inch WORM disks and 20 percent as much storage as medium-capacity, double-sided 5.25-inch WORM and erasable optical disks.

3. The QIC-150 format, which was adopted in 1987, specifies 18-track serpentine recording at a linear density of 10,000 bits per linch. With an effective track density of 72 tracks per inch, the areal recording density is 720,000 bits per square inch. With approximately 150 megabytes per 600-foot data cartridge (3M DC6150 or equivalent), the QIC-150 format offers 65 percent as much storage as the lowest-capacity, double-sided 5.25-inch WORM disks and 25 percent as much storage as medium-capacity, double-sided 5.25-inch WORM and erasable optical disks. When a 1,000-foot data cartridge (3M DC6250 or equivalent) is used, the QIC-150 format can store 250 megabytes -- 20 megabytes more than the lowest capacity, double-sided 5.25-inch WORM disks but 50 megabytes less than the single-sided capacity of medium-capacity WORM and erasable optical disks.

4. The QIC-525 format, which was adopted in 1989, specifies 26-track serpentine recording at a linear density of 16,000 bits per inch. It was formerly designated the QIC-320 format. With an effective track density of 104 tracks per inch, the QIC-525 format's areal recording density exceeds 1.6 million bits per square inch. With approximately 320 megabytes per 600-foot data cartridge (3M DC6320 or equivalent), the QIC-525 format offers about fifty percent as much storage as medium-capacity, double-sided 5.25-inch WORM and erasable optical disks. When 1,000-foot data cartridges (3M DC6525 or equivalent) are used, the QIC-525 format provides 525 megabytes of storage capacity -- 75 megabytes less than the medium-capacity, double-sided 5.25-inch WORM and optical disks.

5. The QIC-1350 format was approved in 1989, but products based on it were not commercially available at the time this report was prepared. The QIC-1350 format specifies 30-track serpentine recording at a linear density of 38,000 bits per inch. With an effective track density of 120 tracks per inch, the QIC-525 format's areal recording density exceeds 4.5 million bits per square inch. As their name suggests, QIC-1350 format data cartridges (3M DC9135 or equivalent) will store 1.35 gigabytes -- approximately 100 megabytes more than the highest-capacity, double-sided 5.25-inch WORM and erasable optical disks.

Several vendors have developed systems that employ data compression algorithms to further increase the capacities of quarter-inch data cartridges. When data compression is utilized, the QIC-525 format supports gigabyte-level storage capacities. Among non-standard technologies, Verbatim Corporation has demonstrated a prototype version of a quarter-inch cartridge system with two gigabytes of storage capacity. When it becomes commercially available, it will offer recording capacities comparable to some 12-inch write-once optical disks.

QIC recording formats for mini data cartridges are designed for quarter-inch magnetic tape drives that employ the 3.5-inch form factor. Such systems have proven especially popular in IBM PS/2 and other equipment configurations that feature 3.5-inch storage peripherals. They are sometimes collectively termed DC2000 drives because they utilize 3M DC2000 or equivalent mini data cartridges. At the time this report was prepared, five QIC formats for mini data cartridges had been approved. As a group, they offer less storage capacity than their standard data cartridge counterparts:

1. The QIC-40 format, which was approved in 1987, specifies 20-track serpentine recording at a linear density of 10,000 bits per inch. With an effective track density of 80 tracks per inch, the areal recording density is 800,000 bits per square inch. As discussed above, cartridge capacities varies with tape length: 205-foot mini data cartridges, such as the 3M DC2000 or equivalent, provide approximately 40 megabytes of storage capacity -- less than one-fifth the amount supported by the lowest-capacity, 5.25-inch WORM disks.

Irwin Magnetics offers a proprietary mini data cartridge system with 40 megabytes of storage capacity per DC2000 cartridge. Although it does not conform to QIC standards, it is widely utilized.

2. The QIC-80 format, which was approved in 1988, specifies 28-track serpentine recording at a linear density of 14,700 bits per inch. With an effective track density of 112 tracks per inch, the areal recording density is approximately 1.65 million bits per square inch. When used with 205-foot mini data cartridges (3M DC2080 or equivalent), the QIC-80 format provides approximately 80 megabytes of storage capacity -- approximately 35 percent of the amount supported by the lowest-capacity, double-sided 5.25-inch WORM disks. When used with 308-foot mini data cartridges (3M DC2120 or equivalent), the QIC-80 format provides approximately 120 megabytes of storage capacity -- slightly more than half as much as the lowest-capacity, double-sided 5.25-inch WORM disks. Among non-standard products, Irwin Magnetics offers a proprietary mini data cartridge drive with 80 megabytes of recording capacity per DC2000 cartridge.

3. The QIC-100 format, which was approved in 1989, specifies 24-track serpentine recording at a linear density of 10,000 bits per inch. With an effective track density of 96 tracks per inch, the areal recording density is 960,000 bits per square inch. When used with 205-foot mini data cartridges (3M DC2000 or equivalent), the QIC-100 format provides approximately 86 megabytes of storage capacity -- approximately 37 percent of the amount supported by the lowest-capacity, double-sided 5.25-inch WORM disks.

4. The QIC-110 format, which was approved in 1988, specifies 26-track serpentine recording at a linear density of 18,000 bits per inch. With an effective track density of 104 tracks per inch, the areal recording density is approximately 1.9 million bits per square inch. When used with 205-foot mini data cartridges (3M DC2110 or equivalent), the QIC-110 format provides approximately 110 megabytes of storage capacity -- slightly less than half of the amount supported by the lowest-capacity, double-sided 5.25-inch WORM disks.

5. The QIC-128 format, which was approved in 1989, specifies 32-track serpentine recording at a linear density of 18,000 bits per inch. With an effective track density of 128 tracks per inch, the areal recording density is approximately 2.3 million bits per square inch. When used with 205-foot mini data cartridges (3M DC2086 or equivalent), the QIC-128 format provides 86 megabytes of storage capacity. When used with 308-foot mini data cartridges (3M DC2128 or equivalent), the QIC-128 format provides 128 megabytes of storage capacity -- approximately one-half the amount supported by the lowest-capacity, double-sided 5.25-inch WORM disks.

The earliest microcomputer systems utilized modified audio cassette recorders as data storage peripherals, but such devices were hampered by low recording capacities and marginal performance characteristics. As prices of floppy disk drives declined, they virtually disappeared from use. Teac Corporation of America, however, offers digital cassette recorders as an alternative to half-inch and quarter-inch data cartridge drives for magnetic disk backup and data archiving. The Teac MT-2ST product line uses 4mm computer-grade tape packaged in standard Philips-type cassettes in 600-foot lengths. The MT-2ST/4S records 60 megabytes of data in nine tracks at a linear density of 8,000 bits per inch. With a nominal track density of 58 tracks per inch, its areal recording density is 464,000 bits per square inch. The MT-2ST/N series records 155 megabytes of data in nine tracks at a linear density of 12,800 bits per inch. It can store about one-fourth as much data as medium-capacity, double-sided 5.25-inch WORM and erasable optical disks.

An increasingly popular group of computer storage products utilizes helical scan technology to record large amounts of machine-readable data on magnetic tape packaged in video or audio cassettes. The quarter- and half-inch magnetic tape drives described above employ longitudinal recording methods. Stationary magnetic heads record and read data in parallel tracks which run the entire length of the tape. Helical scan systems, in contrast, use two or more heads to record data in narrow tracks that are positioned at an acute angle with respect to the edges of tape. Depending on the system, start/ stop or streaming operation may be utilized. Precise head positioning permits high track densities which, combined with high linear recording densities, yield areal recording densities that are unattainable with longitudinal tape recording systems. The characteristics and advantages of helical scan technology are discussed, in varying levels of technical detail, by Ebstein (1983), Podmore (1983), Proper (1983), Hayakawa et al (1985), Sugaya (1986), Balue and Koliopoulos (1987), Hinz (1987), Nelson and Rymer (1987), Sano et al (1987), Barron (1988), Carr and Wachenschwanz (1988), Domshy (1988), Eiberger (1988), Oelschlaeger (1988, 1988a), Platte et al (1988), Rodriguez (1988), Urrows and Urrows (1988, 1988a), Wright (1988), and Yeh et al (1988).

Offering storage capacities that exceed those of 5.25-inch optical disk systems and compare favorably with 12-inch WORM disks, some helical scan systems

record computer processible data on half-inch magnetic tape packaged in video cassettes. While they have only recently been widely publicized, data storage products based on video tape technology have been utilized for more than a decade. Their characteristics are discussed by Curtis and Rolfe (1971), Schneidewind and Syms (1974), Wade (1983), Baugh et al (1986), and Hales (1987). Among commercially available products, the Gigastore disk drives, sold by Digi-Data Corporation, illustrate the enormous storage capacity offered by data-oriented video cassette recorders. As its name suggests, the Gigastore 2.5 system can record 2.5 gigabytes on a T-120 VHS cassette. Its linear recording density of 17,345 bits per inch is much higher than that of the densest nine-track magnetic tape reels but only half that of 3480 cartridge systems. With 650

A helical scan magnetic tape system that records digital data on VHS cassettes. (Courtesy: Digi-Data Corporation)

tracks per inch, the areal recording density is 11.3 million bits per square inch. Where greater storage capacity is required, the Gigastore 5.4 system can record 5.4 gigabytes per T-120 cassette. With a linear recording density of 34,870 bits per inch and 650 tracks per inch, its areal recording density is 22.7 million bits per square inch. Magnetic tape cassettes recorded by the Gigastore 2.5 system can store twice as much data as

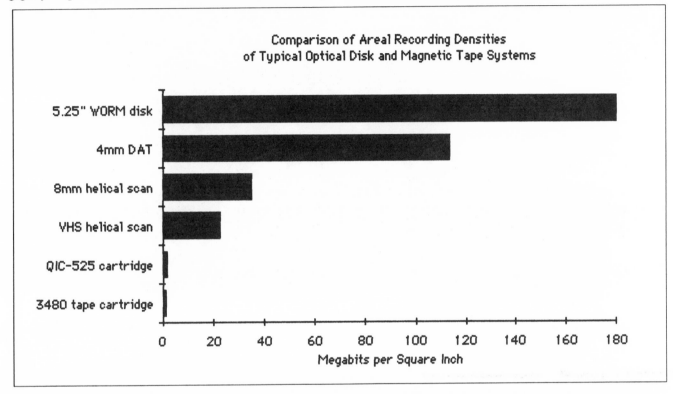

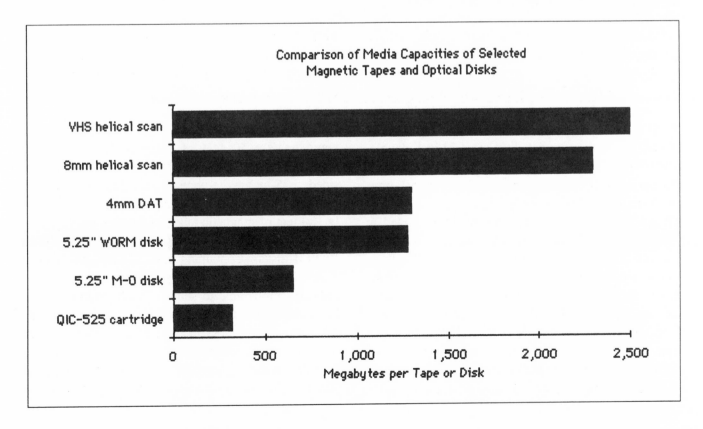

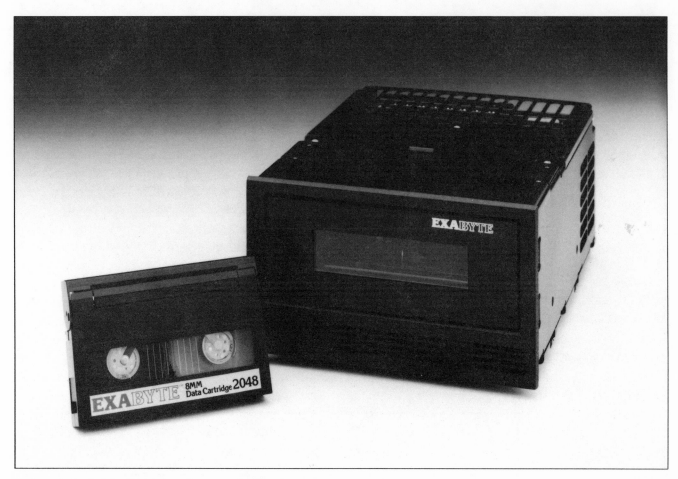

An 8mm helical scan tape unit. (Courtesy: Exabyte)

the double-sided 1.28-gigabyte optical disks utilized by the ISI 525GB, the highest capacity 5.25-inch WORM drive available at the time this report was prepared. Gigastore 2.5-gigabyte cassettes offer as much storage capacity as many 12-inch, double-sided WORM disks. Cassettes recorded by the Gigastore 5.4 system can store more data than most 12-inch double-sided WORM disks, and they provide 80 percent of the storage capacity offered by double-sided, 14-inch optical disks.

As an alternative to half-inch media packaged in VHS-format cassettes, several helical scan recording systems employ 8mm cassettes patterned after 8mm videocassette products but containing a metallic tape that is specifically designed for high density data recording. Products like the EXB-8200 from Exabyte Corporation and the File Safe Series 2100 tape unit from Mountain Computer can record 43,200 bits per linear inch. With 819 tracks per inch, their areal recording densities exceed 35 million bits per square

inch. Termed 8mm data cartridges, the cassettes themselves measure 3.7 inches wide by 2.5 inches high by 0.6 inches deep. Storage capacities range from 291 megabytes to 2.3 gigabytes per cartridge, depending on tape length.

The lowest-capacity 8mm cartridges, which contain approximately 50 feet of magnetic tape, can store about half as much data as a medium-capacity, double-sided, 5.25-inch write-once or erasable optical disk. A medium-length cartridge, which contains approximately 180 feet of magnetic tape, can store about 1.2 gigabytes -- as much as the highest capacity, 5.25-inch WORM disks. Containing approximately 350 feet of magnetic tape, the 2.3-gigabyte cartridge offers storage capacity comparable to some 12-inch WORM disks. For applications requiring backup of very large data bases or online access to sequentially-structured data sets, Exabyte Corporation has announced an automated cartridge handling system, a jukebox-type retrieval unit that provides unattended selection and mounting of designated 8mm cartridges. Supporting 120 cartridges, the system provides unattended access to 276 gigabytes of data -- a total that compares favorably with the highest capacity optical disk jukeboxes.

Based on audio rather than video recording products, one of the newest computer storage technologies utilizes helical scan techniques to record machine-readable data on 4mm magnetic tape packaged in a digital audio tape (DAT) cassette. As discussed by Nakajima and Odaka (1983), Hayashi et al (1986), Hitomi and Taki (1986), Itoh et al (1986), Nagaki et al (1986), Odaka et al (1986), Ohtake et al (1986), Shimpuku et al (1986), Adachi et al (1987), Dare and Katsumi (1987), Doi et al (1987), Iwashita (1987), Arai et al (1988), Hitomi (1988), Mori et al (1988), Ogiro et al (1988), Wood (1988), Motoyama et al (1989), Parker (1989), Vanker (1989), and others, digital audio tape systems were originally developed for super high fidelity audio applications, but they can also record computer processible data. At the time this report was prepared, at least a dozen companies had announced their intention to market such data-oriented products.

DAT cassettes measure three inches wide by two inches high by 0.4 inches deep. DAT drives are available as standalone units or in internal configurations based on the 5.25-inch form factor. At 61,000 bits per inch, DAT's linear recording density was the highest of any magnetic tape system available at the time this report was prepared. When multiplied by a track density of 1,869 tracks per inch, the resulting areal recording density exceeds 1144 million bits per square inch. Recognizing the importance of standardization, two groups of equipment manufacturers have proposed DAT recording formats for industry adoption. The format proposed by the DDS Manufacturers Group can store 1.3 gigabytes of data; the competing Data/DAT committee has proposed a format with one-gigabyte of storage capacity. The two formats employ different error correction schemes and operating modes. In the absence of finalized specifications for either format, several

A digital audio tape (DAT) subsystem. (Courtesy: Wangtek)

manufacturers have introduced DAT systems based on proprietary technologies. At the time this report was prepared, available DAT drives could store approximately 1.2 gigabytes of data per 200-foot cassette. That amount is comparable to the highest capacity 5.25-inch optical disk systems.

PERFORMANCE CHARACTERISTICS

Regardless of format, magnetic tape systems are primarily utilized in applications -- such as data archiving, file backup, file restoration, and software distribution -- where information will be recorded and retrieved sequentially, starting at the beginning of a tape and proceeding through to the end, without reversing direction. Half-inch and quarter-inch tape cartridge systems, as discussed above, employ serpentine recording with multiple tracks laid down in reverse directions, but such tapes are not reversed until the end of the cartridge is reached.

The nine-track magnetic tapes that have historically dominated mainframe and minicomputer installations do not include synchronizing tracks or other mechanisms that define the physical locations of recorded data. As previously noted, data is separated by interblock gaps, but there is no way to address individual bytes within a block. Instead, an entire block is transferred to the host computer's memory where more specific addressing techniques can be applied. Performance comparisons based on access times to randomly requested bytes are consequently inappropriate. As discussed in Part One of this report, optical disk drives provide direct access to stored records, and -- while their access times are slower than their magnetic disk counterparts -- optical disk drives are invariably faster than magnetic tape systems.

Even where direct addressing of data is supported, the necessity of physically transversing many feet of tape makes disk-like access speeds unattainable. Assuming that a typical retrieval operation involves data recorded in the middle of a 2,400-foot reel of nine-track magnetic tape, for example, access times for data recorded at the end of a reel can approach 2.5 minutes (150,000 milliseconds) at a tape movement speed of 100 inches per second. Examination of access times supported by those cartridge tape systems that offer direct addressing of specific data files confirms the foregoing generalization. Several quarter-inch cartridge units, 8mm helical-scan cartridge drives, and 4mm digital audio tape systems can optionally store a directory of file locations in a separate partition at the beginning of each tape. In combination with a fast-forward command, such directory information can be used to rapidly advance the tape to a specific location, quickly passing over data that precedes a desired file. The resulting access times depend on the location of the file and the speed of tape movement. DAT drives, for example, advance the tape at about 30 to 60 inches per second -- 100 to 200 times the normal reading and recording rate -- in the file search mode, but they still require 20 to 40 seconds (20,000 to 40,000 milliseconds) to reach a file recorded in the middle of a 1.2-gigabyte, 200-foot cassette. By way of comparison, a Hitachi 301-A1 WORM drive loaded with a 12-inch optical disk having a single-sided capacity of 1.3 gigabytes supports an average access time of 250 milliseconds -- 80 to 160 times faster than the DAT system.

Once a particular data area is located on a magnetic tape or optical disk, the desired information must be transferred between the storage device and the host computer. As discussed in Part One of this report, data transfer rates are typically measured in multiples of bytes per second. With magnetic tape systems, data transfer rates are determined by a tape drive's velocity and linear recording density. The transfer rate supported by a given product can be calculated by the formula:

$$T = V \times D$$

where:

T = the data transfer rate in kilobytes or megabytes per second;

V = the tape velocity in inches per second; and

D = the linear recording density in bytes per inch (converted from the customary bits per inch as required).

As previously discussed, linear bit and byte densities are identical with nine-track, reel-to-reel tape systems, since the bits that encode individual characters are recorded in parallel tracks across the width of the tape. Thus, a nine-track, reel-to-reel magnetic tape drive operating at 100 inches per second will have a transfer rate of 160 kilobytes per second for data recorded at 1,600 bits per inch and 625 kilobytes per second for data recorded at 6,250 bits per inch.

As might be expected of such a well developed technology, magnetic tape transfer rates have increased steadily and significantly since the 1950s. A historical survey of nine-track, reel-to-reel tape drives intended for IBM mainframe installations indicates that improvements in data transfer rates have been largely attributable to the previously discussed improvements in linear recording densities, which increased by a factor of 62.5 between 1953 and 1973. During the same period, tape velocities increased by a factor of just 2.6.

When it was introduced in 1953, the IBM 726 magnetic tape unit could transfer just 7.5 kilobytes per second, based on a tape velocity of 75 inches per second and a linear recording density of 100 bits per inch. With the introduction of the IBM 727 magnetic tape unit in 1955, linear recording density doubled to 200 bits per inch, and the data transfer rate likewise dou-

bled to 15 kilobytes per second. Velocity was unchanged. By 1962, the IBM 729, Model IV tape unit supported a transfer rate of 90 kilobytes per second, based on a tape velocity of 112.5 inches per second and a linear recording density of 800 bits per inch. When the IBM 2401-6 tape drive was introduced in 1966, it supported a linear recording density of 1,600 bits per inch and a transfer rate of 180 kilobytes per second. The IBM 3420-7 tape drive, which was introduced in 1971, operated at 200 inches per second and supported a transfer rate of 320 kilobytes per second for data recorded at 1,600 bits per inch. With the introduction of the IBM 3420-8 tape drive in 1973, the linear recording density increased to 6,250 bits per inch, and the transfer rate correspondingly increased to 1.25 megabytes per second.

Since the mid-1980s, as previously discussed, IBM has emphasized cartridge tape systems for large mainframe installations. It continues to offer nine-track, reel-to-reel drives, however, as medium-performance devices intended for intermediate-size mainframe and minicomputer sites. The IBM 3422 Magnetic Tape Subsystem, for example, operates at 125 inches per second and supports a transfer rate of 200 kilobytes per second for data recorded at 1,600 bits per inch and 780 kilobytes per second for data recorded at 6,250 bits per

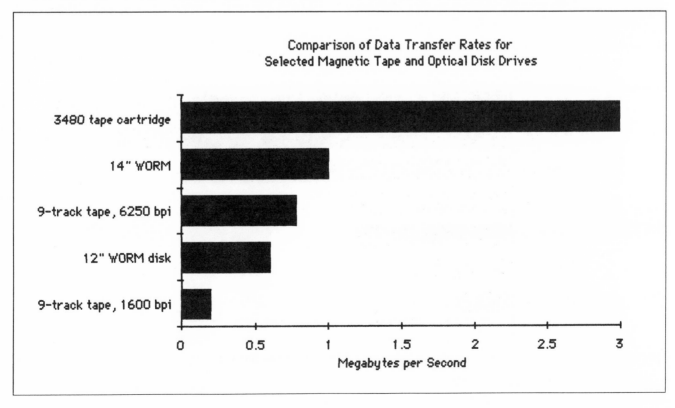

Comparison of Data Transfer Rates for
Selected Magnetic Tape and Optical Disk Drives

inch. Nine-track, reel-to-reel magnetic tape drives offered by minicomputer equipment manufacturers support similar transfer rates. Digital Equipment Corporation's Model TA97, a high-performance reel-to-reel tape unit for VAX installations, likewise operates at 125 inches per second and supports transfer rates of 200 kilobytes per second for data recorded at 1,600 bits per inch and 780 per second for data recorded at 6,250 bits per inch. In HP-9000, HP-3000, and HP-1000 minicomputer installations, Hewlett-Packard's HP-7980A magnetic tape unit supports identical data transfer capabilities.

For data recorded at 1,600 bits per inch, the nine-track, reel-to-reel magnetic tape drives discussed above are slower than optical disk drives, which -- as discussed in Part One of this report -- routinely transfer data at rates exceeding 400 kilobytes per second. For data recorded at 6,250 bits per inch, however, a magnetic tape transfer rate of 780 kilobytes per second is comparable to or faster than the transfer rates supported by most WORM and erasable optical disk drives. Several newer WORM drives can transfer one megabyte of data per second, but high-performance IBM-compatible tape drives -- such as StorageTek's Model 4670 -- exceed those capabilities. Operating at 200 inches per second, its transfer rate is 1.25 megabytes

per second for data recorded at 6,250 bits per inch. Similar nine-track magnetic tape drives intended for non-IBM mainframe installations include the Bull MTU 8205, 8206, and 8208 for DPS 8 computers; the Unisys Model BT328X for V Series mainframes, and Control Data's Model 698 and Model 5698 for Cyber 180, 960, 992, and 992 configurations.

Data transfer rates supported by entry-level, nine-track magnetic tape units are typically much slower than their optical disk counterparts. The IBM 3430 -- a low-velocity tape drive for IBM 303x, 4300, and System/38 installations -- operates at just 50 inches per second and supports transfer rates of 80 kilobytes per second for data recorded at 1,600 bits per inch and 312 kilobytes per second for data recorded at 6,250 bits per inch. The IBM 2440, which is intended for IBM 9370 installations, operates at 75 inches per second and supports transfer rates of 120 kilobytes per second for data recorded at 1,600 bits per inch and 468 kilobytes per second for data recorded at 6,250 bits per inch. Digital Equipment Corporation's TA81, an entry-level device that operates at just 25 inches per second, supports transfer rates of 40 kilobytes per second for data recorded at 1,600 bits per inch and 156 kilobytes per second for data recorded at 6,250 bits per inch. Low-cost nine-track tape drives designed for microcomputer in-

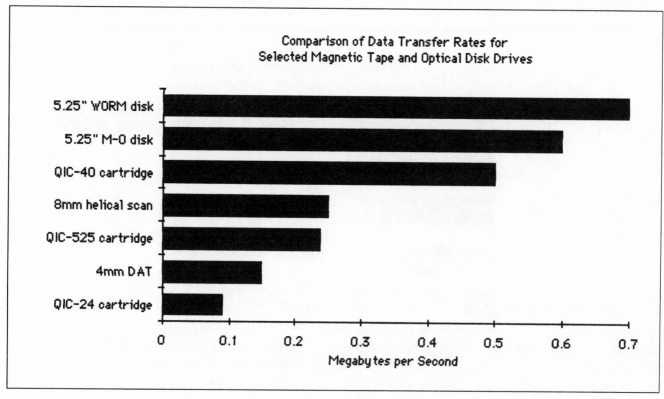

Comparison of Data Transfer Rates for
Selected Magnetic Tape and Optical Disk Drives

stallations likewise operate at 25 inches per second in the start/stop mode, but some models also support a streaming mode at faster speeds.

As a high-performance, high-density storage product designed to meet the most demanding requirements of large-scale mainframe installations, the IBM 3480, Model B22 cartridge drive transports tape at 79 inches per second and supports a data transfer rate of three megabytes per second. As such, it compares favorably with the fastest magnetic disk drives. Identical transport speeds and transfer rates are supported by other 3480-type cartridge drives, including the StorageTek 4480 and 4780, the NAS 7480 from Hitachi Data Systems, the TA90 from Digital Equipment Corporation, the Memorex 5480, and the Unisys 5073. The IBM 3480 Model B11 transports tape at 39.5 inches per second and supports a data transfer rate of 1.5 megabytes per second -- 1.5 times faster than sustained data transfer rates supported by the fastest optical disk drives.

Reflecting their importance in hard disk backup operations, data transfer rates for streaming tape units are variously expressed as the number of megabytes that can be transferred per minute or as the number of minutes required to transfer a specified number of megabytes. For half-inch streaming tape drives that utilize 3480-type cartridges, the previously discussed HI/TC-1 standard specifies a transfer time of 17 minutes for either 240 or 480 megabytes. The resulting data transfer rates of 250 or 500 kilobytes per second are comparable to rates supported by older optical disk drives. Some non-standard cartridge tape systems can operate at transfer rates approaching one megabyte per second, allowing them to back up one gigabyte of data in less than 20 minutes.

For quarter-inch data cartridge systems, transfer rates vary with the recording format, but most are considerably slower than 5.25-inch write-once and erasable optical disk drives. The QIC-24 and QIC-120 formats, for example, support a sustained data transfer rate of 86.7 kilobytes per second. They will consequently require about 12 minutes to back up a 60-megabyte hard disk. At a transfer rate of 600 kilobytes per second, a magneto-optical disk drive can perform the same backup operation in less than two minutes. Supporting a sustained data transfer rate of 108.4 kilobytes per second, drives that employ the QIC-150 format can back up 60 megabytes in less than 10 minutes.

The QIC-525 format supports a sustained data transfer rate of 240 kilobytes per second. It can back up 60 megabytes in about four minutes. Mini data cartridge systems that employ the QIC-40 and QIC-80 format can support data transfer rates up to 500 kilobytes per second.

With helical scan systems, tape moves at very slow speeds, but rapidly rotating read/write heads yield relatively high effective speeds for head-to-tape motion. With 8mm data cartridge drives, for example, the tape moves at just 0.43 inches per second, but a head speed of 1,800 revolutions per minute produces an effective head-to-tape speed of 150 inches per second. Despite this relatively high velocity, however, most helical scan systems transfer data more slowly than optical disk drives. The Gigastore 2.5 described above, for example, can transfer data at 120 kilobytes per second -- about half the speed of the slowest optical disk drives. Its higher density counterpart, the Gigastore 5.4, supports a sustained transfer rate of 250 kilobytes per second which is much slower than rates sustained by newer optical disk drives. A typical 8mm data cartridge systems likewise supports a sustained transfer rate of 250 bits per second. Typical DAT transfer rates range from 140 to 185 kilobytes per second. Given the relative newness of 8mm and DAT technologies, however, future products should offer improved performance.

One potentially time consuming characteristic of magnetic tape drives -- rewind speed -- has no optical disk counterpart. Rewind rates vary from product to product. With nine-track, reel-to-reel tape systems, typical rewind speeds range from 200 to 400 inches per second. 140 inches per second is a typical rewind rate for half-inch, 3480-type cartridge drives. Quarter-inch data cartridge systems rewind tape at 90 inches per second. Among helical scan products, the VHS-based Gigastore drives require six minutes to rewind a T-120 cassette. 8mm helical scan systems rewind tape at about 30 inches per second, while DAT rewind tape at about twice that rate.

STORAGE COSTS

As discussed in Part One of this report, write-once and erasable optical storage media are far less expensive than removable magnetic disk media when costs are calculated on a per-megabyte basis. Typical optical disk media costs, as previously computed, range between 16 and 50 cents per megabyte. Measured by media prices alone, however, magnetic tape is the least expensive computer storage technology. At the time this report was prepared, a high-quality 2400-foot reel of nine-track magnetic tape could be purchased for about $15. When recorded at 6,250 bits per inch, it can store approximately 150 megabytes of data at a cost of just 10 cents per megabyte. A half-inch, IBM 3480-type magnetic tape cartridge, with 200 megabytes of storage capacity, can be purchased for about $12 or six cents per megabyte. By way of contrast, the optical disk-based magnetic tape replacement systems developed for mainframe and minicomputer installations typically utilize high-capacity, 12-inch WORM media that costs as much as 20 cents per megabyte.

Media costs for quarter-inch magnetic tape systems vary with storage capacity, which itself depends on the recording format employed by a given drive. In some cases, quarter-inch media storage costs can prove higher than their optical media counterparts. For quarter-inch tape drives that utilize the 60-megabyte QIC-24 format, for example, 3M DC600A or equivalent data cartridges can be purchased for $25 each or 42 cents per megabyte. Similarly, quarter-inch tape drives that utilize the 40-megabyte QIC-40 format record information on 3M DC2000 or equivalent mini data cartridges that cost $27 each or 55 cents per megabyte. Such tape cartridges are more expensive than 5.25-inch write-once and erasable optical disk systems which routinely offer media costs lower than 40 cents per megabyte. A 650-megabyte magneto-optical disk cartridge, for example, can be purchased for $250 or 38 cents per megabyte.

Higher-capacity quarter-inch tape systems generally fare much better in cost comparisons with optical media. Quarter-inch tape drives that employ the 80-megabyte QIC-80 format, for example, record information on 3M DC2000 or equivalent data cartridges at a cost of 28 cents per megabyte, making them competitive with magneto-optical and lower-capacity WORM media. For quarter-inch tape drives that utilize the 150-megabyte QIC-150 format, 3M DC6150 or equivalent data cartridges can be purchased for $27 each or 18 cents per megabyte. At 16 cents per megabyte, the dye-based, 800-megabyte WORM cartridges utilized by the Maxtor RXT-800S drive are slightly less costly. Quarter-inch tape drives that utilize the 320-megabyte QIC-525 format likewise employ 3M DC6150 or equivalent data cartridges, but their higher recording capacities reduce media costs to about 8.5 cents per

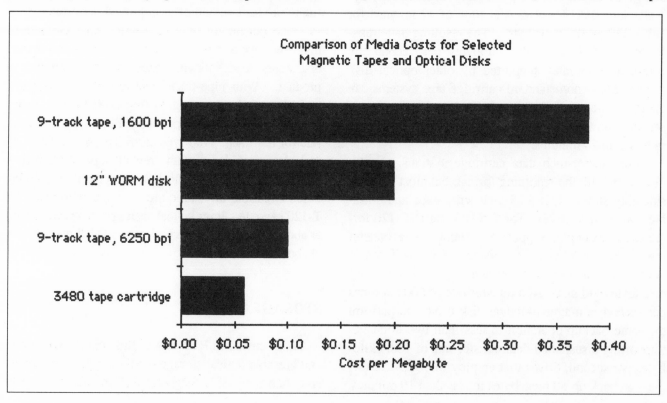

megabyte.

With their very high capacities, the magnetic tape media employed by helical scan systems offer the lowest cost per megabyte of any data storage media. Utilizing magnetic tapes designed for consumer video products, VHS-type helical scan devices offer megabyte storage costs that no currently available optical disk system can approach. The Gigastore 2.5 system, for example, can record 2.5 gigabytes of data on a high-quality VHS-type video cassette that can be purchased for less than $10. The resulting media cost is less than half a cent per megabyte. The Gigastore 5.4 system can record 5.4 gigabytes of data on a Super-VHS (S-VHS) video cassette that can be purchased for less than $20. The resulting media cost is about one-third of a cent per megabyte.

More expensive but still very competitive with optical storage media, 8mm helical scan systems can record approximately two gigabytes of data on a cartridge that costs $40 or two cents per megabyte. DAT systems can record approximately 1.3 gigabytes on a cassette that costs about $20 or 1.5 cents per megabyte. These 8mm and DAT media prices can be expected to decline as additional products become available and installations increase.

The foregoing storage cost comparisons are based on media costs alone and do not reflect differences in the prices of magnetic tape and optical disk equipment. They are consequently incomplete. As noted in Part One of this report, write-once and erasable optical disk cartridges are typically less expensive than removable magnetic disk media, but the resulting savings may be offset by the higher prices of optical disk drives. When comparing optical disk and magnetic tape systems, the opposite situation sometimes prevails; magnetic tape reels and cartridges are generally less costly than optical storage media, but optical disk drives may be lower priced than their magnetic tape counterparts.

A comparison of Digital Equipment Corporation's magnetic tape and optical disk storage systems for VAX installations illustrates this point. As previously discussed in Part Two of this report, Digital's RV20 write-once optical disk subsystem can be purchased for $38,250 in a configuration that includes one 12-inch WORM drive, a controller, cabinet, cables, and software. Double-sided, two-gigabyte WORM cartridges are priced at $400 each or 20 cents per megabyte. The company's top-of-the-line TA79 magnetic tape subsystem, including a nine-track magnetic tape drive and data channel interface, can be purchased for $77,150 -- about twice as much as the optical disk hardware configuration. For data recorded at 6,250 bits per inch

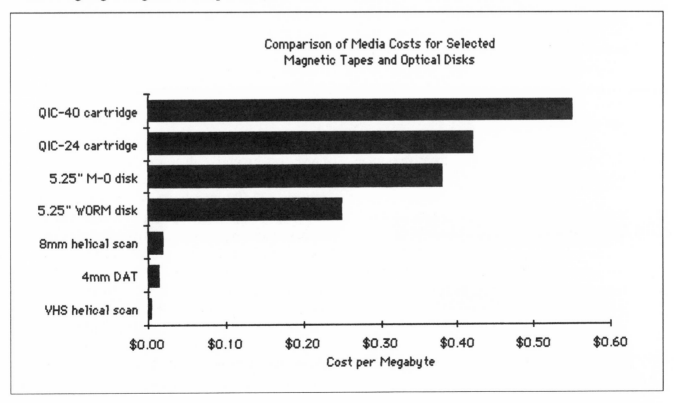

Comparison of Media Costs for Selected
Magnetic Tapes and Optical Disks

(150 megabytes per 100-foot reel), however, magnetic tapes -- as previously noted -- cost just $15 each or 10 cents per megabyte, half as much as optical storage media. Given these prices, the TA79 magnetic tape subsystem will prove less expensive than the RV20 optical storage subsystem when and if the accumulated savings in media costs exceed the substantial hardware cost differential.

As a general rule, computer storage products with low hardware costs but high media costs will prove most economical in low-volume applications; systems with high hardware costs but low media costs enjoy an increasing advantage as the amount of data to be stored increases. The point at which a given computer storage system with high equipment costs but low media costs will become less expensive than a computer storage system with low equipment costs but high media costs can be calculated by the following formula:

$$V = \frac{E_1 - E_2}{M_2 - M_1}$$

Where:

$V =$ the data storage volume, in megabytes, required for a system with high equipment costs but low media costs to be less expensive than a system with low equipment costs but high media costs;

$E_1 =$ the purchase price of the more expensive storage equipment;

$E_2 =$ the purchase price of the less expensive storage equipment;

$M_2 =$ the cost per megabyte for media to be used by the less expensive storage equipment; and

$M_1 =$ the cost per megabyte for media to be used by the more expensive storage equipment.

Applying this formula to the magnetic tape and optical disk costs outlined above, the calculation:

$$V = \frac{77,100 - 38,250}{0.20 - 0.10}$$

indicates that the TA79 magnetic tape subsystem will prove less expensive than the RV20 optical disk subsystem where the amount of data to be stored exceeds 388,500 megabytes (388.5 gigabytes). For nine-track magnetic tape reels containing 150 megabytes of data each, that total represents 2,590 tapes.

A comparison of 3480-type cartridge systems with optical disk drives also indicates an advantage for optical storage in all but the highest volume mainframe and minicomputer installations. Digital Equipment Corporation's TA90 cartridge tape subsystem, for example, can be purchased for $125,000, including dual tape drives and controller. Because the TA90 includes two tape units, it will be compared with a dual-drive RV20 optical disk subsystem. As discussed in Part Two of this report, such a dual-drive configuration can be purchased for $63,750. 3480-type cartridges, as previously noted, cost $12 each or six cents per megabyte, while write-once optical disks cost 20 cents per megabyte. Applying the formula described above, the calculation:

$$V = \frac{125,000 - 63,750}{0.20 - 0.06}$$

indicates that the TA90 cartridge tape subsystem will prove less expensive than a dual-drive RV20 optical disk subsystem where the amount of data to be stored exceeds 437,500 megabytes (437.5 gigabytes). For 3480-type cartridges containing 200 megabytes of data each, that total represents 2,188 cartridges.

These calculations are product-specific and do not imply an invariable advantage for optical disk drives over magnetic tape units in VAX installations at the indicated storage levels. It must also be emphasized that the foregoing examples are based on high-performance magnetic tape equipment. As a less expensive alternative to the TA79 and TA90, Digital Equipment Corporation offers the TA81, an entry-level nine-track magnetic tape drive that can be purchased for $38,100. Offering both lower hardware and lower media costs, it will prove less expensive than the RV20 optical storage subsystem, regardless of the volume of data to be stored. Similar comparisons can be made between various magnetic tape and optical disk subsystems offered by other mainframe and minicomputer equipment manufacturers.

Among smaller data storage devices intended for microcomputer installations, optical disk drives are typically more expensive than quarter-inch magnetic tape cartridge units that employ the QIC-24, QIC-40, QIC, 80, and QIC-150 formats. In some cases, however, optical storage media is less expensive than quarter-inch magnetic tape. At the time this report was prepared, for example, a QIC-24 cartridge tape drive suitable for use with IBM-compatible or Macintosh computers could be purchased for approximately $1,600. As previously discussed, data cartridges with 60 megabytes of recording capacity could be purchased for $25 each or 42 cents per megabyte. Among 5.25-inch write-once optical disk drives, a Corel Model 600 could be purchased for about $3,800. WORM disks, with 600 megabytes of double-sided recording capacity, cost $145 each or 24 cents per megabyte. Applying the formula outlined above, the calculation:

$$V = \frac{3{,}800 - 1{,}600}{0.42 - 0.24}$$

indicates that the Corel Model 600 optical disk drive will prove less expensive than a QIC-24 magnetic tape system where the amount of data to be stored exceeds 12,220 megabytes (12.22 gigabytes). For QIC-24 magnetic tape cartridges containing 60 megabytes of data each, that total represents 203 cartridges.

At the time this report was prepared, a QIC-40 mini data cartridge drive could be purchased for approximately $1,000. Mini data cartridges with 40 megabytes of recording capacity could be purchased for $22 each or 55 cents per megabyte. Comparing a QIC-40 drive to a Corel Model 600 optical disk drive, the calculation:

$$V = \frac{3{,}800 - 1{,}000}{0.55 - 0.24}$$

indicates that the optical disk system will prove less expensive than a QIC-40 tape system where the amount of data to be stored exceeds 9,032 megabytes (9.032 gigabytes). For QIC-40 magnetic tape cartridges containing 40 megabytes each, that total represents 226 cartridges. Similar calculations can be performed for other optical disk and magnetic tape configurations.

Part Three: The Role of Optical and Magnetic Media in Storage Hierarchies

The view that new computer storage technologies compete with and ultimately replace older ones is well established in published literature and is supported by the history of data processing. Semiconductor components, for example, have replaced magnetic cores as the technology of choice for computer main memories, just as magnetic cores previously displaced the vacuum tubes employed by the earliest computers. Among peripheral devices, magnetic storage has entirely supplanted such paper media as punched cards and punched tape. Recent attempts to revive paper-based computer storage media -- the Cauzin Soft Strip System, for example, which was marketed as an alternative to floppy disks for software publication -- have not succeeded.

As a means of comparing and contrasting their most important characteristics, Part One and Part Two of this report treated optical and magnetic storage as competing technologies. As outlined in the preceding discussion, optical disks can perform more effectively than magnetic media in certain information management applications. With their high recording capacities, for example, optical disks can store digitized images, voluminous data bases, large text files, and other information which magnetic disks cannot accommodate at reasonable cost. Optical disks are consequently preferred to their magnetic counterparts in various situations, including electronic document imaging systems, medical picture archiving and communication systems (PACS), and high-capacity file server installations in local area networks. Optical disks similarly offer a high performance alternative to magnetic tape for data backup and archiving. As noted in Part Two of this report, such magnetic tape replacement has been an important market for optical disk products since the mid-1980s.

No information storage technology is perfect, however, and certain characteristics of optical disk systems limit the range of applications which they can successfully address. Given their slow access times relative to magnetic disk systems, for example, optical disk drives are poorly suited to online transaction processing. When measured by the cost-per-megabyte online, optical disks -- as discussed in detail in Part One of this report -- can prove more expensive than magnetic disks in certain computer configurations. For data backup, magnetic tape systems are more widely available than optical disk products, and -- as noted in Part Two of this report -- they can prove less costly in some situations. As a potential advantage over write-once optical disks, magnetic tape can be erased and reused.

Competition between optical and magnetic storage technologies is not inevitable, however. In fact, optical disk drives are rarely the only storage devices in those computer configurations that utilize them. In most installations, optical disk systems supplement or complement magnetic storage devices. In electronic document imaging systems, for example, digitized document images are recorded on optical disk cartridges but the data base records that serve as an index to those images typically reside on magnetic disks. Where optical disks replace magnetic tape for data backup and archiving, magnetic disks remain the principal direct access storage devices. Even the much publicized NeXT computer system, which originally featured a storage configuration based solely on magneto-optical technology, subsequently became available in a version equipped with a fixed magnetic disk drive as standard equipment and a magneto-optical disk drive as an optional accessory.

When selecting computer storage components, information specialists must match product capabilities to application requirements. While either optical or magnetic technology may enjoy an operational or economic advantage in specific situations, some applications may be best served by a hierarchical storage configuration that incorporates both optical and magnetic components. Broadly defined, a computer storage hierarchy -- sometimes termed a computer memory hierarchy -- combines two or more storage technologies and/or devices in order to accommodate information processing requirements that cannot be successfully addressed by one technology alone. The following discussion introduces the concept of storage hierarchies, describes the most important characteristics of hierarchical implementations, and examines the potential of storage hierarchies that combine optical and magnetic devices. In so doing, it will also review the most important points raised in preceding sections of this report.

HIERARCHICAL CONCEPTS

The concept of a storage hierarchy based on media capacity, access time, cost, or other characteristics and capabilities of specific devices and media is well established in information management theory and practice. Data processing textbooks have long differentiated primary storage -- represented by main memory circuits located within or very close to the central processing unit -- from the auxiliary storage facilities provided by external peripheral devices. Among the storage peripherals themselves, secondary systems -- direct access storage devices suitable for online information processing applications -- are commonly distinguished from tertiary systems, such as magnetic tape drives,

that store media offline until the data files or other information they contain are needed for specific data processing tasks.

Such hierarchical storage concepts and configurations are outlined, in varying levels of detail, by Ramamoorthy and Chandy (1970), Mattson et al (1970), Pugh (1971), Lin and Mattson (1972), Mattson (1974), Matick (1977, 1986), Smith (1978, 1981, 1985, 1986), Strecker (1978), Welch (1978, 1979, 1979a), Hoagland (1979), Coughlen et al (1980), Fujiwara (1980), Lehmann (1980), Guerin (1981), Keyes (1981), Pohm and Smay (1981), Strasser (1981), Cote (1982), Wasserman (1983), Christodoulakis (1985), Fujino et al (1985), Grossman (1985), Kryder (1985), Peskin (1985), Ferguson (1986), Kinouchi et al (1986), Langendorfer et al (1986), Nieves (1986), Raimondi et al (1986), Satyanarayanan (1986), Lavington et al (1987), Moore (1987), Olken et al (1987), Keele (1988), Oelschlaeger (1988), Knight (1989), Gelb (1989), and Ramakrishnan and Emer (1989), among others. Computer equipment manufacturers increasingly support storage products and methodologies that are based on hierarchical concepts. Examples are discussed by Finnegan (1984), Itao et al (1986), Sugiura and Hayakawa (1986), Kaneko (1988), Kuduo et al (1988), and Cohen et al (1989). Thorndyke (1985) and

Typical Characteristics of Magnetic and Optical Storage Products

	Areal Density*	Online Capacity**	Access Time***
Fixed magnetic disks	20-60	20-3700	16-65
Removable magnetic disks	0.15-25	0.36-50	60-300
9-track magnetic tapes	0.014-0.112	40-150	†
Half-inch tape cartridges	1-4	90-500	†
Quarter-inch tape cartridges	0.29-4.5	40-1350	†
VHS helical scan cassettes	11-23	2500-5400	†
8mm helical scan cassettes	35	290-2300	†
4mm DAT cassettes	114	1000-1300	†
Optical disks	170-420	115-4100	90-500

```
   *  Megabits per square inch
  **  Megabytes
 *** Milliseconds
   †  Access time varies with tape length,
      other factors; typically ranges from
      30 to 300 seconds
```

Gentzsch (1987) discuss the role of storage hierarchies in supercomputer installations.

Taking advantage of the special attributes of particular technologies, computer storage hierarchies assign specific media and devices to the applications for which they are presumably best suited. Based on the primary, secondary, and tertiary layers outlined above, typical discussions of computer storage hierarchies define a pyramidal ranking of technologies that is principally based on access time, with storage capacity and cost as additional considerations. At the top of the pyramid, semiconductor-based main memories support access times measured in nanoseconds but provide very limited storage capacity and are quite expensive. Low-

drives or other removable magnetic disk systems for direct access storage. The importance of fixed magnetic disk drives as secondary storage devices is secured by their impressive performance characteristics relative to competing technologies. As discussed in Part One of this report, average access times for fixed magnetic disk drives range from less than 20 milliseconds to more than 60 milliseconds, with most newer products supporting access times lower than 30 milliseconds. Storage capacities range from about 20 megabytes for entry-level, microcomputer-based hard disk drives to almost four gigabytes for the newest mainframe-based products. As previously noted, multi-drive configurations can provide formidable storage capacity. Main-

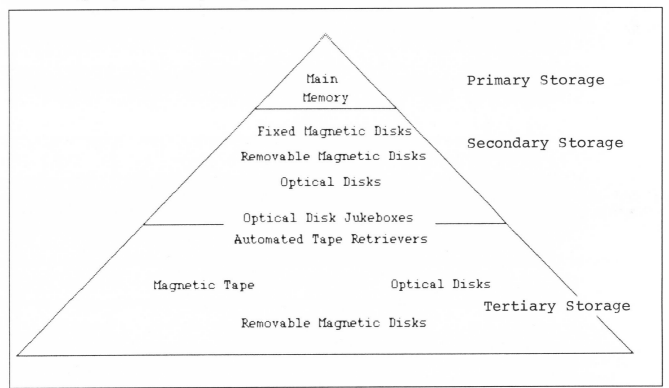

A typical storage hierarchy.

er hierarchical layers are occupied by magnetic and optical devices of decreasing speed, increasing capacity, and decreasing cost. The hierarchical roles played by particular magnetic and optical devices are defined by their specific characteristics.

As the principal direct access storage devices in most computer installations, fixed magnetic disk drives are the mainstay of the secondary layer in a typical storage hierarchy, although the least expensive small computer systems continue to rely on floppy disk

frame and large minicomputer installations with more than 50 gigabytes of fixed magnetic disk storage are possible.

In some storage hierarchies, fixed magnetic disk drives share the second pyramidal layer with write-once and erasable optical disk drives, which can also operate as direct access storage devices. As previously noted, optical storage media support much higher areal recording densities than their magnetic counterparts. As presented in Part One of this report, areal recording densities supported by magnetic disk technology range from less than 20 million bits per square inch for 5.25-inch floppy disks to approximately 60 million bits per square inch for the newest fixed magnetic disk systems. Areal recording densities supported by optical disk drives range from about 170 million bits per square inch to more than 400 million bits per square inch. Such formidable areal densities yield much higher storage capacities for optical disk cartridges when compared to magnetic media with equivalent surface areas. With average access times ranging in the 90-to-500-milliseconds, however, optical disk drives are too slow for many online computing applications, especially those characterized by high-volume transaction processing. In most computer storage hierarchies, optical disk drives are consequently relegated to the tertiary layer which has historically been dominated by magnetic tape.

Tertiary-layer peripherals -- such as magnetic tape units, floppy disk drives, and optical disk drives -- record information on removable media that can be stored offline when not in use. While specific media capacities vary, such devices can store virtually any quantity of data -- assuming, of course, that offline storage of some files or other information is acceptable to the applications which must utilize them. Compared to magnetic tape units, optical disk drives offer the substantial advantages of higher areal recording densities and much faster access times. Ranging from less than 15,000 bits per square inch for nine-track reels to more than 100 million bits per square inch for digital audio tape cassettes, areal recording densities supported by available magnetic tape systems are a fraction of their optical disk counterparts.

As discussed in Part Two of this report, the performance of magnetic tape units is constrained by their serial access characteristics. Average access times are measured in seconds or minutes rather than milliseconds. When a magnetic tape reel, cartridge, or cassette required by a particular computer program is stored offline, several additional minutes will be required to locate, retrieve, and mount it. Similar limitations apply to removable magnetic disks and optical disk cartridges in applications where jukebox units are not utilized.

In the pyramidal storage scheme outlined above, optical disk jukeboxes and automated tape retrievers fall between the secondary and tertiary layers. Sometimes described as mass storage systems, such devices provide unattended access to gigabytes or even terabytes of data, but -- with average access times that are meas-

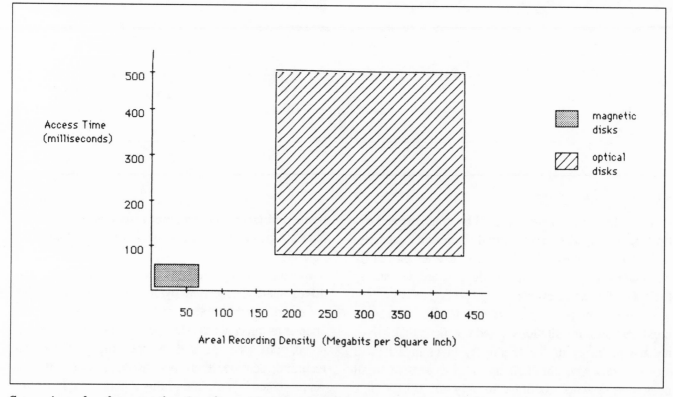

Comparison of performance domains of magnetic and optical disks.

ured in seconds -- they are much slower than conventional online devices. As noted in Part Two of this report, they are best characterized as nearline rather than online devices. Optical disk jukeboxes and automated tape retrievers offer much faster access, however, than magnetic tape units and standalone optical disk drives which require manual retrieval and mounting of media. In many applications, optical disk jukeboxes -- and, to a lesser extent, automated tape retrievers -- offer a higher-performance alternative to offline storage for data files that are referenced occasionally. They free magnetic disk space for applications that require rapid access but allow more information to be retained online or nearline for longer periods of time.

IMPLEMENTATIONS

Recognizing that no single computer storage technology provides an ideal combination of functional characteristics and operating capabilities, hierarchical configurations are designed to take advantage of the unique strengths of different devices and media. In the typical storage hierarchy, semiconductor-based main memory is reserved for data and programs which are under immediate execution by the central processor.

Magnetic disks are utilized for information which will be referenced frequently and which must be accessed quickly. Optical disk jukeboxes and automated tape retrievers provide high capacity storage for information which may be referenced at any time and which must consequently be conveniently available, but which need not be accessed instantaneously. Tertiary-level storage devices are typically utilized for backup operations and archiving of inactive information. In such applications, access times are relatively unimportant, and information recorded on magnetic tapes or optical disk cartridges can be stored offline until needed.

Hierarchical concepts are implicitly implemented in any computer configuration that includes two or more storage technologies, and hierarchical storage procedures are employed every day in mainframe, minicomputer, and microcomputer installations. When different magnetic and optical storage devices are combined in a given computer configuration, a system manager or individual users can use operating system commands or utility programs to transfer infrequently referenced data files, text files, or other information between fixed magnetic disks and removable magnetic disks, optical disks, or magnetic tape. Such file transfer procedures require manual intervention, however.

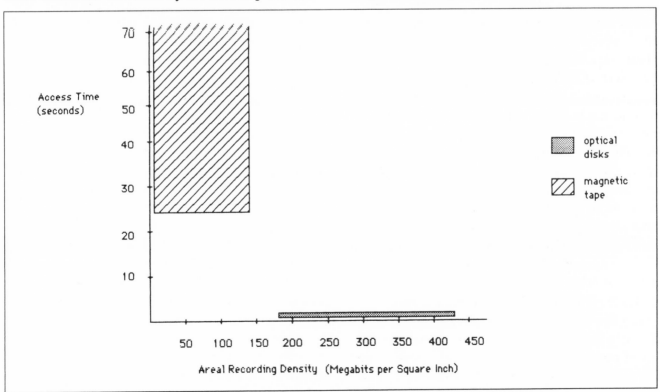

Comparison of performance domains of optical disks and magnetic tape.

The system manager or user must keep track of the storage locations of particular information and must specify the desired device when a given file is required by an application program.

In a fully automated storage hierarchy, the location of specific information is transparent to users, and file transfers are performed without operator involvement. Since the 1960s, virtual memory systems have utilized paging techniques to create the illusion that an unlimited amount of main memory is available to individual application programs. The characteristics of such virtual memory systems have been reviewed in many publications, including Denning (1970) and Doran (1976). The disk caching techniques discussed briefly in Part One of this report operate in similar fashion.

Applying virtual memory concepts to secondary and tertiary storage devices, fully automated hierarchical configurations give users the impression that an unlimited amount of magnetic disk space is at their disposal. All files are assumed to be stored on fixed magnetic disk drives, regardless of their actual locations. The user's logical view of the system's data storage facilities consequently differs from its physical organization. Employing file migration algorithms, hierarchical storage software automatically transfers selected data, text, or other files from magnetic disks to optical disks or magnetic tape for storage in jukeboxes and/or offline locations. Such automatic transfers are typically based on a file's reference history, but additional factors -- such as the need to free magnetic disk space for other purposes -- may also be considered. Files transferred to jukeboxes or offline media are similarly returned to magnetic disks, without operator intervention, when requested. The migration algorithms that support file transfers are discussed in many publications, including Foster and Browne (1976), Franaszek and Bennett (1978), Fujiwara et al (1980, 1980a), Smith (1981), Trivedi and Sigmond (1981), Geist and Trivedi (1982), Hartung et al (1982), Lawrie et al (1982, 1982a), Baboglu (1983), Wong (1983), Kagakawa et al (1987), Deshpande and Bunt (1988), Sato and Tsuda (1988), Hac (1989), and Kure (1989).

Fully automated hierarchical storage configurations have been implemented on a customized basis in a variety of applications. Among published discussions of such installations, Wimmer (1978) describes a hierarchical mass storage system at the DESY Computer Centre in West Germany, while Collins et al (1982) and McLarty et al (1984) discuss a similar configuration implemented by the Los Alamos National Laboratory. Gray et al (1984) describe a hierarchical storage system for large meteorological data bases at the European Centre for Medium Range Weather Forecasts. Choy and O'Lear (1983) and Thanhardt and Harano (1988) discuss the role of hierarchical storage components, including magnetic and optical disks, at the National Center for Atmospheric Research. Guru Prasad (1984), De Valk et al (1985), Mankovich et al (1986), Dallas et al (1987), and Reijns et al (1988) describe systems that combine magnetic and optical storage components for digital radiographs and other medical imagery. Narayan (1988) describes a system that combines magnetic and optical disk storage at the U.S. Patent and Trademark Office.

As an alternative to such customized installations, several systems integrators and peripheral equipment vendors have introduced preconfigured hierarchical storage systems based on combinations of magnetic and optical technologies. As discussed by Burgess (1985, 1987), Burgess and Ramsey (1988), and Owen (1988), the Storage Machine from FileTek Incorporated is a specialized database processing system that provides high-capacity, hierarchical storage facilities for mainframe and larger minicomputer installations. The FileTek Storage Machine can support a variety of peripheral devices, including fixed magnetic disk drives, write-once and erasable optical disk drives, optical disk jukeboxes, and magnetic tape units. Following the typical hierarchical pattern outlined above, fixed magnetic disk drives are the Storage Machine's principal direct access storage devices. One or more optical disk jukeboxes provide nearline access to infrequently referenced data. Inactive data files can be stored offline on optical disk cartridges or magnetic tapes. An integral processor -- typically, a MicroVAX II -- controls access to data files, file transfers, and other processing operations. FileTek's Storage Machine Software automatically migrates data through the hierarchy of available devices, based on access requirements, reference patterns, and available storage space.

Designed for file server applications in local area network installations, the Epoch-1 product line from Epoch Systems likewise combines magnetic and optical storage components in a hierarchical configuration.

As described by Olsen (1988) and Olsen and Kenley (1989), Epoch's Infinite Storage Architecture employs high-capacity optical disks as application-transparent staging media for data transferred from high-performance magnetic disk drives. Files are automatically moved between magnetic and optical storage, based on their activity levels. Aged files are transferred to optical disks when they have not been referenced for a specified period of time or when magnetic disks reach a predetermined level of capacity. The physical storage locations of individual files are transparent to users. The Epoch-1 server -- which can be configured with magnetic disk drives and optical disk jukebox units totalling almost one terabyte of storage -- appears to the user as a magnetic disk system that never becomes full. When a data file stored on an optical disk is requested by an application program, it is automatically returned to magnetic disk storage.

Bibliography

Abbott, S.J. (1988). Digital paper: flexible optical data storage media. Polymer Preprints, vol. 29, no. 2, pp. 213-14.

Abbott, S.J. (1988a). Digital paper: flexible optical data storage media. In Proceedings of the ACS Division of Polymeric Materials Science and Engineering, vol. 59. Washington, DC: American Chemical Society, p. 1220.

Abe, S. et al (1987). The correlation of pit shape with the valence state of Ti in Te-Se-Ti alloy thin films for optical recording disks. Journal of Vacuum Science and Technology, vol. 5, no. 4, pp. 1966-67.

Abe, Y. (1985). Magnetic materials for magnetic recording and magnetic heads. Denki Seiko, vol. 56, no. 3, pp. 198-203.

Adachi, T. et al (1987). Fast random accessing scheme for R-DAT. IEEE Transactions on Consumer Electronics, vol. 33, no. 3, pp. 275-85.

Adachi, O. and Yano, N. (1983). A new high-density mini flexible disk drive system. IEEE Transactions on Magnetics, vol. MAG-19, no. 5, pp. 1704-1706.

Addelson, R. (1986). Nine-track tape systems. PC Tech Journal, vol. 4, no. 8, pp. 94-108.

Adler, R.L. et al (1985). A rate 1/3 (5,12) RLL code. IBM Technical Disclosure Bulletin, vol. 27, no. 8, pp. 4722-24.

Adler, R.L. et al (1985a). A rate 2/3 (1,6) RLL code. IBM Technical Disclosure Bulletin, vol. 27, no. 8, pp. 4727-29.

Ahearn, G.R. et al (1972). Design innovations of the IBM 3830 and 2835 storage control units. IBM Journal of Research and Development, vol. 16, no. 1, pp. 11-18.

Akashi, G. (1982). The development of metal powder for magnetic recording. In Ferrites: Proceedings of the Third International Conference on Ferrites. Dordrecht, The Netherlands: Reidel, pp. 548-52.

Allin, P.J. (1989). Optical or magnetic drives: which way is the mass storage market going? In IEE Coloquium on New Advances in Optical Recording Technology. London: IEE, pp. 6/1-5.

Altman, L., ed. (1978). Memory Design: Microcomputers to Mainframes. New York: McGraw-Hill.

Altman, W.P. et al (1986). Optical storage for high performance applications in the late 1980s and beyond. RCA Engineer, vol. 31, no. 1, pp. 46-55.

Alvarez, D.C. and Burland, D.M. (1982). Room temperature optical frequency domain memory system. IBM Technical Disclosure Bulletin, vol. 25, no. 3A, p. 1090.

Ammon, G.J. and Siryj, B.W. (1983). Automatic handling mechanisms for an optical disc mass memory system. In Proceedings of the Society of Photo-Optical Instrumentation Engineers. Bellingham, WA: SPIE, vol. 385, pp. 14-16.

Ando, R. et al (1988). High density magneto-optical disk capable of overwriting magnetic field modulation. IEEE Translation Journal on Magnetics in Japan, vol. 3, no. 8, pp. 633-41.

Aoyama, S. et al (1988). Recording characteristics of tapes prepared using iron oxide particles treated with organic titanate. Journal of Applied Physics, vol. 63, no. 8, pt. 2A, pp. 3443-45.

Arai, K. et al (1988). Basic technologies for DATs. National Technical Report, vol. 32, no. 2, pp. 29-39.

Armbrust, S. and Forgeron, T. (1985). Moving up to tape. PC Tech Journal, vol. 3, no. 11, pp. 62-83.

Arnoldussen, T.C. (1986). Thin-film recording media. Proceedings of the IEEE, vol. 74, no. 11, pp. 1526-39.

Asano, M. et al (1987). Magneto-optical recording media with new protective films. IEEE Transactions on Magnetics, vol. 23, no. 5, pp. 2620-22.

Asari, S. et al (1987). Preparation of magneto-optical disk using a rare earth-transition metal alloy target. Journal of Vacuum Science and Technology, vol. 5, no. 4, pp. 1949-51.

Aseo, J. (1983). Memory systems: QIC no guarantee for compatibility. Computer Design, vol. 22, no. 7, pp. 48-56.

Aseo, J. (1984). Half-inch tape drives cry out for greater compabitility. Computer Design, vol. 23, no. 5, pp. 29-34.

Ashley, J.J. and Siegel, P. (1987). A note on the Shannon capacity of run-length-limited codes. IEEE Transactions on Information Theory, vol. IT-33, no. 4, pp. 601-605.

Babbitt, W. and Mossberg, T. (1988). Time-domain frequency-selective optical data storage in a solid-state material. Optical Communications, vol. 65, no. 3, pp. 185-88.

Baboglu, O. (1983). Hierarchical replacement decisions in hierarchical stores. Performance Evaluation Review, vol. 11, no. 4, pp. 11-19.

Balue, T. and Koliopoulos, P. (1987). Data-transfer speed extracts mileage from 5.2 gigabyte tape. Electronic Design, vol. 35, no. 25, pp. 95-99.

Banks, M. (1983). From magnetic to optical. Systems International, vol. 11, no. 5, pp. 67-68.

Barron, J.L. (1988). Helical scan provides economical, high capacity backup storage. Computer Design, vol. 27, no. 2, pp. 30-32, 35.

Bartholomeusz, B.J. (1989). Thermomagnetic marking of rare-earth transition-metal thin films. Journal of Applied Physics, vol. 65, no. 1, pp. 262-68.

Bashe, C.J. et al (1986). IBM's Early Computers. Cambridge, MA: MIT Press.

Bate, G. (1980). Improvements in flexible disk media. In Conference Record/Electro 80. El Segundo, CA: Electronic Conventions Incorporated, pp. 7.2-7.10.

Bate, G. (1987). Materials challenges in metallic, reversible optical recording media: a review. IEEE Transactions on Magnetics, vol. MAG-23, no. 1, pp. 151-61.

Bate, G. (1988). Non-magnetic properties of magnetic recording media. In Proceedings of the ACS Division of Polymeric Materials, vol. 59. Washington, DC: American Chemical Society Books and Journals Division, p. 1226.

Bate, G. (1989). Alternative storage technologies. In Digest of Papers: COMPCON Spring '89, Thirty-Fourth IEEE Computer Society International Conference. Washington, DC: IEEE Computer Society Press, pp. 151-57.

Baugh, R.A. et al (1986). Extremely low error rate digital recording with a helical scan recorder. IEEE Transactions on Magnetics, vol. MAG-22, no. 5, pp. 1179-81.

Becker, J.C. et al (1985). Low-cost, highly reliable tape backup for Winchester disc drives. Hewlett-Packard Journal, vol. 36, no. 3, pp. 34-35.

Bell, A.E. (1988). Materials for magneto-optic data storage. Journal of Applied Physics, vol. 63, no. 8, pt. 2B, p. 3648.

Bell, A.E. and Marrello, V. (1984). Magnetic and optical data storage: a comparison of the technological limits. In Digest of Papers: Twenty-Eighth IEEE Computer Society International Conference. New York: IEEE, pp. 512-17.

Bernards, J. et al (1987). Material and recording properties of perpendicular CoCr media. IEEE Transactions on Magnetics, vol. MAG-23, no. 1, pp. 125-27.

Bernstein, P. and Rio, F. (1987). Properties of amorphous TbFe and GdFe thin films for perpendicular recording. IEEE Transactions on Magnetics, vol. MAG-23, no. 1, pp. 143-45.

Berry, B.S. and Pritchet, W.C. (1988). Elastic and viscoelastic behavior of a magnetic recording tape. IBM Journal of Research and Development, vol. 32, no. 5, pp. 882-94.

Bhushan, B. (1990). Tribology and Mechanics of Magnetic Storage Devices. New York: Springer-Verlag.

Bianchi, M.J. et al (1989). Data compression in a half-inch reel-to-reel tape drive. Hewlett-Packard Journal, vol. 40, no. 3, pp. 26-31.

Bican, F. (1988). Mass storage devices: the WORM turns. PC Magazine, vol. 7, no. 6, pp. 199-226.

Bjorklund, G.C. (1984). Progress in frequency domain optical storage. In Topical Meeting on Optical Data Storage: Technical Digest. Washington, DC: Optical Society of America, pp. THC-D5/1-5.

Bjorklund, G.C. et al (1981). Cryogenic frequency domain optical mass memory. In Proceedings of the SPIE, vol. 298. Bellingham, WA: SPIE, pp. 107-14.

Bjorklund, G.C. et al (1982). Evaporated polycrystalline thin film materials for optical memories based upon photochemical hole burning. IBM Technical Disclosure Bulletin, vol. 24, no. 11B, p. 6188.

Bjorklund, G.C. et al (1984). Progress in frequency domain optical storage. In Topical Meeting on Optical Data Storage: Technical Digest. Washington, DC: Optical Society of America, pp. THC-D5/1-5.

Bloom, M. (1989). Don't throw away your Winchester . . . yet. ESD: Electronic System Design Magazine, vol. 19, no. 4, pp. 42-50.

Bohl, M. (1981). Introduction to IBM Direct Access Storage Devices. Chicago: Science Research Associates.

Bolzoni, F. et al (1986). Cobalt alloys for perpendicular magnetic recording. In Second Congress on Cobalt Metallurgy and Uses. Brussels: Cobalt Development Institute, pp. 480-87.

Bonini, D. (1985). Design of a modular, high-capacity optical disk subsystem. In Digest of Papers — IEEE Symposium on Mass Storage Systems. New York: IEEE, pp. 91-93.

Bostwick, S. et al (1988). Multi-vendor system extensions take a big byte out of the VAX. Hardcopy, vol. 8, no. 2, pp. 33-36.

Bowers, D. (1977). Floppy disk drives and systems. Mini-Micro Systems, vol. 10, no. 3, pp. 12-17.

Boyer-Chamard, M. and Moussy, L. (1983). Digital optical disk: the data processing medium of the coming years. In Proceedings of the 17th International Symposium on Remote Sensing of the Environment. Ann Arbor, MI: Environmental Research Institute of Michigan, pp. 1283-90.

Bradshaw, R. et al (1986). Chemical and mechanical performance of flexible magnetic tape containing chromium dioxide. IBM Journal of Research and Development, vol. 30, no. 2, pp. 203-16.

Brady, J.T. (1987). DASD cache and expanded storage. In Proceedings of the SEAS Spring Meeting 1987: Systems Architecture. Nijmegen, The Netherlands: SEAS, pp. 267-79.

Brindza, S. (1989). Magnetic media attracts many applications. Modern Office Technology, vol. 34, no. 2, pp. 64-68.

Brown, D.T. et al (1970). Error correction for IBM 800-bit-per-inch magnetic tape. IBM Journal of Research and Development, vol. 14, no. 4, pp. 384-89.

Budo, Y. and Hasler, S. (1984). Mobius loop system for data storage. IBM Technical Disclosure Bulletin, vol. 27, no. 4A, pp. 2237-39.

Bruun, R.J. (1973). When will core, drum, and disk systems be just a memory. Infosystems, vol. 20, no. 5, pp. 40-43.

Burgess, J.G. (1985). A system approach using optical data disks to solve the mass data storage problem. In Digest of Papers: Seventh IEEE Symposium on Mass Storage Systems. Washington, DC: IEEE Computer Society Press, pp. 74-78.

Burgess, J.G. (1987). Virtual library system: a general purpose mass storage archive. In Digest of Papers: Eighth IEEE Symposium on Mass Storage Systems. New York: IEEE, pp. 72-76.

Burgess, J.G. and Ramsey, N. (1988). FileTek storage machine applications. In Digest of Papers: Ninth IEEE Symposium on Mass Storage Systems. Washington, DC: IEEE Computer Society Press, pp. 98-102.

Camras, M. (1988). Magnetic Recording Handbook. New York: Van Nostrand Reinhold.

Camras, M., ed. (1986). Magnetic Tape Recording. New York: Van Nostrand Reinhold.

Cannon, D.M. (1986). Design and performance of a magnetic head for a high-density tape drive. IBM Journal of Research and Development, vol. 30, no. 2, pp. 270-77.

Carr, T. and Wachenschwanz, D. (1988). A 107-kbpi, 16-mu m track width recording channel. IEEE Transactions on Magnetics, vol. MAG-24, no. 6, pp. 2961-63.

Carringer, M.W. (1988). Real world jukebox implementation for Digital's VAX/VMS. Computer Technology Review, vol. 8, no. 10, pp. 47-54.Castera, J.P. and Lehureau, J. (1986). Optical readout of magnetic tapes. In Proceedings of the SPIE, vol. 702. Bellingham, WA: SPIE, pp. 321-28.

Cavellin, C.D. and Callu, J. (1988). 500 tpi thin film magnetic tape recording heads. IEEE Transactions on Magnetics, vol. MAG-24, no. 6, pp. 2829-31.

Chadwick, D. (1986). Optical or magnetic? Systems International, vol. 14, no. 5, pp. 23-24.

Chen, G. (1986). New longitudinal recording media for high rate static magnetron sputtering system. IEEE Transactions on Magnetics, vol. MAG-22, no. 5, pt. 1, pp. 334-36.

Chen, M. et al (1985). Reversibility and stability of tellurium alloys for optical data storage applications. Applied Physics Letters, vol. 46, no. 4, pp. 734-36.

Chen, M. et al (1988). Effects of sputtering conditions on the recording characteristics of iron oxide thin film media. IEEE Transactions on Magnetics, vol. MAG-24, no. 6, pp. 2988-90.

Chen, T. and Yamashita, T. (1988). Physical origin of limits in the performance of thin-film longitudinal recording media. IEEE Transactions on Magnetics, vol. MAG-24, no. 6, pp. 2700-2705.

Choy, J.H. and O'Lear, B. (1983). Proposal for the integration of digital optical storage into the mass storage system (MSS) at the National Center for Atmospheric Research (NCAR). In Proceedings of the SPIE, vol. 382. Bellingham, WA: SPIE, pp. 59-62.

Christener, J.A. et al (1988). Low-noise metal medium for high-density longitudinal recording. Journal of Applied Physics, vol. 63, no. 8-IIA, pp. 3260-62.

Christodoulakis, S. (1985). Issues in the architecture of a document archiver using optical disk technology. SIGMOD Record, vol. 14, no. 4, pp. 34-50.

Chu, K. (1985). Streaming tape subsystem. In Fourth International Conference: Phoenix Conference on Computers and Communications. Silver Spring, MD: IEEE Computer Society Press, pp. 142-47.

Chubachi, R. and Tamagawa, N. (1984). Characteristics and applications of metal tape. IEEE Transactions on Magnetics, vol. MAG-20, no. 1, pp. 45-57.

Cohen, E.I. et al (1989). Storage hierarchies. IBM Systems Journal, vol. 28, o. 1, pp. 62-76.

Collinson, D. (1986). Magnetic tape storage: a 3480 media. Systems International, vol. 14, no. 9, p. 51.

Collins, W. et al (1982). A network file storage system. In Digest of Papers: Fifth IEEE Symposium on Mass Storage Systems. New York: IEEE, pp. 99-102.

Connell, G. (1986). Magneto-optics and amorphous metals: an optical storage revolution. Journal of Magnetism and Magnetic Materials, vol. 54, pt. 3, pp. 1561-66.

Conti, R. (1986). Bi-level tape path provides small size for 9-track streaming tape. Computer Technology Review, vol. 6, no. 3, pp. 113-15.

Cope, J.R. et al (1977). Bernoulli disk decoupler and stabilizer. IBM Technical Disclosure Bulletin, vol. 20, no. 3, pp. 916-17.

Corradi, A. et al (1987). Reversible coercivity vs. temperature losses in activated cobalt adsorbed iron oxides. IEEE Transactions on Magnetics, vol. MAG-23, no. 1, pp. 48-52.

Cote, H. (1982). New horizons in accessing large amounts of on-line data. In Digest of Papers: Fifth IEEE Symposium on Mass Storage Systems, Hardware and Software Issues for Mass Storage Systems. New York: IEEE, pp. 71-75.

Coughlen, B. et al (1980). System evolution of MSS hierarchies. In Digest of Papers: Fourth IEEE Symposium on Mass Storage Systems. New York: IEEE, pp. 22-25.

Couture, J.J. and Lessard, R. (1988). Modulation transfer function measurements for thinlayers of azo dyes in PVA matrix used as an optical recording material. Applied Optics, vol. 27, no. 18, pp. 3368-74.

Cox, C. and Taylor, M. (1986). Magnetic tape storage: half inch cartridge. Systems International, vol. 14, no. 9, pp. 59-63.

Crane, B.A. (1989). Disk drive technology improvements in the RA90. Digital Technical Journal, no. 8, pp. 46-60.

Crasemann, J. et al (1989). Thermomagnetic switching on rare-earth transition-metal alloy magneto-optic disks. Journal of Applied Physics, vol. 66, no. 3, pp. 1273-78.

Curtis, D. and Rolfe, J. (1971). High density digital recording with video techniques. In International Telemetry Conference Proceedings, vol. 7. Washington, DC: ISA, pp. 410-19.

Cutler, D.S. (1986). Quarter and half inch streaming tape drives. In Video, Audio, and Data Recording: Sixth International Conference. London: IERE, pp. 95-104.

Cutler, D.S. (1986a). Streaming tape drives for computer systems. In Colloquium on Mass Storage Devices for Computers. London: IEE, pp. 1.1-1.5.

Dallas, W.J. et al (1987). A prototype totally digital radiology department: conception and initiation. In Proceedings of the SPIE, vol. 767. Bellingham, WA: SPIE, pp. 700-707.

Dallmann, H. and Hasback, P. (1987). Base films with advanced properties for magnetic recording media. IEEE Transactions on Magnetics, vol. MAG-23, no. 1, pp. 118-21.

Dancygier, M. (1987). Magnetic properties of TbFe amorphous alloys deposited on Kapton: optical tape feasibility. IEEE Transactions on Magnetics, vol. MAG-23, no. 5, pp. 2608-10.

Dare, P.A. and Katsumi, R. (1987). Rotating digital audio tape (R-DAT): a format overview. SMPTE Journal, vol. 96, no. 10, pp. 943-48.

Davies, K. (1986). Working towards higher data densities in disk storage. New Electronics, vol. 19, no. 4, pp. 66-73.

Davis, R. (1987). Optical data storage for space sensing applications. In International Geoscience and Remote Sensing Symposium. New York: IEEE, p. 899.

Denning, P.J. (1970). Virtual memory. Computing Surveys, vol. 2, no. 3, pp. 153-89.

Deshpande, M. and Bunt, R. (1988). Dynamic file management techniques. In Proceedings of the Seventh Annual Phoenix Conference. New York: IEEE, pp. 86-92.

Desmarais, N. (1988). Experiments increase optical storage densitites. Optical Information Systems, vol. 8, no. 3, pp. 120-22.

Desmarais, N. (1989). Write on: the advantages of digital paper. Computers in Libraries, vol. 9, no. 5, pp. 37-38.

Desserre, J.R. (1985). Magnetic recording technology. Journal of Physics, vol. 46, supp. C6, pp. C6.85-92.

De Valk, J.P. et al (1985). Simulation of a feasible medical image storage hierarchy within the Dutch IMAGIS project. In Proceedings of the SPIE, vol. 529. Bellingham, WA: SPIE, pp. 240-45.

Deverell, A. (1989). Optical storage technology: the wave of the future. IMC Journal, vol. 25, no. 3, pp. 8-11.

Devoy, J.C. et al (1988). Media, file management schemes facilitate WORM utilization. Computer Technology Review, vol. 8, no. 13, pp. 48-49.

DiFede, M. (1986). Beyond QIC-24: tape interchange requires additional engineering. Computer Technology Review, vol. 6, no. 1, pp. 93, 96-97.

DiGiulio, M. et al (1988). Reactively sputtered TeO/sub x thin films for optical recording systems. Journal of Vacuum Science and Technology, vol. 6, no. 2, pp. 243-45.

Dodge, J.M. (1988). Disk arrays: here come the disk drive sextuplets. Electronic Business, vol. 14, no. 21, pp. 126-30.

Doi, M. et al (1987). Development of a rotary head digital audio tape recorder (R-DAT). Sanyo Technical Review, vol. 19, no. 2, pp. 3-17.

Dolivo, F.B. (1980). Effects of miniaturization in magnetic recording. In Proceedings of the Journees d'Electronique et de Microtechnique 1980 on the

Subject Limits to Miniaturization. Lausanne: Swiss Federal Institute of Technology, pp. 307-11.

Domshy, L.C. (1983). Built for speed: quarter-inch streaming tape drives. Computer Design, vol. 22, no. 6, pp. 247-57.

Domshy, L.C. (1986). Tape cartridge backup gains more capacity in a standard form factor. Computer Technology Review, vol. 6, no. 3, pp. 116-19.

Domshy, L.C. (1988). The pros and cons of helical scan technology. Computer Technology Review, vol. 8, no. 7, pp. 26-27.

Dong, J. et al (1985). Streaming tape drive hardware design. Hewlett-Packard Journal, vol. 36, no. 3, pp. 25-29.

Donsbach, D.L. (1988). System integration without host computer changes: the use of emulation system software in a VMS environment. In OIS International 1988: Proceedings of the Fifth Annual Conference on Optical Information Systems. London: Meckler Corporation, pp. 100-104.

Donsbach, D.L. (1988a). Transparent optical disk jukebox support for the VAX/VMS environment. In Electronic Imaging '88: International Electronic Image Exposition and Conference. Boston: Institute for Graphic Communication, vol. 2, pp. 880-81.

Doran, R.W. (1976). Virtual memory. Computer, vol. 9, no. 10, pp. 27-37.

Drexler, J. (1981). Drexon optical memory media for laser recording and archival data storage. Journal of Vacuum Science and Technology, vol. 18, no. 1, pp. 87-91.

Drexler, J. (1983). Drexon optical storage for digital picture archiving applications. In Proceedings of the Second International Conference and Workshop on Picture Archiving and Communication Systems (PACS II) for Medical Applications. New York: IEEE, pp. 30-35.

Drexler, J. (1983a). The Drexon product family for laser recording and digital data storage: a status report. In Proceedings of the SPIE, vol. 420. Bellingham, WA: SPIE, pp. 57-59.

Dy, B. (1983). Increasing disk densities with perpendicular recording. Mini-Micro Systems, vol. 16, no. 2, pp. 189-92.

Ebstein, S. (1983). Digital recording on video cassette. Review of Scientific Instrumentation, vol. 54, no. 7, pp. 883-85.

Eiberger, B. (1988). Digital recording of large quantities of data on magnetic tape. ITG-Fachberichte, vol. 102, no. 2, pp. 113-25.

Eiling, A. and Pott, R. (1985). Transverse magnetic field stability of magnetic pigments. IEEE Transactions on Magnetics, vol. MAG-21, no. 5, pp. 1497-99.

Elliott, J. (1987). DEC disks and tapes. In 1987 DEC User Conference. London: EMAP Conferences, pp. 7-10.

Elphick, M. and Parker, R. (1983). Winchester disk technology spins into new orbits. Computer Design, vol. 22, no. 1, pp. 89-102.

Engh, J.T. (1981). The IBM diskette and diskette drive. IBM Journal of Research and Development, vol. 25, no. 5, pp. 701-10.

Enoki, Y. et al (1984). Large capacity 3-inch compact floppy disk. National Technical Reports, vol. 30, no. 3, pp. 372-79.

Feig, E. (1989). Linear models for high-density magnetic recording of data. IEEE Transactions on Magnetics, vol. MAG-25, no. 3, pp. 2769-79.

Ferebee, M. and Kibler, J. (1989). The Earth radiation budget experiment optical disk archival system. Optical Information Systems, vol. 9, no. 1, pp. 2-8.

Ferguson, T.E. (1986). Data storage: picking the right media. ComputerData, vol. 11, no. 10, p. 10.

Finnegan, L.J. (1984). Mass storage devices. DEC Professional, vol. 3, no. 2, pp. 122-23.

Fisher, F.M. et al (1983). IBM and the U.S. Data Processing Industry: an Economic History. New York: Praeger.

Foster, D. and Browne, J. (1976). File assignment in memory hierarchies. In Modelling and Performance Evaluation of Computer Systems: Proceedings of the International Workshop. Amsterdam: North-Holland Publishing Company, pp. 110-27.

Franaszek, P.A. and Bennett, B.T. (1978). Adaptive variation of the transfer unit in a storage hierarchy. IBM Journal of Research and Development, vol. 22, no. 4, pp. 405-12.

Francis, B. (1988). PC back-up's optical understudy. Datamation, vol. 34, no. 25, pp. 57-60.

Freedman, D.H. (1983). Searching for denser disks. Infosystems, vol. 30, no. 9, p. 56.

Freeman, R.C., Jr. (1985). IBM spurs high-end tape drive market. Mini-Micro Systems, vol. 18, no. 8, pp. 137-42.

Freese, R.P. et al (1982). Characteristics of bubble-forming optical direct-read-after-write (DRAW) media. In Proceedings of the SPIE, vol. 329. Bellingham, WA: SPIE, pp. 174-80.

Fujino, M. et al (1985). Magnetic disk storage. Fujitsu Science and Technology Review, vol. 21, no. 4, pp. 395-407.

Fujita, K. and Kakuse, K. (1987). H-6485 magnetic tape subsystem. Hitachi Review, vol. 36, no. 4, pp. 193-200.

Fujiwara, T. (1985). Barium ferrite media for perpendicular recording. IEEE Transactions on Magnetics, vol. MAG-21, no. t, pp. 1480-85.

Fujiwara, T. (1985a). Perpendicular magnetic recording technology. Toshiba Review, no. 154, pp. 6-9.

Fujiwara, T. (1987). Magnetic properties and recording characteristics of barium ferrite media. IEEE Transactions on Magnetics, vol. MAG-23, no. 5, pt. 2, pp. 3125-30.

Fujiwara, T. et al (1982). Recording performances of Ba-ferrite coated perpendicular magnetic tapes. IEEE Transactions on Magnetics, vol. MAG-18, no. 6, pp. 1200-1202.

Fujiwara, Y. et al (1980). Hierarchical external storage configuration. Electronic Communication Laboratory Technical Journal, vol. 29, no. 6, pp. 1129-38.

Fujiwara, Y. et al (1980a). Performance evaluation of hierarchical external storage. Transactions of the Institute of Electronic and Communications Engineers of Japan, vol. E63, no. 7, pp. 560-61.

Fukizawa, A. (1987). Fabrication of high density magnetic recording media by a new sputtering method. Journal of the Metal Finishing Society of Japan, vol. 38, no. 9, pp. 372-77.

Fuld, S. (1988). Amperif cache disk system. In Digest of Papers: 33rd IEEE Computer Society International Conference. New York: IEEE, pp. 156-57.

Fuller, S.H. (1975). Analysis of Drum and Disk Storage Units. New York: Springer-Verlag.

Funkenbusch, A.W. et al (1987). Magneto-optics technology for mass storage systems. In Digest of Papers: IEEE Symposium on Mass Storage Systems. Washington, DC: IEEE Computer Society Press, pp. 101-106.

Furukawa, T. et al (1988). High density recording method for magneto-optical disk. IEEE Transactions on Magnetics, vol. MAG-24, no. 6, pp. 2536-38.

Futamoto, M. et al (1985). Microstructure and magnetic properties of CoCr thin films formed on Ge layer. IEEE Transactions on Magnetics, vol.

MAG-21, no. 5, pp. 1426-28.

Geist, R.M. and Trivedi, K. (1982). Optimal design of multilevel storage hierarchies. IEEE Transactions on Computers, vol. 31, no. 3, pp. 249-60.

Gelb, J.P. (1989). System-managed storage. IBM Systems Journal, vol. 28, no. 1, pp. 77-103.

Gentzsch, W. (1987). Memories in supercomputers. In Proceedings of the SEAS Spring Meeting 1987: Systems Architecture. Nijmegen, Netherlands: SHARE European Association, pp. 353-62.

Gills, D. (1989). Reliability assessment of a quarter-inch cartridge tape drive. Hewlett-Packard Journal, vol. 40, no. 4, pp. 74-78.

Gittleman, J. and Arie, Y. (1984). High performance Al: polymer: Al: trilayer optical disk. Applied Optics, vol. 23, no. 4, pp. 3946-49.

Gittleman, J. et al (1986). High performance Al: polymer: Al: trilayer optical disk. RCA Review, vol. 47, no. 1, pp. 67-77.

Glass, B. (1989). Disk caching. Byte, vol. 14, no. 10, pp. 297-302.

Glass, B. (1989a). Hard disk interfaces. Byte, vol. 14, no. 2, pp. 293-97.

Goldman, S. (1984). Caching disk controller relieves system bottlenecks. Digital Design, vol. 14, no. 9, pp. 102-104.

Graham, R.C. (1987). Kodak optical storage system. In Topical Meeting on Optical Data Storage: Summaries of Papers. Washington, DC: Optical Society of America, pp. 78-81.

Graubart, L. (1988). Magnetic tape trends. In Video, Audio, and Data Recording: Seventh International Conference. London: IERE, pp. 75-84.

Grau, W. (1988). Prospects of technical development of magnetic information storage devices with particular reference to digital stores for large quantities of information: a survey. ITG-Fachberichte, vol. 102, pp. 3-14.

Gravesteijn, D.J. (1987). New material developments for write-once and erasable phase-change optical recording. In Topical Meeting on Optical Data Storage: Summary of Papers. Washington, DC: Optical Society of America, pp. 40-43.

Gravesteijn, D.J. (1988). Materials developments for write-once and erasable phase-change optical recording. Applied Optics, vol. 27, no. 4, pp. 736-38.

Gravesteijn, D.J. and Van der Veen, J. (1984). Organic dye films for optical recording. Philips Technical Review, vol. 41, no. 2, pp. 325-33.

Gravesteijn, D.J. et al (1987). Phase-change optical data storage in GaSB. Applied Optics, vol. 26, no. 22, pp. 4772-76.

Gray, P. et al (1984). Large databases in a meteorological environment. In Proceedings of the SPIE, vol. 490. Bellingham, WA: SPIE, pp. 34-38.

Green, I. (1988). The new face of C-O-M: Arkive IV/CRS. Optical Information Systems, vol. 8, no. 2, pp. 84-85.

Grossman, C.P. (1985). Cache-DASD storage design for improving system performance. IBM Systems Journal, vol. 24, no. 3, pp. 316-24.

Guerin, M. (1981). Architecture and evolution of memory hierarchies. In Convention Informatique 1981: the Means of Computerization. Paris: Convention Informatique, pp. 9-10.

Gupta, M.C. (1984). Laser recording on an overcoated organic dye-binder medium. Applied Optics, vol. 23, no. 4, pp. 3950-55.

Guru Prasad, D.K. (1984). A hierarchical storage and imaging display system for picture archiving and communication systems (PACS). In Proceedings of the SPIE, vol. 454. Bellingham, WA: SPIE, pp. 99-102.

Haarer, D. (1979). Frequency domain storage. In Proceedings of the SPIE, vol. 177. Bellingham, WA: SPIE, pp. 97-103.

Haarer, D. (1987). Photochemical hole burning: a high density storage scheme. Japan Journal of Applied Physics, vol. 26, suppl. 26-4, pp. 227-32.

Haas, G. (1988). Modern storage disks in large computers: state of the art and trends in the development of head, disk, and read/write track. ITG-Fachberichte, vol. 102, pp. 15-26.

Hac, A. (1989). A benchmark for performance evaluation of a distributed file system. Journal of System Software, vol. 9, no. 4, pp. 273-85.

Hage, P. (1987). 3480 sets pace for half-inch magnetic tape. Computer Technology Review, vol. 7, no. 9, pp. 66-67.

Hales, J.C. (1987). Video cassette recording of standard PCM data. In Instrumentation in the Aerospace Industry, vol. 33. Washington, DC: ISA, pp. 421-27.

Halper, S.D. (1988). Optical disk backup library facilities for microcomputers. EDPACS, vol. 15, no. 11, pp. 5-7.

Hansen, P. et al (1989). Magnetic and magneto-optical properties of rare-earth transition-metal alloys containing Gd, Tb, Fe, Co. Journal of Applied Physics, vol. 66, no. 2, pp. 756-67.

Hara, S. et al (1988). Hardware design for high performance 130mm optical disk storage system. Review of the Electronic Communications Laboratory, vol. 36, no. 2, pp. 253-60.

Harker, J.M. et al (1981). A quarter century of disk file innovation. IBM Journal of Research and Development, vol. 25, no. 5, pp. 677-89.

Harman, J.H. (1979). IBM compatible disk drives. Byte, vol. 4, no. 10, pp. 100-106.

Harris, J.P. et al (1975). The IBM 3850 mass storage system: design aspects. Proceedings of the IEEE, vol. 63, no. 8, pp. 1171-76.

Harris, J.P. et al (1981). Innovations in the design of magnetic tape subsystems. IBM Journal of Research and Development, vol. 25, no. 5, pp. 691-99.

Hartmann, M. et al (1984). Erasable magneto-optical recording media. IEEE Transactions on Magnetics, vol. MAG-20, no. 4, pp. 1013-18.

Hartung, M.H. et al (1982). Maintaining status in a storage hierarchy. IBM Technical Disclosure Bulletin, vol. 25, no. 5, pp. 2495-96.

Harvey, R. (1985). PC/T format gives tape a new lease on life. New Electronics, vol. 18, no. 19, pp. 58-65.

Hatano, S. and Hashimoto, T. (1988). Disk media. NEC Technical Journal, vol. 41, no. 15, pp. 36-40.

Hattori, S. et al (1979). Magnetic recording characteristics of sputtered gamma-ferric-oxide thin film disks. IEEE Transactions on Magnetics, vol. MAG-15, no. 6, pp. 1549-51.

Hayashi, K. et al (1986). Error correction method for R-DAT and its evaluation. In ICASSP 86: Proceedings of the International Conference on Acoustic Speech Signal Processing. New York: IEEE, pp. 9-12.

Hecht, J. (1987). Optical memories vie for data storage. High Technology, vol. 7, no. 8, pp. 43-47.

Heitmann, H. et al (1985). Amorphous rare earth transition metal films for magneto-optical storage. Journal of Physics, vol. 46, supp. C6, pp. C6.9-C6.18.

Henry, S. and Niquette, M. (1985). PC/T tape format makes data backup easier, more reliable. Computer Technology Review, vol. 5, no. 4, pp. 107-14.

Herda, D.J. (1985). Computer Peripherals. New York: F. Watts.
Hibst, H. (1988). Magnetic pigments for recording information. Journal of Magnetism and Magnetic Materials, vol. 74, no. 2, pp. 193-202.

Highland, J.H. (1988). Anatomy of a DOS disk. Computers and Security, vol. 7, no. 4, pp. 357-60.

Hinz, H. (1987). Helical scan recording paves the way for new cartridge tape designs. Computer Technology Review, vol. 7, no. 9, pp. 58-64.

Hirayama, Y. (1987). Magnetic recording disk substrates and their materials. Journal of the Metal Finishing Society of Japan, vol. 38, no. 9, pp. 378-85.

Hirota, F. et al (1982). Recent development of ferrite heads and their materials. In Ferrites: Proceedings of the ICF Third International Conference on Ferrites. Dordrecht, The Netherlands: Reidel, pp. 667-74.

Hirshon, B. (1984). Designer's guide to flexible disk drives. Digital Design, vol. 14, no. 2, pp. 58-70.

Hitomi, A. (1988). Advances in magnetic and optical recording: digital audio tape recorder. Journal of the Institute of Television Engineers of Japan, vol. 42, no. 4, pp. 347-53.

Hitomi, A. and Taki, T. (1986). Servo technology of R-DAT. IEEE Transactions on Consumer Electronics, vol. 32, no. 3, pp. 425-32.

Hitzfeld, M. et al (1987). CoNiCr thin film flexible disk for longitu–dinal recording. IEEE Transactions on Magnetics, vol. MAG-23, no. 5, pt. 2, pp. 3417-19.

Hoagland, A.S. (1963). Digital Magnetic Recording. Malabar, FL: Krieger. (1983 reprint with new preface).
Hoagland, A.S. (1979). Storage technology: capability and limitations. Computer, vol. 12, no. 5, pp. 12-18.

Hoagland, A.S. (1985). Information storage technology: a look at the future. Computer, vol. 18, no. 7, pp. 60-67.

Hoekstra, B. (1983). Optical disk systems. Physics Technology, vol. 14, no. 5, pp. 241-48.

Hoffman, H. (1986). Thin film media. IEEE Transactions on Magnetics, vol. MAG-22, no. 5, pp. 472-77.

Honda, K. et al (1988). Surface oxidation of CoCr evaporated films. IEEE Transactions on Magnetics, vol. MAG-24, no. 6, pp. 2664-66.

Honda, K. et al (1989). Composition control for evaporated CoCr thin films. IEEE Transactions on Magnetics, vol. MAG-25, no. 3, pp. 2612-16.

Honda, Y. et al (1987). Observation of magnetization structure on Co-Cr perpendicular magnetic recording media by bitter and electron holography methods. Japanese Journal of Applied Physics vol. 2, no. 6, pp. 923-25.

Hopkins, D. (1981). Eight-inch Winchester disk system design considerations. In Digest of Papers: 22nd IEEE Computer Society International Conference. New York: IEEE, pp. 19-24.

Hosokawa, T. et al (1989). 5.25-inch erasable optical disk system. National Technical Reports, vol. 35, no. 2, pp. 144-50.

Hospodor, A. (1988). New look at analyzing peripheral performance. Computer Design, vol. 27, no. 6, pp. 94-97.

Howard, J.K. (1986). Thin films for magnetic recording technology: a review. Journal of Vacuum Science and Technology, vol. 4, no. 1, pp. 1-13.

Howe, D.G. and Marchant, A. (1983). Digital optical recording in infrared sensitive organic polymers. In Topical Meeting on Optical Data Storage: Summaries of Papers. Washington, DC: Optical Society of America, pp. 23-25.

Howell, T.D. (1989). Statistical properties of selected recording codes. IBM Journal of Research and Development, vol. 33, no. 1, pp. 60-73.

Hume, A. (1988). The file-motel: an incremental backup system for Unix. In Proceedings of the Summer 1988 USENIX Conference. Berkeley, CA: USENIX Association, pp. 61-72.

Hyakawa, A. et al (1985). FACOM 1750/6475 magnetic tape subsystem. Fujitsu, vol. 36, no. 6, pp. 618-23.

Iijima, T. et al (1989). Magnetic and magneto-optical properties of In-alloyed TbFe amorphous films. Applied Physics Letters, vol. 54, no. 23, pp. 2376-77.

Inagaki, N. et al (1976). Ferrite thin films for high recording density. IEEE Transactions on Magnetics, vol. MAG-12, no. 6, pp. 785-87.

Inamura, M. et al (1985). Barium ferrite perpendicular recording floppy disk. Toshiba Review, no. 154, pp. 18-22.

Imamura, M. et al (1986). Barium ferrite perpendicular recording flexible disk drive. IEEE Transactions on Magnetics, vol. MAG-22, no. 5, pp. 1185-87.

Inoue, K. et al (1987). Co-Cr-W-C alloy thin films for perpendicular recording media. IEEE Transactions on Magnetics, vol. MAG-23, no. 5, pt. 2, pp. 3651-53.

Inouye, Y. and Hatayama, S. (1988). FACOM 6443 magneto-optic disk sub-system. In Proceedings: Supercomputing '88. New York: IEEE, pp. 266-71.

Irwin, J.W. et al (1971). The IBM 3803/3420 magnetic tape subsystem. IBM Journal of Research and Development, vol. 15, no. 5, pp. 391-400.

Isasaka, K. et al (1989). The application of high-coercivity cobalt iron oxide tape for digital video recording. SMPTE Journal, vol. 98, no. 3, pp. 168-72.

Ishi, Y. et al (1982). Sputtered ferrite disks for high density magnetic recording. In Ferrites: Proceedings of the ICF Third International Conference on Ferrites. Dordrecht, The Netherlands: Reidel, pp. 584-87.

Ishibashi, H. et al (1987). Magneto-optic disk drive of high speed track accessibility. Japan Journal of Applied Physics, vol. 26, suppl. 26-4, pp. 167-70.

Ishii, O. et al (1987). High coercivity sputter-deposited maghemite thin-film disk. IEEE Transactions on Magnetics, vol. MAG-23, no. 4, pp. 1985-94.

Ishii, O. et al (1989). Double-layered overwritable magneto-optic disk with magnetic recording and magneto-optic reproducing. Journal of Applied Physics, vol. 65, no. 12, pp. 5245-47.

Itao, K. et al (1986). Automated magnetic tape memory system: systems design. Review of the Electronic Communication Laboratory, vo. 34, no. 5, pp. 603-609.

Itao, K. et al (1987). High data transfer rate and high speed accessing optical disk drive technology. In Topical Meeting on Optical Data Storage: Technical Digest Series. Washington, DC: Optical Society of America, pp. 164-67.

Itao, K. and Hosokawa, S. (1985). An automated mass storage system with magnetic tape cartridges. In Digest of Papers: Seventh IEEE Symposium on Mass Storage Systems. Washington, DC: IEEE Computer Society Press, pp. 87-90.

Ito, M. et al (1988). Magnetic heads. NEC Technical Journal, vol. 41, no. 15, pp. 41-44.

Ito, O. et al (1987). High speed write once optical memory using 130mm disk for computer use. Japanese Journal of Applied Physics, vol. 26, suppl. 26-4, pp. 211-14.

Ito, Y. (1980). DIPS mass memory system development. Electric Communications Laboratory Technical Journal, vol. 29, no. 2, pp. 141-50.

Ito, Y. et al (1980). Development of DIPS mass memory system. Electric Communications Laboratory Technical Journal, vol. 28, no. 5-6, pp. 415-23.

Itoh, F. et al (1986). Magnetic tape and cartridge of R-DAT. IEEE Transactions on Consumer Electronics, vol. 32, no. 3, pp. 441-52.

Itoh, U. and Tani, T. (1988). Research activities on materials for wavelength-multiplexed optical recording in Japan. In Topical Meeting on Optical Data Storage: Summaries of Papers. Washington, DC: Optical Society of America, pp. 147-50.

Iwasaki, S. (1989). A change in concept: some experiences in the research of magnetic recording. Journal of the Institute of Electronics Information and Communication Engineers, vol. 72, no. 2, pp. 188-91.

Iwashita, R. (1987). The outline of DAT standardization. Journal of the Institute of Electronic Information and Communication Engineers, vol. 70, no. 1, pp. 63-66.

Izumi, T. (1985). Materials for magnetic recording media. Jitsumu Hyomen Gijutsu, vol. 32, no. 10, pp. 549-54.

Jacobs, B. (1985). Thin film requirements for optical recording. Vacuum, vol. 35, no. 3, pp. 445-46.

Jalics, P.J. and McIntyre, D. (1989). Caching and other disk access avoidance techniques on personal computers. Communications of the Association for Computing Machinery, vol. 32, no. 2, pp. 246-55.

Jarrett, T. (1983). The new microfloppy standards. Byte, vol. 8, no. 9, pp. 166-76.

Jeanniot, D. (1988). Flying height influence on vertical recording on rigid disks. IEEE Transactions on Magnetics, vol. MAG-24, no. 6, pp. 2476-78.

Jipson, V.B. (1987). Erasable optical recording technologies. In Topical Meeting on Optical Data Storage: Technical Digest Series. Washington, DC: Optical Society of America, p. 146.

Johnson, C.T. (1975). The IBM 3850: a mass storage system with disk characteristics. Proceedings of the IEEE, vol. 63, no. 8, pp. 1166-70.

Jorgensen, F. (1988). Handbook of Magnetic Recording. Third edition. Blue Ridge Summit, PA: Tab Books.

Kagakawa, K. et al (1987). The optimal file selection policy for two level hierarchical auxiliary storage. Transactions of the Information Processing Society of Japan, vol. 28, no. 5, pp. 516-24.

Kanazawa, Y. et al (1984). Development of large capacity optical disk. In Proceedings of the SPIE, vol. 490. Bellingham, WA: SPIE, pp. 12-19.

Kaneko, R. (1985). Future of hard disk technology. In Proceedings of the SPIE, vol. 529. Bellingham, WA: SPIE, pp. 190-97.

Kaneko, S. (1988). Consideration of Fujitsu mass storage systems. In Digest of Papers: Ninth IEEE Symposium on Mass Storage Systems. Washington, DC: IEEE Computer Society Press, pp. 83-87.

Katayama, T. (1988). Magneto-optical memory materials. Kino Zairyo, vol. 8, no. 8, pp. 45-51.

Katoh, Y. et al (1983). High density magnetic recording on a 3.5-inch micro floppy disk drive system. IEEE Transactions on Magnetics, vol. MAG-19, no. 5, pp. 1707-1709.

Katz, E. and Brechtlein, R. (1988). Perpendicular recording increases data density. Mini-Micro Systems, vol. 21, no. 3, pp. 85-91.

Keele, R.V. (1988). Optical storage: terabytes online for IBM mainframes. In Proceedings of the SPIE, vol. 899. Bellingham, WA: SPIE, pp. 262-71.

Kehr, W.D. et al (1988). Integrated thin-film head for flexible disks. IEEE Transactions on Magnetics, vol. MAG-24, no. 6, pp. 2615-2616.

Kendall, C. (1988). Cimarron user experience. In Digest of Papers: Ninth IEEE Symposium on Mass Storage Systems. Washington, DC: IEEE Computer Society Press, pp. 93-97.

Keyes, R.W. (1981). Fundamental limits in digital information processing. Proceedings of the IEEE, vol. 69, no. 2, pp. 267-78.

King, C.B. (1983). Data storage shortage: optical disks will solve it. Data Management, vol. 21, no. 11, pp. 12-13.

Kinouchi, Y. et al (1986). Cost evaluation for on-line storage system. Transactions of the Information Processing Society of Japan, vol. 27, no. 6, pp. 621-29.

Kishi, H. et al (1988). The design and fabrication of a thin-film perpendicular magnetic head. Mitsubishi Denki Giho, vol. 62, no. 121, pp. 998-1001.

Knight, A. (1989). Storage configuration issues. EDP Performance Review, vol. 17, no. 10, pp. 3-4.

Kobayashi, H. (1984). Perpendicular magnetic recording medium using the continuous sputtering system. In Recent Magnetics for Electronics. Amsterdam: Elsevier Science Publishers, pp. 67-75.

Kobayashi, K. et al (1983). High density perpendicular magnetic recording on rigid disks. Fujitsu Science and Technology Journal, vol. 19, no. 1, pp. 99-126.

Kobayashi, K. et al (1987). Thin film head for perpendicular magnetic recording. IEEE Translation Journal on Magnetics in Japan, vol. TJMJ-2, no. 1, pp. 35-47.

Kohlmann, J. and Frohmader, K.P. (1987). Thin film head for high density storage on flexible disks. IEEE Transactions on Magnetics, vol. MAG-23, no. 5, pp. 2937-39.

Koiwa, I. et al (1986). Effect of film thickness on the magnetic properties of electroless cobalt alloy plating films for perpendicular magnetic recording media. Journal of the Electrochemical Society, vol. 133, no. 3, pp. 597-600.

Koiwa, I. et al (1986a). The structure of electroless cobalt alloy films for perpendicular magnetic recording media. Journal of the Electrochemical Society, vol. 133, no. 4, pp. 685-89.

Koiwa, I. and Osaka, T. (1987). A study on initial deposition films of electroless plated Co-Ni-Re-P alloy for perpendicular magnetic recording media. Journal of the Metal Finishing Society of Japan, vol. 38, no. 9, pp. 434-38.

Kokubu, A. et al (1987). Recording characteristics of magneto-optical TbFeCo NiFe films. IEEE Transactions on Magnetics, vol. 23, no. 5, pp. 2692-94.

Komatsu, S. et al (1988). Recent recording technology: from AV to digital data. Journal of the Society of Instrumentation Control Engineers, vol. 27, no. 6, pp. 515-22.

Koshimoto, Y. et al (1987). Film heads for large-capacity fast-access magnetic disk storage. IEEE Transactions on Magnetics, vol. MAG-23, no. 5, pt. 2, pp. 2940-42.

Koshimoto, Y. et al (1988). Magnetic head design for large-capacity fast-access magnetic disk storage. Review of the Electronic Communication Laboratory, vol. 36, no. 1, pp. 97-102.

Kouvatsos, D.D. and Wong, S.K. (1984). On optimal blocking of sequential files. Computing Journal, vol. 27, no. 4, pp. 321-27.

Krass, P. (1983). Which microfloppy is right? Datamation, vol. 29, no. 5, pp. 207-208.

Kryder, M.H. (1985). Magneto-optic recording technology. Journal of Applied Physics, vol. 57, no. 8, pt. 2B, pp. 3913-18.

Kryder, M.H. (1985a). Trends in magnetic information storage technologies. In Proceedings of the IEEE International Conference on Computer Design: VLSI in Computers. Washington, DC: IEEE Computer Society Press, pp. 7-11.

Kuan, F.Y. (1987). A sensitivity approach to the choice of optimal block sizes for magnetic tape files. In Proceedings of the International Conference on Optimization: Techniques and Applications. Singapore: National University of Singapore, pp. 170-79.

Kudou, R. et al (1988). FACOM 6443 magneto-optic disk drive subsystem, vol. 39, no. 3, pp. 237-43.

Kure, O. (1989). File migration in distributed file systems without replication. Performance Evaluation Review, vol. 17, no. 1, p. 229.

Kurokawa, H. et al (1987). Applicationof diamond-like carbon films to metallic thin film magnetic recording media (by plasma injection CVD). IEEE Transactions on Magnetics, vol. MAG-23, no. 5, pt. 1, pp. 2410-12.

Langendorfer, H. et al (1986). Multimedia filing and retrieval based on optical and magnetic mass storage technologies. Microprocessing and microprogramming, vol. 18, no. 5, pp. 505-12.

Langveld, W.G. (1987). Optical storage and its possible use in high-energy physics. Computational Physics Communications, vol. 45, nos. 1-3, pp. 395-402.

Larson, D.D. et al (1987). StorageTek 4400 automated cartridge system. In Digest of Papers: Eighth IEEE Symposium on Mass Storage Systems. Washington, DC: IEEE Computer Society Press, pp. 112-17.

Laskodi, T. et al (1988). A Unix file system for a write-once optical disk. In Proceedings of the Summer 1988 USENIX Conference. Berkeley, CA: USENIX Association, pp. 51-60.

Lavington, S.H. et al (1987). Hardware memory management for large knowledge bases. In PARLE — Parallel Architectures and Languages Europe: Proceedings. Berlin: Springer-Verlag, vol. 1, pp. 226-41.

Lawrie, D.H. et al (1982). Simulation of automatic file migration. Computer, vol. 15, no. 7, pp. 45-55.

Lawrie, D.H. et al (1982a). Simulation of automatic file migration policies. In Digest of Papers: Fifth IEEE Symposium on Mass Storage Systems. New York: IEEE, pp. 27-32.

Lee, K. (1973). Magnetic thin films for optical storage. Journal of Vacuum Science and Technology, vol. 10, no. 5, pp. 631-39.

Lee, T.C. et al (1979). Development of thermoplastic photoconductor tape for optical recording. Applied Optics, vol. 17, no. 4, pp. 2802-11.
Lehmann, A. (1980). Performance evaluation and prediction of storage hierarchies. Performance Evaluation Review, vol. 9, no. 2, pp. 43-54.

Lemke, J.U. (1979). Ultra-high density recording with new heads and tapes. IEEE Transactions on Magnetics, vol. MAG-15, no. 6, pp. 1561-63.

Lemke, J.U. (1982). Tape in the mass storage system environment. In Digest of Papers: Hardware and Software Issues for Mass Storage Systems: Fifth IEEE Symposium on Mass Storage Systems. New York: IEEE, pp. 67-69.

Lenth, W. et al (1986). High-density frequency domain optical recording. In Proceedings of the SPIE, vol. 695. Bellingham, WA: SPIE, pp. 216-23.

Levenson, M.D. (1981). Time domain optical information storage in systems capable of photochemical hole burning. IBM Technical Disclosure Bulletin, vol. 24, no. 6, p. 2797.

Levenson, M.D. et al (1980). Photochemical hole burning storage material. IBM Technical Disclosure Bulletin, vol. 23, no. 7A, p. 2953.

Lin, Y.S. and Mattson, R. (1972). Cost-performance evaluation of memory hierarchies. IEEE Transactions on Magnetics, vol. MAG-8, no. 3, pp. 390-92.

Lin, Y. and Wolf, J.K. (1988). Combined ECC/RLL codes. IEEE Transactions on Magnetics, vol. MAG-24, no. 6, pp. 2527-29.

Liou, S.H. and Chien, C.L. (1988). Granular metal films as recording media. Applied Physics Letters, vol. 52, no. 6, pp. 512-14.

Lipoff, S.J. (1985). High-capacity storage: dealing with the information overload. Today's Office, vol. 19, no. 11, pp. 16, 18.

Loeschner, F. (1968). Techniques of digital recording. Computer Design, vol. 7, o. 11, pp. 44-51.

Loovenstijn, J.V.M. (1984). Fifty years of magnetic tape recording. Polytechnisch Tijdschrift: Elektrotechniek/Elektronica, vol. 39, no. 12, pp. 37-41.

Lowenthal, L.B. (1987). Integration of optical disk into mainframe system software. In Digest of Papers: Compcon Spring 87. New York: IEEE, pp. 138-41.

Lowman, C.E. (1972). Magnetic recording. New York: McGraw-Hill.

Machrone, B. (1986). Tape backup: measuring speed and cost per megabyte. PC Magazine, vol. 5, no. 3, pp. 106-39.

Maggio, T. (1984). Comparing specs: easier said than done. Computer Design, vol. 23, no. 4, pp. 259-64.

Majumder, D. (1983). Digital Computers' Memory Technology. New York: Wiley.

Mallinson, J.C. (1971). Theory of Magnetic Recording Systems. In AIP Conference Proceedings. New York: IEEE, vol. 5, pt. 1, pp. 743-63.

Mallinson, J.C. (1985). The next decade in magnetic recording. IEEE Transactions on Magnetics, vol. MAG-21, no. 3, pp. 1217-20.

Mallinson, J.C. (1987). The Foundations of Magnetic Recording. San Diego: Academic Press.

Mankovich, N.J. et al (1986). The software architecture of an integrated optical disk archive for digital radiographic images. In Proceedings of the SPIE, vol. 695. Bellingham, WA: SPIE, pp. 407-11.

Mansuripur, M. et al (1985). Erasable optical disks for data storage: principles and applications. Industrial and Engineering Chemistry: Product Research and Development, vol. 25, no. 1, pp. 80-84.

Matick, R.E. (1977). Computer Storage Systems and Technology. New York: Wiley.

Matick, R.E. (1986). Impact of memory systems on computer architecture and system organization. IBM Systems Journal, vol. 25, no. 3, pp. 274-305.

Matsuda, H. et al (1985). Preparation of magnetic recording tape by electroless Co-P plating. Journal of the Metal Finishing Society of Japan, vol. 36, no. 3, pp. 124-30.

Matsuda, N. et al (1986). Three-inch high recording density floppy disk. IEEE Transactions on Magnetics, vol. MAG-22, no. 5, pp. 1176-78.

Mattson, R. (1974). Role of optical memories in computer storage. Applied Optics, vol. 13, no. 4, pp. 755-60.

Mattson, R. et al (1970). Evaluation techniques for storage hierarchies. IBM Systems Journal, vol. 9, no. 2, pp. 78-117.

Mayer, J.H. (1988). Quarter-inch tape drives follow desktop directions. Computer Design, vol. 27, no. 10, pp. 88-95.

McArthur, D. (1981). Thin film recording. Systems International, vol. 9, no. 5, pp. 33-34.

McFarlane, R. et al (1977). Optical disc data recorder. In Proceedings of the SPIE, vol. 220. Bellingham, WA: SPIE, pp. 45-47.

Mclarty, T. et al (1984). A functional view of the Los Alamos central file system. In Digest of Papers: Sixth IEEE Symposium on Mass Storage Systems. New York: IEEE, pp. 10-16.

McMahon, P. (1988). Eight and 5.25-inch drives compared. Computer Technology Review, vol. 8, no. 3, p. 20.

McNeil, K. (1985). 322-megabyte, eight-inch Winchester advances disk drive technology. Computer Technology Review, vol. 5, no. 2, pp. 81-83.

Mee, C.D. (1964). The Physics of Magnetic Recording. Amsterdam: North-Holland.

Mee, C.D. (1986). The Physics of Magnetic Recording. Amsterdam: North-Holland.

Mee, C.D. and Daniel, E., eds. (1987). Magnetic Recording. New York: McGraw-Hill.

Mee, C.D. and Daniel, E., eds. (1989). Magnetic Recording Handbook: Technology and Applications. New York: McGraw-Hill.

Meiklejohn, W.H. (1986). Magneto-optics: a thermomagnetic recording technology. Proceedings of the IEEE, vol. 74, no. 11, pp. 1570-81.

Menon, J. and Hartung, M. (1988). The IBM 3990 disk cache. In Digest of Papers: 33rd IEEE Computer Society International Conference. New York: IEEE, pp. 146-51.

Miceli, J. et al (1987). Head media interface tolerancing Kodak optical head and Kodak LWR media. In Topical Meeting on Optical Data Storage: Summaries of Papers. Washington, DC: Optical Society of America, pp. 86-89.

Miller, C.D. (1989). DC2000 tape drives: backup on a personal scale. PC Magazine, vol. 8, no. 22, pp. 189-239.

Miller, S.H. and Freese, R. (1983). Recording densities push the limits. Mini-Micro Systems, vol. 16, no. 11, pp. 287-88.

Miller, S.W., ed. (1977). Memory and storage technology. Montvale, NJ: AFIPS Press.

Mitsuya, Y. and Takanami, S. (1987). Technologies for high recording density in large-capacity fast-access magnetic disk storage. IEEE Transactions on Magnetics, vol. MAG-23, no. 5, pt. 1, pp. 2674-79.

Mitsuya, Y. et al (1987). 8.8-gigabyte capacity magnetic disk storage system. In Digest of Papers: Eighth IEEE Symposium on Mass Storage Systems. Washington, DC: IEEE Computer Society Press, pp. 118-23.

Miyazaki, M. and Nishi, K. (1985). Hitachi optical disk subsystems. In Digest of Papers — IEEE Symposium on Mass Storage Systems. New York: IEEE, pp. 62-68.

Moerner, W.E. (1985). Molecular electronics for frequency domain optical storage: persistent spectral hole burning — a review. Journal of Molecular Electronics, vol. 1, no. 2, pp. 55-71.

Moerner, W.E. et al (1987). Frequency domain optical storage: the importance of photon-gated materials. In Topical Meeting on Optical Data Storage: Summaries of Papers. Washington, DC: Optical Society of America, pp. 151-54.

Molaire, M.F. (1988). Influence of melt viscosity on the writing sensitivity of organic dye-binder optical-disk recording media. Applied Optics, vol. 27, no. 4, pp. 743-46.

Moore, F. (1987). Report of large systems storage hardware. In UKCMG Conference Proceedings. Reading, England: United Kingdom Computer Measurement Group, pp. 1-16.

Moore, S. (1984). The mass storage squeeze. Datamation, vol. 30, no. 16, pp. 68-79.

Moran, R. (1988). Optical drives meet mainframes. Computer Decisions, vol. 20, no. 10, pp. 36-37.

Mori, K. et al (1988). Properties of DAT cassette-tape AXIA DA. IEEE Translation Journal on Magnetics in Japan, vol. 3, no. 5, pp. 388-98.

Morisako, A. et al (1985). Recording characteristics of BaM thin films. IEEE Translation Journal on Magnetics in Japan, vol. TJMJ-1, no. 9, pp. 1157-58.

Morisako, A. et al (1986). Ba-ferrite thin film rigid disk for high density perpendicular magnetic recording. IEEE Transactions on Magnetics, vol. MAG-22, no. 5, pp. 1146-48.

Morisako, A. et al (1987). Sputtered Mn-Al-Cu films for magnetic recording media. IEEE Transactions on Magnetics, vol. MAG-23, no. 5, pt. 1, pp. 2470-72.

Morita, A. (1984). There is no limit to creativity: the development of magnetic recording technology in Japan. IEEE Transactions on Magnetics, vol. MAG-20, no. 5, pt. 1, pp. 648-50.

Morris, R.M. (1986). Half-inch tape cartridges provide more capacity for disk drive backup. Computer Technology Review, vol. 6, no. 2, pp. 95-99.

Motoyama, Y. et al (1989). Digital audio tape recorder (DAT) file. NEC Research and Development, no. 92, pp. 77-80.

Muller, R. (1986). Magnetic tape development. BKSTS Journal, vol. 68, no. 4, pp. 204-10.

Muller, R. (1988). Magnetic film: developments in coating technology. Image Technology, vol. 70, no. 6, pp. 207-16.

Muller-Raab, E. (1977). Experience with the mass data storage system IBM 3850. IBM Nachrichten, vol. 27, no. 238, pp. 341-46.

Mulvany, R.B. (1974). Engineering design of a disk storage facility with data modules. IBM Journal of Research and Development, vol. 18, no. 6, pp. 489-505.

Mulvany, R.B. and Thompson, L. (1981). Innovations in disk file manufacturing. IBM Journal of Research and Development, vol. 25, no. 5, pp. 711-23.

Muratomi, Y. et al (1987). Simultaneous measurement of head-disk spaciong and reproduced output in flexible perpendicular magnetic recording disk drive. IEEE Transactions on Magnetics, vol. MAG-23, no. 5, pt. 2, pp. 3444-46.

Murphy, J.A. (1974). Floppy disc drives and storage. Modern Data, vol. 7, no. 2, pp. 47-52.

Myers, E. (1984). Making floppies smaller. Datamation, vol. 30, no. 15, pp. 60, 64.

Myers, E. (1989). High-density magnetic challenges optical. Inform, vol. 3, no. 4, pp. 30-31, 41.

Nagaki, T. et al (1986). Magnetic contact duplication for R-DAT with barium ferrite media. IEEE Transactions on Magnetics, vol. MAG-22, no. 5, pp. 1191-93.

Nagatani, K. (1986). Compact mass storage subsystem with magnetic tape auto-handling. Japan Telecommunications Review, vol. 28, no. 3, pp. 205-10.

Nakagawa, T. et al (1985). Sputtered disks for high density recording. In 1985 International Symposium on VLSI Technology, Systems, and Applications: Proceedings of Technical Papers. Hsinchu, Taiwan: ERSO, pp. 81-85.

Nakajima, H. and Odaka, K. (1983). Rotary head, high density digital audio tape recorder. IEEE Transactions on Consumer Electronics, vol. 29, no. 3, pp. 430-37.

Nakamura, K. et al (1986). Perpendicular read/write performance of ferrite heads on vacuum-deposited CoCr single-layer media. IEEE Transactions on Magnetics, vol. MAG-22, no. 5, pp. 1182-84.

Nakamura, K. et al (1987). High density perpendicular magnetic recording by ring head and vacuum-deposited Co-Cr single-layer media. IEEE Translation Journal on Magnetics in Japan, vol. TJMJ-2, no. 1, pp. 69-70.

Nakamura, Y. (1985). Systems and materials for high density magnetic recording. Bulletin of the Japanese Institute of Metals, vol. 24, no. 8, pp. 646-52.

Nakamura, Y. and Iwasaki, S. (1984). Recording and reproducing characteristics of perpendicular magnetic recording. In Recent Magnetics for Electronics. Amsterdam: Elsevier Science Publishers, pp. 3-17.

Nakane, Y. et al (1985). Principle of laser recording mechanism by forming an alloy in the trilayer of thin metallic films. In Proceedings of the SPIE, vol. 529. Bellingham, WA: SPIE, pp. 76-82.

Nakayama, Y. et al (1984). Large capacity floppy disk drive using perpendicular magnetic recording. National Technical Reports, vol. 30, no. 3, pp. 405-13.

Nakayama, Y. et al (1984a). Sputtered Co-Cr magnetic recording media and their recording characteristics. In International Magnetics Conference '84: Intermag Digest. Amsterdam: North-Holland, p. 150.

Naoe, M. et al (1987). Recording characteristics of semi-hard Mn-Zn ferrite sputtered disks. IEEE Transactions on Magnetics, vol. MAG-23, no. 5, pt. 2, pp. 3429-31.

Narayan, A. (1988). Thirty terabyte mass storage architecture. In Digest of Papers: Ninth IEEE Symposium on Mass Storage Systems. New York: IEEE, pp. 103-107.

Naruse, J. and Nakagoshi, K. (1988). A product family of large-scale magnetic disk drives with 9.5-inch platters. Hitachi Review, vol. 37, no. 5, pp. 275-82.

Nasu, S. et al (1989). Magnetic properties and recording characteristics of partially oxidized Fe-Co medium. IEEE Translation Journal on Magnetics in Japan, vol. 4, no. 1, pp. 20-25.

Natarajan, B.R. and Murdock, E. (1988). Magnetic and recording properties of sputtered Co-P/Cr thin film media. IEEE Transactions on Magnetics, vol. MAG-24, no. 6, pp. 2724-26.

Nathanson, M. et al (1980). Advanced six-megabyte flexible disk drive. In Electro/80 Conference Record. El Segundo, CA: Electronic Conventions, pp. 7-3/1-3.

Neary, D.R. (1982). Optical disk: part of tomorrow's media picture. Modern Office Procedures, vol. 26, no. 2, pp. 52-53, 56-57.

Nelson, R. and Rymer, J. (1987). Mega/giga micro mass storage. Computer and Communications Decisions, vol. 19, no. 12, pp. 21-23.

Newton, M. (1981). GCR increases recording rates and reliability. Digital Design, vol. 11, no. 7, pp. 34-39.

Nicholson, E.L. and Khan, M.R. (1986). Microstructure and magnetic properties of electroless plated Co-Ni-P and Co-P thin films for magnetic recording. Journal of the Electrochemical Society, vol. 133, no. 11, pp. 2342-45.

Nieves, E. (1986). Storage solutions: a management perspective. In CMG 86: International Conference on Management and Performance Evaluation of Computer Systems. Alexandria, VA: Computer Measures Group, pp. 516-19.

Nine, J. (1986). 40-megabyte QIC-40 standard uses floppy controller interface. Computer Technology Review, vol. 6, no. 4, pp. 91-93.

Nishigaki, T. and Yamamoto, A. (1984). Performance analysis of disk cache systems for sequential data access. Transactions of the Information Processing Society of Japan, vol. 25, no. 2, pp. 313-20.

Nishikawa, Y. et al (1987). Anti-corrosion thin protective film for vacuum deposited Co-Ni-O layers. IEEE Transactions on Magnetics, vol. MAG-23, no. 5, pt. 1, pp. 2389-91.

Noguchi, K. et al (1985). Half-inch streaming magnetic tape drive. NEC Technical Journal, vol. 38, no. 7, pp. 55-58.

Nunnelley, L.L. (1984). Media noise considerations: determination of particle noise limit from particulate disk coatings. IEEE Transactions on Magnetics, vol. MAG-20, no. 5, pp. 763-64.

Oba, H. et al (1986). Organic dye materials for optical recording media. Applied Optics, vol. 25, no. 22, pp. 4023-26.

Odaka, K. et al (1986). Digital audio magnetic recording: progress in packing density and key technology. In ICASSP 86: Proceedings of the International Conference on Acoustic Speech Signal Processing. New York: IEEE, pp. 1-4.

Oelschlaeger, J. (1988). Helical scan recording sets sights on mass data storage. Canadian Datasystems, vol. 20, no. 2, pp. 32-33.

Oelschlaeger, J. (1988a). Rethinking DP automation with helical scan. Computer Technology Review, vol. 8, no. 4, p. 22-24.

Oelschlaeger, J.R. (1988). Relieving the strain applications place on disk storage systems. Computer Technology Review, vol. 8, no. 6, pp. 60-67.

Ogawa, M. et al (1987). Fast access method of optical disk memory. In Proceedings of the SPIE, vol. 817. Bellingham, WA: SPIE, pp. 17-23.

Ogiro, K. et al (1988). A high functional compact and lightweight mechanism for R-DAT. IEEE Transactions on Consumer Electronics, vol. 34, no. 4, pp. 873-79.

Ohtake, N. et al (1986). Magnetic recording characteristics of R-DAT. IEEE Transactions on Consumer Electronics, vol. 32, no. 4, pp. 707-12.

Ohura, M. et al (1987). Design of high recording density thin-film heads for particulate rigid disks. Journal of Applied Physics, vol. 61, no. 8, pt. 2B, pp. 4182-84.

Oka, T. and Ishikawa, H. (1984). Streaming magnetic tape subsystem. Hitachi Review, vol. 33, no. 3, pp. 133-36.

Okuwaki, T. (1985). 5.25-inch floppy disk drive using perpendicular magnetic recording. IEEE Transactions on Magnetics, vol. MAG-21, no. 5, pp. 1365-67.

Olken, F. et al (1987). Data management for high energy physics experiments: preliminary proposals. Computer Physics Communications, vol. 45, no. 3, pp. 379-83.

Olsen, R.P. (1988). Workstations change role of file servers. Computer-Aided Engineering, vol. 7, no. 10, p. 88.

Olsen, R.P. and Kenley, G. (1989). Virtual optical disks solve the online storage crunch. Computer Decisions, vol. 28, no. 1, pp. 93-96.

Omachi, R. (1988). Hi-tech applications of rare earths. Material Science Forum, vol. 30, no. 1, pp. 147-53.

Oochi, H. (1988). A simple diffraction calculation of magneto-optical disc systems. Journal of Modern Optics, vol. 35, no. 9, pp. 1541-48.

Osaka, T. et al (1987). Correlation between magnetic properties and composition of electroless-plated cobalt alloy films for perpendicular magnetic recording media. Japanese Journal of Applied Physics, vol. 1, no. 10, pp. 1674-79.

Oseroff, S.B. et al (1987). Magnetization time decay in particulate media. IEEE Transactions on Magnetics, vol. MAG-23, no. 5, pt. 1, pp. 2871-73.

Oseroff, S.B. et al (1988). Temperature dependence of magnetization time decay in particulate magnetic media. Journal of Applied Physics, vol. 63, no. 8, pt. 2A, p. 3446.

Osterlund, S. (1987). Optical archiving systems. DEC PROFESSIONAL, vol. 6, no. 6, pp. 66-69.

Ouchi, K. and Iwasaki, S. (1984). Properties of high rate sputtered perpendicular recording media. Journal of Applied Physics, vol. 57, no. 8-IIB, pp. 4013-15.

Ouchi, K. and Iwasaki, S. (1984a). Studies of perpendicular recording media. In Recent Magnetics for Electronics. Amsterdam: Elsevier Science Publishers, pp. 51-66.

Ouchi, K. and Iwasaki, S. (1988). Recent subjects in research on Co-Cr perpendicular magnetic recording medium. IEEE Translation Journal on Magnetics in Japan, vol. 3, no. 4, pp. 322-35.

Owen, D.J. (1988). New breakthroughs in digital paper. Inform, vol. 2, no. 8, pp. 32-34.

Owen, D.J. (1989). ICI Imagedata's digital paper. Optical Information Systems, vol. 9, no. 5, pp. 226-29.

Owen, P.J. (1988). Optical disk systems. In OIS International 1988: Proceedings of the Fifth Annual Conference on Optical Information Systems. London: Meckler Corporation, pp. 105-11.

Ozue, T. et al (1985). Development of a 3.5-inch high-speed and high-capacity FDD. IEEE Translation Journal on Magnetics in Japan, vol. TJMJ-2, no. 7, pp. 589-95.

Parker, C. (1989). Digital audio tape. HP World, vol. 2, no. 4, pp. 65-68.

Parkinson, T. (1988). Data security: the tape solution. In Networking Technology and Architectures: Proceedings of the International Conference. London: Blenheim Online, pp. 243-54.

Patel, A.M. (1985). Adaptive cross-parity (AXP) code for a high-density magnetic tape subsystem. IBM Journal of Research and Development, vol. 29, no. 6, pp. 546-62.

Patel, A.M. and Hong, S.J. (1974). Optimal rectangular code for high density magnetic tapes. IBM Journal of Research and Development, vol. 18, no. 6, pp. 579-88.

Patterson, D.A. et al (1988). A case for redundant arrays of inexpensive disks (RAID). SIGMOD Record, vol. 17, no. 3, pp. 109-16.

Paul, D.I. and Finkelstein, B.I. (1988). Orientation of acicular particles in magnetic tape. Journal of Applied Physics, vol. 63, no. 8, pt. 2A, pp. 3441-42.

Peckham, R.C. and Campbell, M. (1987). Real world disk comparisons. In Proceedings of the Digital Equipment Users Society. Marlboro, MA: Digital Equipment Users Society, pp. 257-79.

Perlman, L. (1988). Can magnetic storage survive new technologies? Electronic Business, vol. 14, no. 18, pp. 133-34.

Perrone, G. (1985). The Bernoulli Box. PC Tech Journal, vol. 3, no. 6, pp. 144-56.

Peskin, A.M. (1985). On the role of optical disk at computing centers. In Proceedings of the SPIE, vol. 529. Bellingham, WA: SPIE, pp. 237-39.

Philips, W.B. (1984). Trends in high-density, digital, magnetic-tape recording. In Digest of Papers: the Mass Storage System Spectrum, a Study in Extremes: Sixth IEEE Symposium on Mass Storage Systems. Silver Spring, MD: IEEE Computer Society Press, pp. 72-75.

Phillips, B.W. (1988). Floptical disk drive stores 20.8 megabytes of data. Electronic Design, vol. 36, no. 18, pp. 65-68.

Pierce, D. et al (1988). A new 2.5-inch thin film disk. Solid State Technology, vol. 31, no. 10, pp. 113-15.

Pingry, J. (1984). Microfloppies squeeze their way into the market. Digital Design, vol. 14, no. 10, pp. 88-94.

Pingry, J. (1984a). Refined media extend magnetic recording capabilities. Digital Design, vol. 14, no. 6, pp. 88-98.

Platte, H. et al (1988). Matrix scan recording: a new alternative to helical scan recording on videotape. IEEE Transactions on Consumer Electronics, vol. 34, no. 3, pp. 606-11.

Podmore, L.W. (1983). Videocassette conversion to gigabyte data archiver. In DIGEST OF PAPERS: IREECON INTERNATIONAL SYDNEY 83, 19TH INTERNATIONAL ELECTRONICS CONVENTION AND EXHIBITION. Sydney: Radion and Electronics Engineers of Australia, pp. 262-64.

Pohm, A.V. and Smay, T.A. (1981). Computer memory systems. Computer, vol. 14, no. 10, pp. 93-110.

Popovich, S. et al (1986). Optical disks compete with magnetic media in many user applications. Computer Technology Review, vol. 6, no. 3, pp. 95-100.

Pountain, D. (1989). Digital paper. Byte, vol. 14, no. 2, pp. 274-80.

Priestley, I. (1985). Half-inch cartridges. Systems International, vol. 13, no. 8, p. 36.

Proper, J. (1983). Video cassette recorders for disk backup. Mini-Micro Systems, vol. 16, no. 4, pp. 179-82.

Pugh, E.W. (1971). Storage hierarchies: gaps, cliffs, and trends. IEEE Transactions on Magnetics, vol. MAG-7, no. 4, pp. 810-14.
Pugh, E.W. (1984). Memories that Shaped an Industry: Decisions Leading to IBM System/360. Cambridge, MA: MIT Press.

Rabinowicz, E. (1988). Size effects in magnetic recording. In Engineered Materials for Advanced Friction and Wear Applications. Metals Park, OH: ASM International, pp. 209-14.

Radman, A. and Cornaby, D. (1985). Bernoulli principle stabilizes flexible media. Computer Technology Review, vol. 5, no. 4, pp. 86-87.

Ragle, H. et al (1978). Position sensing for high track density recording. IEEE Transactions on Magnetics, vol. MAG-14, no. 5, pp. 327-29.

Raimondi, D. et al (1986). Managing data storage. Computerworld, vol. 20, no. 9, pp. 33-50.

Ramakrishnan, K. and Emer, J. (1989). Performance analysis of mass storage service alternatives for distributed systems. IEEE Transactions on Software Engineering, vol. 15, no. 2, pp. 120-33.

Ramamoorthy, C. and Chandy, K. (1970). Optimization of memory hierarchies in multiprogrammed systems. Journal of the ACM, vol. 17, no. 3, pp. 426-45.

Rampil, I. (1977). A floppy disk tutorial. Byte, vol. 2, no. 12, pp. 24-28, 35-36, 40-45.

Ramsay, N.C. (1988). Using optical disk in non-image applications. Optical Information Systems, vol. 8, no. 4, pp. 164-68.

Rasek, E. (1985). On the history of digital data storage on magnetic tape. Rechenanlagen, vol. 27, no. 4, pp. 221-35.

Rasek, E. (1986). On trends and alternatives in the development of magnetic tape data storage. Informationstechnik, vol. 28, no. 2, pp. 97-107.

Rash, W. (1987). A quintet of WORMs. Byte, vol. 13, no. 2, pp. 146-52.

Rebane, K.K. et al (1988). Photo-burning of persistent spectral holes and space-time domain holography of ultrafast events of nana- and pico-second duration. In Laser Optics of Condensed Matter: Proceedings of the Third USA-USSR Symposium. New York: Plenum, pp. 421-26.

Reijns, G.L. et al (1988). Simulation and communication aspects of PACS. In Proceedings of the SPIE, vol. 914. Bellingham, WA: SPIE, p. 1153-58.

Renwick, W. (1964). Digital Storage Systems. New York: Wiley.

Renwick, W. and Cole, A.J. (1971). Digital Storage Systems. London: Chapman and Hall.

Replogle, R.A. (1988). Optical storage (WORM) applications for the PC, PS/2. In OIS International 1988: Proceedings of the Fifth Annual Conference on Optical Information Systems. London: Meckler Corporation, pp. 86-83.

Robbins, W. et al (1981). Bubble forming media for optical recording: a new approach. In CLEO 81: CONFERENCE ON LASERS AND ELECTRO-OPTICS. New York: IEEE, p. 122.

Rodriguez, J.A. (1988). Rotary heads: new directions for tape backup. In Digest of Papers: Compcon Spring 88. New York: IEEE, p. 41.

Roll, K. (1986). The impact of process parameters and coating source on the properties of magnetic recording layers. Journal of Vacuum Science and Technology, vol. 4, no. 1, pp. 14-18.

Rosch, W.L. (1987). DC2000 systems: pocket-size backup. PC Magazine, vol. 6, no. 12, pp. 111-16, 126.

Rosch, W.L. (1987a). WORMs for mass storage. PC Magazine, vol. 6, no. 12, pp. 135-68.

Rosenberry, W. (1986). Storage subsystems performance: 3380E DASD and cache. In Proceedings of the SEAS Spring Meeting 1986: Expert Systems. Nijmegen, The Netherlands: SEAS, pp. 181-96.

Rossum, B. (1989). Magnetic storage remains viable. Computer Technology Review, vol. 9, no. 4, pp. 24-25.

Rossum, B. (1989a). New price and performance upgrades will keep magnetic storage competitive. Computer Technology Review, vol. 9, no. 3, pp. 25-26.

Rubel, M.C. (1986). Four quarter-inch tape backup units. Byte, vol. 11, no. 10, pp. 243-47.

Ruddick, A.J. (1989). Digital paper: a write once optical medium. In IEE Colloquium on New Advances in Optical Recording Technology. London: IEE, pp. 2/1-2/5.

Rugar, D. et al (1987). Submicron domains for high density magneto-optic data storage. Transactions on Magnetics, vol. MAG-23, no. 5, pt. 1, pp. 2263-65.

Rupp, G. and Hulsing, H. (1988). RF-sputtered CoCr film on glass substrate for perpendicular recording. Siemens Forschung Entwicklungsberichte, vol. 17, no. 3, pp. 120-24.

Ruska, D.W. et al (1985). Firmware for a streaming tape drive. Hewlett-Packard Journal, vol. 36, no. 3, pp. 29-31

Russell, R.J. (1987). The need for a low-cost, reliable, open-ended IBM 3850 mass storage system replacement. In Digest of Papers: Eighth IEEE Symposium on Mass Storage Systems. Washington, DC: IEEE Computer Society Press, pp. 61-65.

Ryu, H. et al (1986). Present situation of and future prospects for optical disks. CEER Chemical Economics Engineering Review, vol. 18, no. 12, pp. 26-33.

Saffady, W. (1989). Text Storage and Retrieval Systems: a Technology Survey and Product Directory. Westport, CT: Meckler Corporation.

Saito, A. et al (1988). High storage density optical disks using pit-edge recording on PbTeSe thin films. Applied Optics, vol. 27, no. 20, pp. 4274-78.

Sakata, T. et al (1988). Perpendicular thin film head for rigid disk. IEEE Translation Journal on Magnetics in Japan, vol. 3, no. 12, pp. 830-37.

Salsburg, M.A. (1987). Disk cache performance modelling. Unisphere, vol. 7, no. 9, pp. 40-46, 78.

Salsburg, M.A. (1988). Modeling disk performance options for the A Series with CMF.Disk. Unisphere, vol. 8, no. 6, pp. 28-34.

Sano, T. et al (1987). Moving data storage system. In Proceedings - IECON 87: International Conference on Industrial Electronics, Control, and Instrumentation. New York: IEEE, pp. 934-41.

Sasaki, S. et al (1985). Interaction between double-layer film and recording characteristics of perpendicular recording media. IEEE Translation Journal on Magnetics in Japan, vol. TJMJ-1, no. 3, pp. 312-13.

Sato, H. et al (1988). Magneto-optical rewritable disk drive. Sharp Technical Journal, no. 40, pp. 51-55.

Sato, I. (1987). Thin film media for hard disks. IEEE Translation Journal on Magnetics in Japan, vol. TJMJ-2, no. 1, pp. 4-14.

Sato, I. et al (1988). Magnetic recording media for large capacity fast-access magnetic disk storage. Review of the Electronic Communication Laboratory, vol. 36, no. 1, pp. 103-107.

Sato, M. et al (1987). Reliability of magneto-optical memory disks. IEEE Translation Journal on Magnetics in Japan, vol. TJMJ-2, no. 5, pp. 395-96.

Sato, T. and Tsuda, T. (1988). Permuting information in multi-level storage and the optimization of memory hierarchy. Transactions of the Information Processing Society of Japan, vol. 29, no. 4, pp. 386-96.

Satoh, Y. et al (1988). Preparation of metal particulate smooth tape oriented longitudinally inside and perpendicularly at surface. IEEE Transactions on Magnetics, vol. MAG-24, no. 6, pp. 3021-23.

Satyanarayanan, M. (1986). Modelling Storage Systems. Ann Arbor, MI: UMI Research Press.

Savage, P. (1985). Proposed guidelines for an automated cartridge repository. Computer, vol. 18, no. 7, pp. 49-58.

Scannell, T. (1980). Optical memory disk challenging tape and disk. Computerworld, vol. 14, no. 25, p. 65.

Schaake, R.C. et al (1987). Tensile testing of magnetic tapes. IEEE Transactions on Magnetics, vol. MAG-23, no. 1, pp. 109-11.

Schellenberg, F.M. et al (1986). Technological aspects of frequency domain data storage using persistent spectral hole burning. Applied Optics, vol. 25, no. 18, pp. 3207-16.

Schewe, H. (1988). A new read/write concept for vertical recording. IEEE Transactions on Magnetics, vol. MAG-24, no. 6, pp. 2410-12.

Schewe, M. (1989). Evaluating jukeboxes for optical disk systems. IMC Journal, vol. 25, no. 6, pp. 26-27.

Schmidt, R.C. (1982). Pushing the limits of magnetic disk technology. Data Management, vol. 20, no. 7, pp. 10-13.

Schmitt, F.M. and Lee, T. (1979). Developments in thermoplastic tape for optical recording. In Proceedings of the SPIE, vol. 177. Bellingham, WA: SPIE, p. 89-96.

Schneidewind, N. and Syms, G. (1974). Mass memory system peripherals. In IEEE Computer Society International Conference: Compcon 74. New York: IEEE, pp. 87-91.

Scranton, R.A. et al (1984). The access time myth. In Fifth International Conference on Video and Data Recording. London: IERE, pp. 145-49.

Schultz, M. and Kryder, M. (1989). Erase process in direct overwrite magneto-optic recording material. Applied Physics Letters, vol. 54, no. 14, pp. 1371-73.

Sharrock, M.P. and Bodnar, R. (1985). Magnetic materials for recording: an overview with special emphasis on particles. Journal of Applied Physics, vol. 57, no. 8, pt. 2B, pp. 3919-24.

Shepherd, J.P. (1988). Organic optical storage media for short wavelength systems. In Proceedings of the SPIE, vol. 899. Bellingham, WA: SPIE, pp. 220-25.

Shibaya, H. (1988). History of thin alloy film for magnetic recording head aiming at high density and wide band recording. IEEE Translation Journal on Magnetics in Japan, vol. 3, no. 5, pp. 399-406.

Shimizu, R. et al (1988). Average access time is shortened to 50 ms or less in 5.25-inch magneto-optical disk drive. Nikkei Electronics, no. 445, pp. 211-24.

Shimpuku, Y. et al (1986). R-DAT: a new digital audio recording technique. International Broadcast Engineering, vol. 17, no. 209, pp. 62, 65-68.

Shinohara, M. et al (1979). Sputtered ferrite disks for high density magnetic recording. Fujitsu Science and Technical Journal, vol. 15, no. 3, pp. 99-113.

Shiraki, M. et al (1985). Perpendicular magnetic media by anodic oxidation method and their recording characteristics, IEEE Transactions on Magnetics, vol. MAG-21, no. 5, pp. 1465-67.

Shiroishi, Y. et al (1985). Perpendicular recording characteristics of ring head and Co-Cr/Co-Zr-Mo double-layer media. Journal of Applied Physics, vol. 57, no. 8, pt. 2B, pp. 3964-66.

Shiroishi, Y. et al (1988). Read and write characteristics of Co-alloy/Cr thin films for longitudinal recording. IEEE Transactions on Magnetics, vol. MAG-24, no. 6, pp. 2730-32.

Sidman, M.D. (1989). Control systems technology in Digital's disk drives. Digital Technical Journal, no. 8, pp. 61-73.

Siegel, P.H. (1985). Code design for optical storage: a comparison to magnetic storage. In Topical Meeting on Optical Data Storage: Digest of Technical Papers. Washington, DC: Optical Society of America, pp. AA1/1-4.

Siegel, P.H. (1986). Constrained codes for digital magnetic recording channels. In 1986 IEEE International Symposium on Information Theory. New York: IEEE, pp. 26-27.

Sikorav, S. (1986). Magnetic materials for high density recording. Revue de Physique Appliquee, vol. 21, no. 11, pp. 623-33.

Silva, R. (1985). Magnetic storage media's continuing evolution. Office Administration and Automation, vol. 46, no. 9, pp. 47-54.

Simmons, R.G. and Lee, D.K. (1988). Advanced particulate media for high density DASD. IEEE Transactions on Magnetics, vol. MAG-24, no. 6, pp. 2868-70.

Simpson, D. (1985). IBM shuffles half-inch tape cartridge deck. Mini-Micro Systems, vol. 18, no. 6, pp. 71-75.

Simpson, D. (1989). Is write once the right choice? Systems Integration, vol. 22, no. 5, pp. 42-48.

Slicker, R.J. (1988). A software standard for write-once optical disks. Optical Information Systems, vol. 8, no. 2, pp. 81-83.

Sloane, N.J. (1976). Simple description of an error-correcting code for high-density magnetic tape. Bell System Technical Journal, vol. 55, no. 2, pp. 157-65.

Smith, A.J. (1978). Directions for memory hierarchies and their components: research and development. In Proceedings of COMPSAC 78: Computer Software and Applications Conference. New York: IEEE, pp. 704-709.

Smith, A.J. (1981). Analysis of long term file reference patterns for application to file migration algorithms. IEEE Transactions on Software Engineering, vol. 7, no. 4, pp. 403-17.

Smith, A.J. (1981a). Long term file migration: development and evaluation of algorithms. Communications of the ACM, vol. 24, no. 8, pp. 521-32.

Smith, A.J. (1985). Problems, directions, and issues in memory hierarchies. In Proceedings of the Eighteenth Hawaii International Conference on System Science. North Hollywood, CA: Western Periodicals Company, pp. 468-75.

Smith, A.J. (1986). Research and development trends for memory hierarchies. In Proceedings of the Workshop on Future Directions in Computer Architecture and Software. Washington, DC: IEEE Computer Society Press, pp. 62-71.

Sollman, G. (1978). Evolution of the minifloppy product family. IEEE Transactions on Magnetics, vol. MAG-14, no. 4, pp. 160-66.

Sonu, G.H. (1985). Dropout-error-tate calculations for a maximum-density study. IEEE Transactions on Magnetics, vol. MAG-21, no. 5, pp. 1392-94.

Speliotis, D.E. (1967). Magnetic recording materials. Journal of Applied Physics, vol. 38, no. 3, pp. 1207-14.

Speliotis, D.E. (1980). Maximum recording density obtainable in particulate media. IEEE Transactions on Magnetics, vol. MAG-16, no. 1, pp. 30-35.

Speliotis, D.E. (1987). Digital recording performance of Ba-ferrite media. Journal of Applied Physics, vol. 61, no. 8, pt. 2B, pp. 3878-80.

Speliotis, D.E. (1987a). Distinctive characteristics of barium ferrite media. IEEE Transactions on Magnetics, vol. MAG-23, no. 5, pt. 2, pp. 3143-45.

Speliotis, D.E. and Chi, C.S. (1976). Plated films for digital magnetic recording. Plating and Surface Finishing, vol. 63, no. 1, pp. 31-34.

Speliotis, D.E. and Johnson, C., eds. (1972). Advances in Magnetic Recording. New York: New York Academy of Sciences.

Spencer, K. (1988). Terabyte optical tape recorder. In Digest of Papers: Ninth IEEE Symposium on Mass Storage Systems. Washington, DC: IEEE Computer Society Press, 1988, pp. 144-46.

Spencer, K. (1988a). Terabyte optical tape recorder. In Electronic Imaging '88: International Electronic Imaging Exposition and Conference. Waltham, MA: Institute for Graphic Communications, pp. 957-61

Spinnler, C.J. and Sillers, R. (1981). Tape drives and heads in 1982. Digital Design, vol. 11, no. 12, pp. 26-28.

Spratt, G.W. et al (1988). Static and dynamic experimental studies of particulate recording media. Journal of Magnetism and Magnetic Materials, vol. 75, no. 3, pp. 309-18.

Staals, A. et al (1987). Localization and characterization of sub-surface particles in magnetic tape. IEEE Transactions on Magnetics, vol. MAG-23, no. 1, pp. 112-14.

Stark, C.L. (1986). Tape backup: technologies in competition. PC Magazine, vol. 5, no. 3, pp. 140-48.

Steinbrecher, D. (1987). Optical disks go head to head with traditional storage media. Today's Office, vol. 22, no. 5, pp. 24-30.

Stevens, L.D. (1981). The evolution of magnetic storage. IBM Journal of Research and Development, vol. 25, no. 5, pp. 663-75.

Strasser, W. (1981). Use of optical videodiscs in graphics systems. In CAD/CAM as a Basis for the Development of Technology in Developing Nations: Proceedings of the IFIP WG 5.2 Working Conference. Amsterdam: North-Holland Publishing Company, pp. 37-43.

Strecker, W.D. (1978). Optimal design of memory hierarchies. In Proceedings of the Eleventh Hawaii International Conference on System Sciences. North Hollywood, CA: Western Periodicals Company, pp. 46-56.

Strelitz, M. (1989). Digital paper feeds at OA data banquet. Computer Technology Review, vol. 9, no. 2, pp. 26-29.

Stubbs, D.P. and Alexander, J. (1986). Transition lengths in magnetic recording on particulate disks. IEEE Transactions on Magnetics, vol. MAG-22, no. 5, pp. 382-84.

Sugaya, H. (1986). The videotape recorder: its evolution and the present state of the art of VTR technology. SMPTE Journal, vol. 95, no. 3, pp. 301-309.

Sugita, R. et al (1987). Magnetic properties of vacuum deposited Co-Cr perpendicular media and their recording properties. IEEE Transactions on Magnetics, vol. MAG-23, no. 5, pt. 1, pp. 2449-54.

Sugiura, H. and Hayakawa, A. (1986). External storage devices. Fujitsu, vol. 37, no. 2, pp. 148-54.

Suh, S.Y. (1985). Writing process in ablative optical recording. Applied Optics, vol. 24, no. 3, pp. 868-74.

Surden, E. (1977). Optical mass storage expected to rival disk storage. Computerworld, vol. 11, no. 11, p. 43.

Suzuki, T. (1984). Perpendicular magnetic recording: its basics and potential for the future. IEEE Transactions on Magnetics, vol. MAG-20, no. 5, pt. 1, pp. 675-80.

Swartz, E. (1988). QIC-40 brings flexibility to data/file exchange. Mini-Micro Systems, vol. 21, no. 4, pp. 87-90, 93-96.

Tachiwada, H. (1987). Large-capacity, fast-access magnetic disk storage system: GEMMY. Japan Telecommunications Review, vol. 29, no. 3, pp. 57-61.

Tagami, K. et al (1985). Ferrite thin film disks using electroless-plated Ni-P substrates. IEEE Transactions on Magnetics, vol. MAG-21, no. 2, pp. 1164-69.

Tai-Shung, C. (1987). Laser-induced fluid motion on a dye/polymer layer for optical data storage. AIChE Journal, vol. 33, no. 6, pp. 1041-44.

Takahashi, J. et al (1986). Longitudinal recording on a rigid disk using Ba-ferrite powder. IEEE Transactions on Magnetics, vol. MAG-22, no. 5, pp. 713-15.

Takahashi, T. (1988). Vertical magnetic recording media formed with anode oxide films. Alutopia, vol. 18, no. 5, pp. 14-20.

Takasaki, N. (1988). Flexible disk drives. Mitsubishi Electric Advances, vol. 42, pp. 12-14.

Takeda, T. et al (1987). Bit shift characteristics on perpendicular recording using single-layer Co-Cr media and ring heads. IEEE Translation Journal on Magnetics in Japan, vol. TJMJ-2, no. 1, pp. 66-68.

Takenaga, M. et al (1982). Optical disc memory using tellurium sub-oxide thin films. National Technical Reports, vol. 29, no. 5, pp. 728-33.

Tanaka, K. et al (1988). High-performance data-recording technology for rewritable optical disk memory. Mitsubishi Denki Giho, vol. 62, no. 7, pp. 578-81.

Tani, T. (1983). Photochemical hole burning and its applications. Bulletin of the Electrotechnical Laboratory, vol. 47, no. 12, pp. 1242-52.

Tani, T. et al (1987). Photochemical hole burning materials: dye molecules and matrices. Japan Journal of Applied Physics, vol. 26, suppl. 26-4, pp. 77-81.

Tatsuta, T. and Ishida, G. (1984). Disk drive using perpendicular magnetic recording. In Recent Magnetics for Electronics. Amsterdam: Elsevier Science Publishers, pp. 41-49.

Taugawa, J. (1987). Floppy disks and FDD systems. AEU, no. 135, pp. 58-60.

Tazaki, S. and Osawa, H. (1985). Trends on coding systems for high density recording. Journal of the Institute of Electronics and Communications Engineering of Japan, vol. 68, no. 12, pp. 1301-1306.

Thanhardt, E. and Harano, G. (1988). File migration in the NCAR mass storage system. In Digest of Papers: Ninth IEEE Symposium on Mass Storage Systems. New York: IEEE, pp. 114-21.

Thapar, H.K. and Patel, A. (1987). A class of partial response systems for increasing storage density in magnetic recording. IEEE Transactions on Magnetics, vol. MAG-23, no. 5, pt. 2, pp. 3666-68.

Thomas, G.E. (1987). Thin films for optical recording applications. Journal of Vacuum Science and Technology, vol. 5, pt. A, pp. 1965-66.

Thompson, M.A. et al (1988). The operation and use of a two terabyte optical archival store. In Digest of Papers: Ninth IEEE Symposium on Mass Storage Systems. New York: IEEE, pp. 88-92.

Thorndyke, L.M. (1985). Supercomputers and mass storage: the challenges and impacts. In Digest of Papers: Seventh IEEE Symposium on Mass Storage Systems. New York: IEEE, pp. 27-30.

Thornley, R.F. (1985). The future of digital magnetic tape. In Proceedings of the SPIE, vol. 529. Bellingham, WA: SPIE, pp. 198-202.

Tobin, V.M. et al (1988). Magnetization time decay in chromium dioxide tape. IEEE Transactions on Magnetics, vol. MAG-24, no. 6, pp. 2880-82.

Tomono, Y. and Nishida, H. (1987). 8.8-inch disk drive with large capacity. Hitachi Review, vol. 36, no. 4, pp. 201-204.

Tompham, A.D. (1989). Mechanical design of a new quarter-inch cartridge tape drive. Hewlett-Packard Journal, vol. 40, no. 4, pp. 67-73.

Torawaza, K. et al (1988). Development of magneto-optical diskc using amorphous TbFeCo. Sanyo Technical Review, vol. 20, no. 1, pp. 19-29.

Touchton, J.J. (1982). The evolution of disk drive technology during the 1980s. In Digest of Papers: Fifth IEEE Symposium on Mass Storage Systems. New York: IEEE, pp. 64-66.

Trapp, P. (1988). The WORM jukebox: current and future technological and market development plans. Optical Information Systems, vol. 8, no. 2, pp. 76-77.

Trivedi, K. and Sigmon, T. (1981). Optimal design of linear storage hierarchies. Journal of the Association for Computing Machinery, vol. 28, no. 2, pp. 270-88.

Tsutsumi, K. et al (1987). Fabrication and properties of double layer perpendicular rigid disks. IEEE Translation Journal on Magnetics in Japan, vol. TJMJ-2, no. 3, pp. 194-200.

Tsuya, N. et al (1988). Perpendicular magnetic flexible disc by anodic oxidation. IEEE Transactions on Magnetics, vol. MAG-24, no. 2, pt. 2, pp. 1790-92.

Tyan, Y. et al (1987). Recent advances in phase-change media. In Topical Meeting on Optical Data Storage: Summaries of Papers. Washington, DC: Optical Society of America, pp. 44-49.

Umeda, K. et al (1987). Magnetic properties of iron nitride thin films with high corrosion resistance. IEEE Translation Journal on Magnetics in Japan, vol. TJMJ-2, no. 6, pp. 575-76.

Umehara, M. et al (1985). Application of organic dyes to optical disk memory. Journal of Synthetic Chemistry, vol. 43, no. 2, pp. 334-43.

Urrows, H. and Urrows, E. (1988). Optical disks compete with videotape and magnetic storage media: part 1. Optical Information Systems, vol. 8, no. 2, pp.54-63.

Urrows, H. and Urrows, E. (1988a). Optical disks compete with videotape and magnetic storage media: part 2. Optical Information Systems, vol. 8, no. 2, pp.101-109.

VanderGiessen, A.A. (1973). Magnetic recording tape based on Fe particles. IEEE Transactions on Magnetics, vol. MAG-9, no. 3, pp. 191-94.

Van der Poel, C. et al (1986). Phase-change optical recording in TeSeSb alloys. Journal of Applied Physics, vol. 59, no. 4, pp. 1819-21.

Vanker, A.D. (1989). Digital audio tape: yet another archival media? Laserdisk Professional, vol. 2, no. 5, pp. 46-49.

Vanker, A.D. (1989a). Digital paper: mass storage revolution? Laserdisk Professional, vol. 2, no. 1, pp. 38-41.

Van Maren, D.J. et al (1989). Maximizing tape capacity by super-blocking. Hewlett-Packard Journal, vol. 40, no. 3, pp. 32-34.

Van Tongeren, H. and Sens, M. (1987). Write-once phase-change recording in GaSb. In Topical Meeting on Optical Data Storage: Summaries of Papers. Washington, DC: Optical Society of America, pp. 50-53.

Voelker, J. (1987). Winchester disks reach for a gigabyte. IEEE Spectrum, vol. 24, no. 2, pp. 64-67.

Vogelgesang, P. and Hartmann, J. (1988). Erasable optical tape feasibility study. In Proceedings of the SPIE, vol. 899. Bellingham, WA: SPIE, pp. 172-77.

Volker, S. and Macfarlane, R. (1979). Photochemical hole burning in free-base porphyrin and chlorin in N-alkane matrices. IBM Journal of Research and Development, vol. 23, no. 5, pp. 547-55.

Vriens, L. and Jacobs, B. (1984). Digital optical recording with tellurium alloys. Philips Technical Review, vol. 41, no. 2, pp. 313-24.

Wadatani, S. and Harada, H. (1987). Waveform equivalent circuit to increase recording density of the floppy disk unit. Nikkei Electronics, no. 422, pp. 183-93.

Wade, G.J. (1983). Storing medical images on high density digital tape recorders. In Proceedings of the Second International Conference and Workshop on Picture Archiving and Communication Systems (PACS II) for Medical Applications. Bellingham, WA: SPIE, pp. 36-41.

Waltrip, S. and Blake, R. (1988). The software factor: optical disk software — caveat emptor. Inform, vol. 2, no. 2, pp. 22-24.

Wasserman, R.S. (1983). Storage systems architectural overview. In Proceedings of the IEEE International Conference on Computer Design: VLSI in Computers. Silver Spring, MD: IEEE Computer Society Press, p. 324.

Watson, C.M. (1989). 3480 compatible tape subsystems meet demands for midrange systems. Computer Technology Review, vol. 9, no. 10, pp. 73-75.

Weide, H.G. (1982). Application of thin film metal-coated endless tape in mass data storage. Journal fuer Signalaufzeichnungsmaterialen, vol. 10, no. 6, pp. 445-47.

Weinlein, W. (1988). Thirty years of magnetic image recording in Germany. Rundfunktechnische Mitteilungen, vol. 32, no. 5, pp. 211-28.

Welch, T.A. (1978). Memory hierarchy configuration analysis. IEEE Transactions on Computers, vol. 27, no. 5, pp. 408-13.

Welch, T.A. (1979). Analysis of memory hierarchies for sequential data access. Computer, vol. 12, no. 5, pp. 19-26.

Welch, T.A. (1979a). Effects of sequential data access on memory hierarchy design. In Proceedings of Spring COMPCON 79. New York: IEEE, pp. 65-68.

White, R.M., ed. (1985). Introduction to magnetic recording. New York: IEEE Press.

White, J.W. (1984). On the design of low flying heads for floppy disk magnetic recording. In ASLE Special Publication No. 16. Park Ridge, IL: ASLE, pp. 126-31.

White, R.M. (1983). Magnetic disks: storage densities on the rise. IEEE Spectrum, vol. 20, no. 8, pp. 32-38.

Williams, B. (1988). ICI digital paper: the equivalent of a high riser in storage space on one reel of tape. Information Media and Technology, vol. 21, no. 6, pp. 266-68.

Williams, P. (1987). Recent developments in particulate recording media. IEEE Transactions on Magnetics, vol. 24, no. 2, pp. 1876-79.

Williams, R. and Adkisson, J. (1989). Increasing diskette capacity with FLOPTICAL technology. In Digest of Papers: IEEE Computer Society International Conference. New York: IEEE, pp. 148-50.

Williams, T. (1987). Optical storage opens new applications for system design. Computer Design, vo. 26, no. 16, pp. 37-42.

Williams, T. (1989). Digital paper emerges as loc cost archival storage option. Computer Decisions, vol. 28, no. 7, pp. 41-42.

Wimmer, W. (1978). A mass storage hierarchy as part of the file management system at the DESY Computer Centre. Angewandte Informatik/Applied Informatics, vol. 20, no. 9, pp. 1381-88.

Winarski, D.J. et al (1986). Mechanical design of the cartridge and transport for the IBM 3480 magnetic tape subsystem. IBM Journal of Research and Development, vol. 30, no. 6, pp. 635-44.

Winkler, K. (1988). Magnetic storage tapes for data processing: principles of longer tape instruments and of the streamer. ITG-Fachberichte, vol. 102, no. 1, pp. 27-36.

Wohlfarth, E. (1987). New magnetic materials. In New Materials and their Applications. Bristol, England: IOP Publishing, pp. 293-99.

Wolf, I. and Neuman, T. (1989). Recording at high volumetric packing densities. SMPTE Journal, vol. 98, no. 7, pp. 515-19.

Wong, C.K. (1983). Algorithmic Studies in Mass Storage Systems. Rockville, MD: Computer Science Press.

Wood, R. (1986). Magnetic recording systems.

Proceedings of the IEEE, vol. 74, no. 11, pp. 1557-60.

Wood, R. et al (1984). Experimental eight-inch diskc drive with one-hundred megabytes per surface. IEEE Transactions on Magnetics, Vol. MAG-20, no. 5, pp. 698-702.

Wood, T. (1988). D-1 through DAT. In Digest of Papers: Ninth IEEE Symposium on Mass Storage Systems. Washington, DC: IEEE Computer Society Press, pp. 130-38.

Wright, M. (1985). Cartridge tape drives. EDN, vol. 30, no. 24, pp. 108-20.

Wright, M. (1988). Helical scan drives store gigabytes on tiny tape cartridges. EDN, vol. 33, no. 26, pp. 128-34, 136.

Yamaoka, H. (1989). Magneto-optical rewritable disk system. Sharp Technical Journal, no. 41, p. 7-14.

Yamada, T. et al (1987). 16-megabyte 3.5-inch Ba-Ferrite flexible disk drive with dual track following servo modes. IEEE Transactions on Magnetics, vol. MAG-23, no. 5, pp. 2680-82.

Yamamore, K. et al (1983). Per–pendicular magnetic recording floppy disk drive. IEEE Transactions on Magnetics, vol. MAG-19, no. 5, pp. 1701-1703.

Yamamori, K. et al (1986). High density recording characteristics for Ba-ferrite flexible disks. IEEE Transactions on Magnetics, vol. MAG-22, no. 5, pp. 1188-90.

Yamamoto, S. et al (1988). Dependence of recording and reproducing characteristics on thickness of Co-Cr layer in perpendicular recording. IEEE Translation Journal on Magnetics in Japan, vol. 3, no. 6, pp. 467-70.

Yamamoto, T. et al (1985). Recording characteristics of rigid disks for perpendicular magnetic recording. IEEE Translation Journal on Magnetics in Japan, vol. TJMJ-1, no. 3, pp. 310-11.

Yamanaka, Y. et al (1988). High density magneto-optical recording using 0.67-mu m-band high power laser diode. Transactions on Magnetics, vol. MAG-24, no. 6, pp. 2300-2304.

Yamashita, T. et al (1988). An optical disk-based data-acquisition system for the MX series mini-computers. Mitsubishi Denki Giho, vol. 62, no. 7, pp. 596-99.

Yamazaki, H. et al (1987). Study on high-density recording of an ablative-type optical disk. Journal of Applied Physics, vol. 62, no. 5, pp. 1605-9.

Yasuda, K. and Kaneko, R. (1985). R/W experiment using high-speed flexible disk. IEEE Translation Journal on Magnetics in Japan, vol. TJMJ-2, no. 7, pp. 580-88.

Yeh, N.H. et al (1988). Characteristics of overwrite-induced bit shift. IEEE Transactions on Magnetics, vol. MAG-24, no. 6, pp. 2967-69.

Yencharis, L. (1981). Small Winchester drives move up to mainframe encoding schemes. Electronic Design, vol. 29, no. 21, pp. 51-52.

Yochum, K. (1988). Optical disk jukeboxes: how they work, what they can do. IMC Journal, vol. 24, no. 5, pp. 50-51.

Yokoi, T. et al (1988). The optical disk subsystem of the MELCOM EX series general-purpose computers. Mitsubishi Denki Giho, vol. 62, no. 7, pp. 600-605.

Yonezawa, Y. et al (1988). The characteristics of magnetic recording on the toner image. Electrophotography, vol. 27, no. 2, pp. 301-306.

Yonge, M.A. (1984). Magnetic media market rides on drive advances. Mini-Micro Systems, vol. 17, no. 2, pp. 217-20.

Yoshii, S. (1982). Magnetic thin films for high density digital recording. In Ferrites: Proceedings of the ICF Third International Conference on Ferrites. Dordrecht, The Netherlands: Reidel, pp. 579-83.

Yoshimura, F. and Ishii, O. (1983). Magnetic properties of sputtered gamma ferric oxide thin films. Journal of the Vacuum Society of Japan, vol. 26, no. 8, pp. 663-70.

Zellinger, S. (1987). The optical disk jukebox: issues, choices, and options. Inform, vol. 1, no. 12, pp. 34-38.

Zieren, V. et al (1988). High performance heads for perpendicular recording. IEEE Transactions on Magnetics, vol. MAG-24, no. 6, pp. 2597-2602.

Zschau, E.V. (1973). The IBM diskette and its implications for minicomputer systems, vol. 6, no. 6, pp. 21-26.

Index